Blogging the Revolution

Caracas Chronicles and the Hugo Chávez Era

Francisco Toro | Juan Cristobal Nagel

Blogging the Revolution:
Caracas Chronicles and
the Hugo Chávez Era

Francisco Toro
Juan Cristobal Nagel
© 2013

ISBN 978-1-939393-14-2 (eBook)
ISBN 978-1-939393-15-9

Cognitio
Books & Apps

www.cognitiobooks.com

www.CaracasChronicles.com

Table of Contents

V

Foreword

This is not the story of Venezuela's Hugo Chavez.

These are the chronicles of a generation that, bereft of political role-models and unanchored in prior political traditions, has had to come to grips with a changing national perspective. What the untrained eye might see like a momentous upheaval in its history, perhaps even in global history, the dawning of a true post-soviet socialist utopia, it is in fact the –alas, bombastic- return of Third-World-esque discursive tropes and mismanagement fostered by social and cultural inequalities.

Hugo Chávez, the former Lieutenant-Colonel Paratrooper who led two unsuccessful coup attempts in the early 1990s, looms large in any current recreation of Venezuelan history, as its most famous character in recent decades. His long-winding political career, entering into his fourth consecutive term as President, is often viewed by foreign eyes through mainstream media accounts of his antics. He is either an underestimated and harmless buffoon, or a proto-totalitarian menace. Some, echoing the dream-like and hopeful writings of left-leaning and well-meaning intellectuals and journalists, disappointed by the fall of Socialist countries –or the harsh endurance of its most authoritarian modes- have turned to Venezuela to find its new and fashionable egalitarian revolution. The last decade has witnessed a cottage industry of essays, reports and studies on our country, and its contemporary history has been often reframed through the –dark or rosy- lenses through which the *Barinés* caudillo is seen.

Over two decades ago, Venezuela wasn't viewed either as some topical South American Republic - riddled with coups and colonels - or as a Socialist haven. It was a budding, State-and-capitalist economy, lifted from its XIXth Century morass by oil wealth and then embarked as the steadying example of Latin American democracy. It was imperfect, but competitive; unequal, but with an increasing upward mobility; conservative, yet modernizing at an impressive pace. A peaceful nation –no civil wars since 1903- in a region famous for its upheavals, it also became a beacon of modern State building. This side of China's modernization, Venezuela enjoyed the highest rate of growth of any Western Hemisphere economy throughout a large chunk of the XXth Century.

The notion that this small Godforsaken country -rid of its politics-in-horseback- could be both prosperous and democratic became a blinding panacea, making us both proud and anxious about its shortcomings. The generations that came of age in the booming 60s and 70s became more internationally-minded, and received an intellectual and technical preparation beyond any of its predecessors. With that, came an overabundance of opportunities, and a certain sense of entitlement and complacency, a kind of aloof citizenship. The people from these generations -save perhaps for Comandante Chávez himself- never reached political power: the preceding generations (the founding group of radicalized middle class politicians who led the path toward democratization and party-building) ruled the roost up until 1998, defeating the best and the brightest that the new Venezuela had to offer. As such, this founding generation, fearing chaos and anarchy, and both protective of its legacy and mindful of its social reform commitments, avoided reforming the relationship between the State and civil society. The fact that the most educated and enlightened of our generations has also been the least politically successful is an irony that is not lost on the coming pages.

What about the following generations? Those of us who grew up in the 80s and 90s, and came of age as Mr. Chávez took office, have only witnessed a seemingly endless crisis. Since the crash of Oil prices and the Debt crisis that shook our flush economy in the early 1980s, the riots and coup attempts of the late 1980s and early 1990s, as well as the financial crisis of that decade, all idols were broken. Voter disaffection manifested in low turnout, frequent political impasses, and short-lived booms with even more social deception became the norm during our formative years. Moreover, our own expectations on social mobility and prosperity screeched to a halt, and downward mobility became evident. We were not a prosperous country, let alone a sustainable democracy. The

Venezuela our parents and teachers had taught us about during our childhood was, if not in tatters, in very bad shape.

And, yet, this generation moved on. Mobilized by the joint forces of the centripetal globalization and centrifugal local instability, many viewed foreign lands as a pathway to a brighter future. The rest, perhaps not pining for emigration, live with the realization that this country is increasingly foreign, and that the harmony and national unity our elder statesmen longed for was a grand illusion.

Of course, patriotism remains a strong calling, and with information and intellectual prowess came new attempts to understand this uncanny land we call our own. Needless to say, the challenges posed to its traditional national narrative by the Chávez government (political institutions, social situation, economic structure, racial and cultural habits, our common language, everything...) presented an alternative: you could either entrench yourself in the past, waxing poetically of a stillborn Republic, or try to come to grips with our misgivings and understand the country, and ourselves, better in the process.

It is from the worries and trials of this new generation that this book comes about. The exploits of our redeemer, the Comandante-Presidente, are of course a main focus of these short pieces originally written by the successful Venezuelan blog *Caracas Chronicles*, written by Francisco Toro, Juan Nagel and, as of late, Gustavo Hernandez Acevedo. Their work is a reference for anyone interested in Venezuela, and it is an excellent showcase of the contradictions, hopes and savvy of global Venezuelans. Even though the blog has been, in its run of over a decade, in-and-of-itself critical of Mr. Chávez's experiments and actions, it has never toed a party line. Its critique aims toward a sincere redefinition of opposition politics, from the mere reactionary squabbles and maximalist actions at the turn of this Century (heroic and tragic as they might have been), but also to an honest reappraisal of our society's subsidiary relationship with Oil wealth and State support, that could also lead to a constructive dialogue with the most redeeming features of our XXth Century growth.

It was precisely the chaos and bewilderment facing the beginnings of the Chávez revolution and the political and social responses to it from which this marvelous blog was born. At times elation, sometimes consternation and disbelief, came from the unruly and iconoclastic keyboards of these young writers, as they grew frustrated by the limitations of Venezuela's media and the callous shallowness of foreign outlets, which projected their own sympathies and stereotypes or were channelling official propaganda dollars and messages over a complex political and social situation. *Caracas Chronicles* has strived to create an independent narrative and a singular voice in the Venezuelan blogosphere and, to its English-reading audience, a unique and brave offering.

And how could this be? How dare "these kids" claim to understand the complexities and the vagaries of the Venezuelan experience? "Aporrea for escuálidos", as a former student of mine commented. It is indeed a tall order, but one that has been honed and perfected over its long digital run. No other Venezuelan blog has been as well written and well received among local readers, and they pay generous tribute to their sources and fellow bloggers, often linking to their pieces or translating entire pieces written first in Spanish for the benefit of its demanding audience, filling its own niche in the process. Some of the best short essays of the blog are collected here, bundled in thematically independent chapters: an introduction to Venezuela, its history and politics; an overview of our mores and habits; a look on Oil and the economic distortions it creates; a review of the Venezuelan opposition movements and parties; a gripping account on how Chavismo's ideology has seeped into our public consciousness; a lively chronicle of the 2002-2004 political crisis –perhaps the most publicised but less understood moments in our contemporary history-; and a critical and assessment of our public sphere and a hopeful call to rebuild it.

Poised and independent, this book has a great mixture of styles: from the snarky and liberally-minded Francisco –Quico- Toro, coming from a Political Science background, to the stern and mindful conservatism of economist Juan Nagel. Together with the social and regional sensibility of Gustavo Hernandez Acevedo –

who has almost single-handedly turned the blog into something that goes well beyond chronicling Caracas-, the blog's trio has tackled a myriad of different and, sadly, recurring issues: political encroachment and squabbles, economic and policy fallacies, sovereign debt, pollution, crime and security, drug trafficking, beauty queens, prison conditions and riots, labour issues, historical foibles, and so on. And, of course, the quirks and menace of President Chávez, his heirs and his foes.

Sons of a Venezuela that dreamt of modernization, this trio of young Venezuelan writers provides the reader with an essential collection of essays: non-parochial and yet deeply knowledgeable of Venezuelan mores and traits; academically minded and yet not bookish; serious and yet unfazed by the need for humor; challenging through and through, and a privilege to the public. Now, as we face a critical juncture in the Chavez era –and, of course, for the country at large- this voice needs to be read anew and, if you've been familiar with their work, refreshed.

This is not the story of Venezuela's Hugo Chavez. These are the chronicles of a generation trying to face its future and honestly asses its past. These are the Caracas Chronicles.

Guillermo T. Aveledo
Caracas, December 2012

Introduction

Comprising more than 6,000 posts written over more than 10 years, the full *Caracas Chronicles* archive reads like a blow-by-blow of the most tumultuous period of our recent history. The crazy, unhealthy twist to this... is that we don't live in Venezuela. For Quico and me, the blog is a classic case of the-hobby-that-got-out-of-control-and-consumed-our-lives.

Why do we put ourselves through it? Thinking about this brings to mind a famous story about Miguel Ángel Burelli, an *eminence grise* of the old, pre-Chávez regime. In a meeting with Venezuelan expatriates in New York, Burelli reportedly chastised them for not going back home. "You will die," he scornfully admonished them, "like Pedro Estrada, looking for an *arepa* in every corner of Paris."[1] News from home is just a click away, and at times it seems as if *Harina Pan* – like many other things - is easier to find abroad than in Caracas, so his warnings about *arepas* seem dated. But Burelli had a point in that none of this substitutes the real thing.

For Venezuelans abroad, nostalgia is a permanent deadweight. Ours is like no other country I can think of, and that's not necessarily a good thing. We're like a deeply dysfunctional family; a violent, unruly place full of intractable problems, with enormous potential, and an unlimited capacity for failing to fulfill it. At times, it feels as if the country is overflowing with hatred. We have plenty of reasons for giving up on Venezuela altogether.

But we don't. Something keeps drawing us back, whether it's the laughter shared with friends, the memory of drinking a *Solera* while we smoked away Belmonts in *Playa Parguito*, the sounds of the *Piano Merengue*, or the intellectual challenge of convincing others that this or that policy (like giving away free gas) is terrible.

---

[1] Estrada was the head of former dictator Marcos Pérez Jiménez's secret police. He was exiled in Paris after the fall of the dictatorship in 1958.

I am reminded of the Ibsen Martínez quote: "Cada quién se defiende de Venezuela como puede." Each of us defends himself from Venezuela as best he can.

Me? I gave up defending myself a long time ago. Instead of leaving Venezuela in the past, I just embraced my obsession. Call it the Caracas Stockholm Syndrome.

Once in a while I get the same trite criticism. "What can you know? You don't even live here." That's true, I don't, and neither does Quico. But both of us have always viewed not living in Venezuela as a plus in our writing.

Written in a language other than our own from countries other than our own, *Caracas Chronicles* has always been premised on distance - the kind of remove that sharpens and at the same time deforms. Distance lets us ponder events without the distractions of the latest mugging, of not finding staples in the supermarket, of a *cadena*[2]. Using English allows debates that have grown stale through repetition in Spanish to spring to life, opening up possibilities that get boarded up by the weight of hyper-polarized debate in our native tongue. It also opens the door to non-Spanish speakers - some honest brokers, others not much - whose voices are rarely heard but who have much to contribute.

Deep down, we think Burelli had it all wrong. It's not just *arepas* that are easier to come by abroad than in Venezuela these days, but also, perhaps, an unencumbered understanding of the realities back home.

The world has gotten smaller, and we don't need to look for Venezuela in every corner of Paris. Venezuela comes to us. We find her by writing her critically, whether from Santiago, Montreal, Kyoto, Maastricht, Ann Arbor, or here, at the foot of the Villarrica volcano. That unfulfilled, underfed *saudade* - a proverbial sea without shores - is the fuel that keeps *Caracas Chronicles* going.

---

[2] You will see many references to cadenas in this book. They are forced transmissions of anything the government decides is transmissible by all TV and radio stations in the country, for as long as the government wants to. Hugo Chávez has made practically unlimited use of this power through the years.

This book is for our recent readers who are not familiar with our earlier stuff, as well as for all those interested in Venezuela during the Hugo Chávez years. It is a look back at our first ten years, with what we believe is our best material. The editing was done by me. Mine, too, are the blurbs at the beginning of each chapter and the footnotes. Most of the text in the book, as should be evident, is Quico's.

Rather than chronologically, I've organized the book thematically, seeking to allow lines of argument that took us years to work out to flow naturally through a single chapter. I think it works like this, and it's indicative of the static chaos of Chávez's Venezuela, whereby a topic that was relevant in 2003 probably remained relevant - though often, more dire – in, say, 2009.

There are several people to thank for this book. Mariana Rodríguez and Santiago Schnell first approached me with the idea, and have been heavily involved in the formatting, proof-reading, and designing the book. Alejandro Toro and Alejandro Ramos of *Cognitio Books & Apps* have been remarkably supportive of this project. I thank them for this, and for their friendship. Special thanks to Mariana for taking the picture of me that appears in the back cover of the hard copy version.

Gustavo Hernández Acevedo has been a great help in keeping the content of the blog flowing, and it has been a pleasure watching him blossom into a promising young blogger. His assistance in the ungodly task of selecting the nuggets from the 6,000+ posts we have written proved to be crucial.

It's a cliché, but our readers keep us going. Many thanks to those of you who take the time to comment frequently and keeping things interesting – Syd, Kepler, Omar, Dr Faustus, Juantxon, Paul Challenger, Torres, Donacobius, Feathers, Capablanca, Firepiggette, Lucia, Dorothy, Guido, and many more. A special shout-out goes out to two people: GTAvex, the inimitable Guillermo T. Aveledo, who accepted my invitation to write the Foreword, and Cristina Toro. I'm sure Quico will join me in thanking our families – Katy, Kanako, and our respective daughters – for allowing us the time to write and comment.

Finally, big thanks go to all the reporters, writers, and thinkers that have inspired us and continue to do so: Adriana Arreaza, Alberto Barrera, Alek Boyd, Ana Maria Sanchis, Anabella Abadí, Andrew Sullivan, Ángel Alayón, Bárbara Lira, Benedict Mander, Brian Ellsworth, Brian Nelson, César Batiz, Carolina Romero, Charlie Devereux, Corina Rodríguez, Cristina Marcano, Daniel Duquenal, Daniel Raguá, Dorothy Kronick, Ezequiel Minaya, Francisco Monaldi, Gerardo Blyde, Girish Gupta, Harry Hutton, José Antonio López, Jose Manuel Briceño Guerrero, Juan Forero, Keyal Vyas,Laura Weffer, Laureano Márquez, Luis Pedro España, Marianna Párraga, Marino González, Mayé Primera, Miguel Angel Santos, Miguel Octavio, Nathan Crooks, Omar Bello, Phil Gunson, Ricardo Hausmann, Richard Obuchi, Raul Sanchez Urribarri, Roberto Nasser, Roberto Prego, Rory Carroll, Simón Romero, Steve Bodzin, Teodoro Petkoff, Terry Karl, Toby Bottome, Veronica Suarez, and many more. Through the years we have quoted your stuff and used your ideas – may the freedom of the Internet allow us to continue doing so.

And may the freedom of the Internet continue allowing us to constructively wallow in our nostalgia.

JCN

I

A primer on Venezuela, and on Caracas Chronicles

Part of our job at Caracas Chronicles is to put the daily happenings of chavista madness into a historical context. Foreigners find it easy to get lost in the daily craziness of Hugo Chávez's Venezuela, and they struggle to understand the forces that lie beneath the events they witness or read about. This chapter is a modest attempt at decoding the basics of the country.

Venezuela is like few places on Earth, a poor country with even poorer institutions, and yet blessed with extraordinary riches that seep out of the ground. From time to time, when oil sells at a high price, we live an "illusion of harmony" - as people who are far smarter than us once called it. This illusion, or rather the memory of it, permeates the Venezuelan psyche just as much as the legacy of Simón Bolívar. The periods of relative prosperity, much of it undeserved, lead many to think ours is a very rich nation when, in fact, it is not.

In this chapter, we present a series of posts that provide some background into the factors that shape our daily existence – oil, military strongmen, and our ethnic composition chief among them.

On the blog, we focus a lot on the petrostate, for Venezuela can't be understood as just any other Latin American country, with its social relations guided by agricultural realities or middle-of-the-road industrialization. In Venezuela, oil permeates everything, and it is an essential part of understanding the country, and the Chávez phenomenon in particular.

This chapter also serves to introduce you to our interests. Blogs are deeply personal endeavors, and with some of these posts, you can get a glimpse of the type of stuff we dig, and the ways in which we write about them.

The Petrostate that was and the Petrostate that is.
Posted on February 14, 2003, updated in 2004 by Quico

Too many foreign observers write about the Chávez era in a historical vacuum. But you can't understand *chavismo* without a feel for the political economy of the petrostate.

The Acción Democrática model

Back in 1996, I did some field work for my thesis on the Venezuelan labor movement in Cabimas, a dusty little oil city on the eastern shore of Lake Maracaibo. One day, I saw a bunch of guys playing basketball at a municipal court and thought I'd hang out with them for a while - not that I'm any good at basketball, but I hoped they might offer a different perspective.

Later, when I told my labor movement buddies what I'd been up to, they were horrified. "What!?[3] You were hanging out with those *adeco* basketball players? Oh Jesus, did you give them any information?!" *Adeco* basketball players? I was shocked.

I'd often read about how deeply political parties had penetrated the fiber of everyday life in Venezuela, but the notion that even the guys shooting hoops down the street had a party affiliation struck me as deeply weird.

Undaunted, I went back and asked them about it.

"So, you guys are from AD?"

One of them kind of smiled awkwardly and one of them said, "well, we needed a court and..."

He went on to tell me the story about how they'd always wanted a proper court to play on, and they'd never had enough

---

[3] Acción Democrática, or AD, was Venezuela's preeminent political party during the second half of the XXth Century. Founded by, among others, Romulo Betancourt, who later became Venezuela's first President after the fall of Marcos Pérez Jiménez in 1958, it was initially a left-wing organization, but became center-left as time went by. It basically invented the politics of patronage in the country. Its members are called "adecos."

money for shoes, balls, uniforms, coaching ... all the stuff you need to join a youth league. The mayor of Cabimas was an Acción Democrática politician and one of the guys mentioned his uncle was an AD member, so they asked him for help.

The uncle pointed them to their neighborhood AD party organizer. They asked him if the city would build them a basketball court. The organizer said he would be happy to press their case with the mayor, but told them the mayor would be, cough-cough, much more likely to agree to it if they'd sign up to become party members.

The bargain was simple - a chunk of the municipal recreation budget in return for becoming AD members and helping out with election campaigns and get-out-the-vote drives.

That didn't strike the guys as such a bad deal. So they signed up, and after a year or so they'd gotten their court and some gear...with the slight inconvenience that the whole town started to think of them as "those *adeco* basketball players."

And there you have it: at its core, *that* is the Venezuelan petrostate.

The petrostate is a mechanism that turns oil money into political power - or, more precisely, control of the state's oil money into control of the state - in a self-perpetuating cycle.

The way you do that is by building a huge patronage network. It's Tammany Hall politics on a national basis.

Those kids shooting hoops in Cabimas had never heard of Terry Lynn Karl, but they instinctively grasped how the system worked. So did their neighborhood party organizer: he was able to use his influence over a tiny share of the state's oil revenue – just enough to get a basketball court built - to fund a miniature local patronage network. His clients - the guys - would return the favor on Election Day, not due to any sort of ideological affinity, but simply to keep their access to his influence over funds. And he would use his influence over them - his ability to mobilize them for political purposes - to bolster his position as client to the next patron up the line: the mayor.

That basic, pyramid-like structure was replicated all throughout the country, in every imaginable sphere of life, from multi-billion dollar infrastructure projects to things as petty as a neighborhood basketball court.

The mayor of Cabimas - who was patron vis-à-vis the neighborhood organizer - was in turn client to the next patron up the line: the governor of Zulia state. And the governor played client to *his* higher up, perhaps a politician or a faction in AD's all powerful National Executive Committee.[4] And *that* patron in turn played client to the party secretary general or to the President of the Republic...one neat string of patron-client relationships running all the way from the dusty backstreets of Cabimas up to the presidential palace in Caracas.

Copei, the second party, ran a parallel (if somewhat smaller) patronage pyramid, and MAS, the nominal left-wing party, ran a much smaller and weaker one.[5]

This, basically, was the system Hugo Chávez was elected to dismantle.

By the time the 1998 elections came around, people resented it acutely. But before launching into a (by now redundant) critique of the system, it bears stopping to notice a few of its features.

For one thing, it's important to realize that the system was not totally paralyzed – after all, the basketball court did get built. Undoubtedly, the funds that built it were mercilessly stripped at every step from presidential palace to dusty backstreet as successive layers of patrons took their cut, but the court got built eventually.

---

[4] Until 1989, state governors were appointed by the President directly, without legislative approval. Starting in 1989, governors and mayors were directly elected, and budgets were allocated more or less independently. This process is known as "descentralización."

[5] In pre-Chávez days, COPEI was the country's second-largest party. It was nominally a Christian Democratic party, in theory right-of-center, but in practice center-left.

So while it was inefficient, bloated, antidemocratic, and everything else, the system was not totally useless , and in its own amoral way, corruption served as a rough-and-ready way to spread the oil money around, to make sure it reached many hands, not just a few. The recipients of the final product - the basketball players - were the end-point of a sprawling corruption scheme: it's just that they got paid off for their services in courts and basketball gear rather than cash.

The Petrostate is a state of mind

It's important to note that the petrostate is not simply a system of social relationships; it's also a cultural system, an interlocking set of beliefs. It's a state of mind.

In a typical developing country, the overriding political problem is the problem of production: how to generate enough wealth to pull the nation out of poverty. But in a petrostate, production is not seen as particularly problematic: wealth is just there, all you have to do is pump it out of the ground.

In a petrostate, the basic political problem is distribution: how best to spread around wealth whose existence you take for granted. Success in life depends not on work, not on your capacity to produce wealth, but on connections, on your ability to get your hands on a piece of the resource pie.

This outlook comes to dominate people's relationship with the state. The state comes to be seen as an inexhaustible source of money. People come to believe that whatever problem they have, they state can and should solve it.

Those guys in Cabimas had no doubt that if they wanted a basketball court, it was the state's job to build them one. After all, wasn't the country awash in oil money? Insofar as the petrostate has a culture, that's its central conceit - the idea that the government has so much oil money that it can, and should, bankroll the needs and desires of the entire society. Within the petrostate mental model that's what the state is for and governments are to be judged by how well they deliver on that promise.

That's not just me saying it - polls consistently find that over 90% of Venezuelans think this is a rich country, with over 80% calling it - incongruously - "the richest country on earth."

Those beliefs didn't just appear in popular imagination by accident. The petrostate's founding myth was at the center of the AD political program from the 1920s onward. AD's founding father, Romulo Betancourt, wrote a number of books on the subject.

In his influential book, *The Magical State,* anthropologist Fernando Coronil argues that this petrostate mentality extends backwards in time all the way to the presidency of Eleazar López Contreras in the late 1930s, and is centered on the expectation that the state can magically bring about modernity.

For a while, that redistributive vision worked. So long as the population was relatively small, the state relatively efficient, and the oil revenue stream relatively steady, a simple redistributive strategy went a long way.

Throughout the 40s, 50s, 60s and into the mid-70s, the petrostate model yielded a huge improvement in Venezuelans' living standards. Infrastructure got built, people got jobs, and each generation could reasonably expect to live better than the one before. The country got universal schooling, free universities, hospitals, public housing, sewers, phones, roads, highways, ports, airports, and all kinds of markers of modernity decades before other Latin American countries had them.

Less tangibly, but just perhaps even more importantly, the petrostate bankrolled institutions ranging from paid maternity leave and severance pay, to old age pensions and statutory vacation pay.

By creating sprawling patron-client networks, the political parties became strong enough to make a limited form of democracy viable. The web of social relationships was quite useful in the early decades of democratization. Patronage webs ensured that enough people were socially and economically attached to democratic institutions to have a personal stake in the political system. This loyalty was the key to keeping the country stable and democratic at a time when most of Latin America was not.

And here's the wonder: for a long time, it actually worked. There were elections every five years, AD and COPEI routinely and peacefully alternated in power, Venezuela was an island of democracy and stability in a continent torn apart by Marxist insurgents and coup-plotting generals.

Breakdown

But it didn't last.

There are many reasons why the relatively benign clientelism of the 50s and 60s atrophied into the kleptocratic lunacy of the 80s and 90s. Corruption is the typical reason cited, but the truth is both more complex and less morally satisfying than that.

The underlying reason for the system's breakdown, in my view, has everything to do with the increasing volatility of the world oil market, together with appalling mismanagement and good old demographics.

Until 1973, oil had traded in a relatively narrow price range, making Venezuela's revenues more or less predictable from one year to the next. But starting with the oil embargo in 73 - remembered as the "oil crisis" in importing countries but as the "oil bonanza" here - oil prices started to gyrate wildly, making it impossible to forecast state revenues with any degree of certainty. With each new boom, huge torrents of petrodollars would pour into the Venezuelan economy, only to be followed by busts that were just as marked and unexpected.

This boom and bust cycle was destructive on a number of counts. From a merely macroeconomic point of view, it's clear that economies don't do well under that sort of instability.

More destructive than the cycle, though, was the state's chronic mismanagement of it. Each boom made *politicos* think that high prices would last forever, and so they would take out new debt even as money poured in at record rates. When prices fell, the boom-time excess would only fuel increasingly acute recessions, made all the worse by the new debt burden that had to be financed. This is the famous debt-overhang hypothesis that some observers blame for the onset of Venezuela's economic decline in the 1980s.

I would argue that the most destructive effects of the late petrostate were cultural rather than economic. The massive influx of oil dollars in the 70s shifted public morals in this country. Amidst the abundance of oil dollars, graft became accepted in a way it had never been before. The perception was that only a *pendejo*, a simpleton, would miss out on the opportunities for easy riches that proliferated in those days for the well-connected. A culture of easy-going racketeering, of matter-of-fact robbery, penetrated deep into the Venezuelan psyche. We've never managed to shake it.

At the same time, population growth gradually diluted the oil wealth among a bigger and bigger pool of recipients, making the principle of "petrodollar-funded prosperity for all" ever less feasible. Even if the state redistributed all its oil rents in cash equally to everyone, most Venezuelans would not stop being poor.

By the late 1980s, the petrostate model had broken down irretrievably. Even if the politicians of the day had been a gaggle of angels gifted with Prussian administrative efficiency, there just wasn't enough oil money to go around.

Alas, the politicians we had then were the polar opposite of Prussians and anything but angels.

Patrons' reliance on their patronage networks made the entire system exceedingly difficult to reform, and particularly deaf to calls for change from the outside. Never particularly suited to ideological debate, the petrostate became ossified completely: power itself became its only ideology. The drive to amass more of it, to climb higher and higher in the pyramid, to gain access to ever more lucrative sources of patronage, came to dominate the political system entirely. As the system became more and more dysfunctional, people's resentment of the corruption at the heart of the system grew ever stronger, though very few within the state recognized this.

The late 1980s were a critical moment in the country's history. Venezuela needed massive reform. It needed to reinvent itself, to leave behind a model of governance that was well past its sell-by date and find a way to integrate itself into the world economy, shedding its excessive reliance on oil, not just as a source of money, but as lynchpin of its socio-political and cultural systems. Venezuela needed to ditch clientelism, reinvent social relations at every level, and pry apart the patronage networks that had defined its social relations for so long. We needed to ditch the notion that the state could bankroll everyone's way of life just by distributing the oil money.

We needed to invent a whole new idea of the state, nothing short of a total rethink of society, the state, and the relationship between the two. And we failed.

That failure is the reason Hugo Chávez is in power today. His political success is the inevitable outcome of our inability to cast off the petrostate model.

Our botched attempt at reform

Back in 1989, all you had to do to realize how badly Venezuela needed reform was pick up a phone. On a bad day it could take half an hour or more to get a dial-tone. You'd unhook the phone, go make yourself a sandwich, check for a dial tone, eat the sandwich, check for a dial tone again, wash your dishes and put away the mayonnaise, come back and check for a dial tone again.

But once you'd managed to place the call, your troubles had only started: more often than not you'd have to go through the delightful ritual of the *llamada ligada* - the "linked call." This was a queer little phenomenon where two entirely unrelated conversations would become entwined in the circuitry somehow, and you'd end up sharing your conversation with two complete strangers. Sometimes, these absurd little four-way interchanges would develop, as each set of callers tried to convince the other set to hang up and try their call again: of course, you didn't want to be the one to hang up, because then you'd have to wait who-knows-how-long for a new dial tone.

Ah, the days of the nationalized phone company. Working with 40 year old equipment, CANTV (as the company is called) was far, far behind the technological and service curves. Waiting times for a new phone line could extend into months or years. Predictably, the delays spawned their own little hotbed of corruption: if you needed a new phone line, you had to pay off somebody inside CANTV to bump you to the front of the line.[6]

Phone lines were such a scarce luxury that they carried a premium on the real-estate market: in the classified ads, people selling their apartments would advertise not just location and size, but, proudly, *con teléfono* – an item that would add a good 5% to the price of an apartment. Having a second phone line became the ultimate status-symbol, the height of conspicuous consumption.

State-owned CANTV was prey to all the vices of clientelism run amok. Shielded from competition, the company could get away with bloody murder. As a consumer, you were powerless: a supplicant in the grip of a system that existed more to extract bribes than to provide phone service.

The CANTV-style attitude of total contempt for the user/citizen pervaded the state. Trying to get anything out of the bureaucracy was a nightmare. Registering your car or trying to get a passport or a *cédula* (a national ID card) became an exercise in frustration-control. Notoriously, even paying your taxes became a problem. Tax officials knew that you needed that little shard of official paper they controlled (the certificate that you'd paid your taxes) for a number of reasons – you couldn't sell real estate without it, for instance - so you ended up in the incredible position of having to bribe an official for the privilege of paying your taxes! That's how entrenched the culture of corruption was.

---

[6] In 1991, President Carlos Andrés Pérez privatized CANTV. The company was sold to a group of foreign and national investors. In 2007, Hugo Chávez expropriated CANTV. It is once again a state-owned company.

But the rot wasn't confined to the micro-level: the country was also in serious macroeconomic trouble. In 1989, the Central Bank was more or less out of foreign reserves. Protected by years of tariff barriers and subsidies, both private and state-owned enterprises were inefficient, rent-seeking leeches cranking out substandard goods at inflated prices. Business had been thoroughly assimilated into the pyramid: trading political support for subsidies and tariffs in exactly the same way those kids in Cabimas traded political support for basketball gear.

Thirty years of petrostate clientelism had turned the government into albatross around the nation's neck. The public sector payroll was impossibly bloated. The petrostate had slowly morphed into a full-employment scheme for governing party clients. In 1988, Venezuela had more public employees than Japan, but as the dark joke at the time went, "of course, in Japan they don't get quality public services like we do here." Lots of public sector jobs were "no-show jobs," where clients showed up just twice a month to collect their paychecks, but didn't actually work. Many other officials treated their salaries as a sort of retainer, but everyone understood that the real money was elsewhere – in the kickbacks, commissions and bribes that state jobs gave them access to.

A sprawling state-owned sector of the economy was made up of a single profit-making firm (the oil giant, PDVSA) bankrolling dozens of parasitic, loss-making firms. Money that might have gone to build schools and hospitals went instead to prop up a thousand and one money-holes: state sugar-refineries, banks, mining companies, airlines, even, famously, a fast-food joint in Caracas called "La Sifrina" (que tiempos aquellos!).

People were sick of it, and understandably so. But – and this is a crucial "but" – they didn't see the need for root and branch reform. What they wanted was to see the petrostate fixed, not replaced.

Venezuelans longed for the bonanza days of the 70s, when windfall oil revenues financed a huge and rapid expansion in consumer spending. If they were angry at politicians, it was because they thought politicians had failed to deliver on their basic mission to meet everyone's needs by distributing the oil money fairly and generously. Do that, they figured, and the country could return to the good old days of the 70s.

Here we get back to the mental model that underpins the Venezuelan petrostate, and its founding myth that Venezuela is a fantastically rich country, so all the state has to do is distribute the oil rents for everyone to live comfortably.

If you genuinely believe that, as 90% of Venezuelans still do, but you personally live in poverty, then the obvious inference is that the reason you're poor is that somebody stole your fair share. Those *adeco* bastards!

Let me be clear about this: corruption really was a huge problem back then, and it still is. But Venezuelans had wildly unrealistic notions how much their lives could improve if corruption was stamped out. Few grasped that even without corruption, the petrostate model was unworkable. The complicated structural and demographic reasons that made it fundamentally non-viable were not part of the national debate. They were understood only partially even in academic and technocratic circles. So the perception that corruption was the whole of the problem in fact impeded a deeper examination of the real reasons the state had stopped working.

El Gocho pal '88

Lo and behold, the 1988 presidential election featured a candidate uniquely positioned to play into people's anger at the state of the state: Carlos Andrés Pérez, who had actually been president from 1974 to 1979, when the first big spike in petrodollars reached the country.[7]

CAP, as everyone called him, ran as an old style populist, promising to turn back the clock and govern just as he had the first time around. Venezuelans wanted a revamped petrostate, and he offered a revamped petrostate. Not surprisingly, he won by a landslide.

---

[7] Pérez ran, and won, both times as the AD candidate. He was expelled from the party in 1994, during his impeachment trial.

What CAP was thinking of when he ran his campaign that way is still a subject of debate in Venezuela today. Looking back, it's clear that the state was in no financial position to bankroll the whole of society anymore, and CAP must have known that. Some people think it was all a carefully calculated ploy from the start, that he knew he needed to talk the talk to get elected, but was aware all along that he couldn't walk the walk.

Not everyone agrees. As one delicious anecdote would have it, CAP was certain that he could revamp the petrostate because he had already worked out a preliminary deal with the incoming US administration. The soon-to-be secretary of the treasury was fully on board for a financial rescue package that would allow the Venezuelan government to keep doing business more or less as usual ... and that incoming administration would be run by President Dukakis.

CAP won with a record number of votes, but of course Dukakis went down in flames. Literally weeks after being elected, CAP found himself at the head of a barely functioning, bankrupt state. He had little choice but to renege on pretty much everything he'd stood for during the campaign.

Instead, he announced a program of massive, IMF-sponsored structural reforms – lifting tariff barriers, dropping subsidies, privatizing state assets...a straightforward neoliberal, Washington Consensus type program.

Now, it's easy to rant against the IMF, but context is key here. Given the scale of the mess that state finances were in, and the role petrodollar-funded patronage played in undermining state finances, there's a good case to be made that radical reform was badly needed with or without the IMF. This, in general, is my critique of the standard critique of the IMF: put forward in a context vacuum, it fails to take note of the entirely Venezuelan reasons why reform was necessary to overcome the bottlenecks generated by petrostate clientelism.

Be that as it may, it's also true that CAP's reforms were a bald-faced betrayal of everything he'd stood for just weeks before he announced them.

Venezuelans thought they'd elected CAP to fix the petrostate, instead, he immediately moved to dismantle it. It barely made a difference that the petrostate was badly in need of dismantling: anyone needing a phone-line in those days should have been able to see that. Consensus on the need for reform was confined to technocratic circles - the public sphere just was not on board.

CAP didn't seem to think he had to make the case for dismantling the petrostate. He thought he could just do it, steamroll over all opposition, and present the country with a *fait accompli*. His thinking, apparently, was that the economic benefits of reform would be so evident within a couple of years that the critics of reform would be marginalized.

Alas, he miscalculated badly. First off, CAP was elected on the AD ticket, as the candidate of the party that benefited the most from the petrostate model. In fact, the main source of resistance to CAP's reform push was his own party. CAP might have had a road-to-Damascus moment sometime after the Dukakis campaign imploded, but the rest of AD was still very much wedded to petrostate clientelism. And CAP's reforms were plainly incompatible with their vision of the state.

Take CANTV. Sure, it was a nightmare for consumers, but who cares about consumers? For the AD patrons who ran it, the phone company was a cherished power-base. Not only could they exploit their control over a scarce commodity – phone lines – to demand any number of bribes, enriching themselves and feeding their personal patronage networks, they could also use the company to listen in on their opponent's phone conversations, to distribute CANTV jobs to clients, and, of course, to install multiple phone lines in their own homes. If you privatized the company, the phone system might start working, but the whole patron-client network it sustained would come crashing down.

A similar dynamic was in play in dozens of state institutions CAP wanted to sell off, streamline, or reform. Every ministry and university, every state owned enterprise and autonomous institute, every piece of the petrostate had a powerful set of AD *caciques* dead set against reform.

CAP's reform package would drive a dagger through the heart of the party's whole racket - not surprisingly the *caciques* mobilized furiously against the president they'd just helped to elect.

Soon, CAP found himself engulfed in a rising tide of unmanageable protest and dissent. Every scrap of reform met strong resistance in congress, where the caciques still had a majority. AD patrons exploited people's strong adherence to the petrostate cultural model to fuel resistance to reforms that would undermine their power bases. The IMF was predictably demonized, as was CAP for caving in to its demands.

Many Venezuelans were genuinely outraged at what they saw as an unacceptable onslaught on their petrostate perks. In the end, too many people were too dependent on the cash that flowed through the patron-client networks for reform to be viable – and those who stood to lose the most were particularly easy to mobilize politically, precisely because they were part of a pyramid that made political loyalty to your patron rule #1

From 27F to 4F

The straw that broke the camel's back was laid in the early days of CAP's second term as President. It came when the government cut back its fuel subsidies at the end February 1989. Public transport operators responded to a 10% increase in gas prices by doubling fares, and the shit hit the fan.

On February 27th, 1989, a group of far-left agitators in Guarenas, a Caracas suburb, staged a protest over the fare hikes that soon escalated into a riot. The disturbances spread quickly, first to Caracas itself and then throughout the country. For three days Venezuela went through an unprecedented spasm of rioting, arson, and widespread looting, met with a violent response from State security forces.

The police was helpless in the face of this sudden outburst of anarchy. Eventually, the government called out army troops with orders to shoot looters on sight. At least 600 people were shot dead in the next two days, but by some estimates the real toll was over a thousand. The bodies were dumped into mass graves - a practice Venezuela had not witnessed in many decades.

It was the end of Venezuela's age of innocence.

The effect the 1989 riots – known as the *Caracazo* - had on Venezuela's public life was in some ways analogous to 9/11 in the US, an event so deeply traumatizing it could be summoned just by its date: 27F. Until then, Venezuelans had seen themselves as different, more civilized, more democratic, *better* than their Latin American neighbors. Thirty-one years of unbroken, stable, petrostate-funded democracy had made us terribly cocky. In a sense, the riots marked Venezuela's re-entry into Latin America. The country was no longer exceptional: just another hard-up Latin American country struggling to put its democracy on a stable footing.

CAP's reform program was seriously hobbled by the riots, but it continued, at half-steam, for another 4 years.

Economically, it was a relative success – after a serious recession in 1989 that saw the economy contract by 10.9%, Venezuela experienced real economic growth for the first time since the 70s. Real per capita income was expanding steadily: 3.9% in 1990, 7.1% in '91, 3.6% in '92 - though, again this was helped by the spike in oil prices following Iraq's invasion of Kuwait.

Still, from a narrowly economic point of view, it seemed to be working.

But none of that mattered to the old-style patrons, the 10,000 little *caciques* heading up administrative fiefdoms large and small throughout the state. What they cared about was power, and CAP's program constituted too big a threat to their habitual way of getting it. From their perches in AD's National Executive Committee, in congress, in the courts, the nationalized companies and the labor movement, they were extraordinarily well placed to wreck the reform drive.

It was during the third year of this CAP vs. AD psychodrama that a certain army lieutenant colonel named Hugo Chávez first entered the public scene ... and he did so, literally, with a bang.

On February 4th, 1992, a group of junior officers launched a bloody coup attempt against the elected government. The crazy adventure – the first time someone had tried to overthrow a Venezuelan government by force of arms since the 60s – left about a hundred people dead, and earned its own instantly recognizable date-moniker: 4F.

The coup attempt failed, but it turned its leader into a kind of folk hero – the valiant paratrooper willing to put his life on the line to stop CAP's outrageous drive to dismantle the cherished petrostate, and a rare Venezuelan public figure willing to forthrightly accept responsibility for failure.

The coup-plotting lieutenant colonel went to jail, where he whiled away two years reading (but not understanding) Rousseau, Bolívar and Walt Whitman. In those two years, the government faced a second, even bloodier coup attempt by officers loosely associated with the first. Eventually, CAP was impeached by his fellow AD party members on flimsy charges, and after a brief interim government, the presidency passed to yet another petrostate dinosaur – Rafael Caldera, who had also been president already, but even further back than CAP, in 1969-1974.

Like CAP, Caldera ran as an old style populist. Unlike CAP, Caldera governed like one.

The return of the mummy

By the time he reached power for the second time, Rafael Caldera was over 80 years old. He'd spent 58 of those years in front-line politics. Frail, some would say decrepit, his voice tremulous and often barely audible, he wasn't exactly the kind of leader you'd turn to for bold new ideas. Caldera tried to patch up the old petrostate system – the only one he understood – as best he could.

Predictably, he failed.

Corruption continued unabated, cronyism as well, and much of the banking sector collapsed in 1994, wiping out the lifetime savings of thousands. The economy languished, and the nation's collective impoverishment continued afoot. Eventually, Caldera was persuaded of the need for some reform, including an important overhaul of the criminal system and of social security. But he didn't understand, much less share, the notion that the basic model of the state he had spent a lifetime championing needed a total overhaul.

If the petrostate was well past its sell-by date in 1989, by the end of Caldera's term in 1998 it was rotten to the core. Nobody doubted that the country needed a serious shake-up, a massive jolt to move beyond the stagnation and decay of the last 20 years.

Indeed, all three of the politicians who ever looked to have a serious shot at power that year were anti-establishment figures, people who'd built political careers outside the traditional party system.

The country faced a choice between a one-time Miss Universe turned centrist mayor of a wealthy district of Caracas (Irene Sáez) a Yale graduate and reformist governor from Carabobo State (Henrique Salas Römer), and the aforementioned leftist Lieutenant Colonel (who'd been pardoned by Caldera and released from prison in the interim.)

Disenchantment with the old party structures ran so deep that Copei didn't even bother to try to run a party insider as candidate. Instead, they tried to co-opt the beauty queen, who collapsed in the polls the second she accepted their nomination. As always, AD was the last to get the message: they nominated Luis Alfaro Ucero, a semi-literate 80 year-old *cacique*, a sort of *capo di tutti i capi* sitting at the pinnacle of the party's patronage structure. The guy never got beyond 7% in the polls. The vaunted adeco electoral machine had sputtered to a halt. Soon enough, it was all down to the governor and the coupster, and it was clear that the election would go to the one who best voiced the people's virulent rage at the ongoing failure of the petrostate.

And if *that's* the game you're playing, nobody but nobody beats Hugo Chávez.

From institutional clientelism to the Chavista cult of personality

The scene went down in the middle of one of his infamous, never-ending televised speeches in 2004. President Chávez had barely hit his stride when something caught his eye. His tone changed. Concerned, he looked up at the scaffolding above the stage he was using, where the lights for his speech hung.

"Hey, come down from there," he said in a soft, fatherly tone, "no, don't climb to the front, it's hot there because of the lights ... that's right, climb down towards the back. Don't worry; you'll get to talk to me. I want to hear your problem. I saw you crying earlier, just, just come down from the scaffolding and come up here."

Soon, a 15 year old kid has climbed down from the scaffolding and is walking towards the stage. He's crying. Chávez calls him up to the podium. With the camera's running, millions of people watching, Chávez takes him, hugs him hard and holds him for, oh, 45 seconds or a minute, while he the kid tells him, in between sobs, how his father recently died and his mother is sick and he can't afford the medicines to make her better...Chávez listens at length, pets his hair, assures him that he's going to help him.

The crowd is ecstatic, chanting "that, that, that's the way to govern!"

Welcome to the new era of chavista post-institutional clientelism. This sort of thing is typical of Chávez's governing style. The president works hard to make the entire audience feel how much he wants to help them all, personally, one by one. And he has succeeded brilliantly at selling the image of a president deeply, passionately, personally concerned with the problems of his supporters.

Obviously, this brand of clientelism is quite a different animal from the old *adeco* version. Just as obviously, it's still clientelism.

Chávez's peculiar contribution to the concept has been to cut out the middlemen. In the old system, each client's relationship was with the patron immediately above him. But the chavista patronage system only has two levels: the president and everyone else. These days, the relationships that underpin the system happen are televised; they are mediated rather than personal - the charismatic leader's bond with each of his followers is unique.

Chavistas are, in a sense, imagined clients.

Though Chávez has spent billions of dollars on emergency social programs that effectively re-distribute petro-dollars to his political supporters (the famous social programs called *misiones*) I'd argue that his success has almost as much to do with raw sentiment, with primary identifications. Many chavistas feel deeply, personally, almost mystically wedded to the president - the intensity of their emotions towards him are hard to overstate.

That's a departure from what we'd seen before. In the old system, the relationship between patrons and clients was basically a quid-pro-quo, a matter of mutual interest. Insofar as feelings played into it at all, they didn't go beyond a certain deference born of respect and fear of the boss. With Chávez, the bond comes from the heart. He is so charismatic, and his rhetoric is so powerful, that he makes people want to see him as a savior. They want to cry on his shoulders, they want to redeem themselves through him.

In other words, Chávez's bright idea for moving beyond the outdated system of vertical interpersonal relations is to replace it with a cult of personality.

It's bad news.

In the old system, the state had two fully independent institutions: AD and Copei. It's true, it's regrettable that there were only two real institutions around, that the courts and the elections authorities and the nationalized companies and every other part of the state was subjugated to one party or the other. But at least there were two of them!

To a certain extent, AD and Copei served to balance each other off. No truly transcendent decision could be made without at least a tacit agreement between the two.

Moreover, each of the two big parties was a complex institution in its own right. Their National Executive Committees were composed of factions that had to deliberate with one another to set the party's position on any given issue. Each faction would press the interests of a given constituency - the pro-business faction would haggle with the labor bureau to agree on the party's minimum wage policy and the peasant representatives would hash out the party's position on agricultural imports in talks with the technocrat wing. Each party had its own internal deliberative process. It was hardly a model of tocquevilian pluralism, granted, but at least some deliberation and interest-aggregation took place.

In the chavista state, there is only one institution: Hugo Chávez. Note that I'm not talking about an abstraction - about "the presidency of the republic" - I'm talking about a man. When an important policy decision has to be made, the only deliberations that matter take place between his ears.

All loyalties are directed at him personally. Supporters guide their gratitude for the *misiones* not at the State in some abstract sense, or to a patron they know personally, but at Chávez personally. With the president locked in a circle of relentlessly sycophantic collaborators, all dissent is equated with treason. So the one man who makes every relevant decision personally is never confronted with a view of the world that differs one iota from his own.

The post-institutional petrostate flattens the distinctions between state, government, party, presidency and president. The result is an accelerated decay in the state's institutional structure, to the point where no part of the state can act independently of Hugo Chávez personally.

Clearly, some aspects of the petrostate model have changed - everyone recognizes this. What I'd like to highlight, though, are the elements of continuity - elements that are often underestimated in commentary about Chávez. If the basic petrostate trick is to turn control of the state's oil dollars into control of the state, Chávez has merely brought the system up to date, yielding a petrostate for the 21st century.

Of course, Chávez thinks of himself as the pre-eminent critic of the post-1958 state. But his critique is based on ideas that have been at the heart of the petrostate's cultural model all along. Chávez certainly thinks he's rebuilding Venezuela's political and social structures from the ground up. But like so many self-described revolutionaries before him, he's blind to how much his vision has in common with the old regime.

The central conceit of the petrostate cultural model is the idea that the state can and should use its oil wealth to bankroll society. Rather than a critique of the petrostate as such, what Chávez provides is a critique of the way it went astray in the 1970s and 1980s, and particularly of "neoliberalism," understood here as CAP's attempts to dismantle it.

Chávez doesn't realize it, but that outlook places him squarely in the intellectual tradition pioneered by Romulo Betancourt more than 50 years ago. Ultimately, Chávez is just peddling a very old petrostate line - the old longing to fix the petrostate, to reform what cannot be reformed.

That longing has been the key to his political success. In beating the old petrostate drum, Chávez taps into a rich vein of Venezuelan culture. In the end, breaking the petrostate as social system is child's play compared to the monumental task of breaking the petrostate as an idea, as a collective understanding of what the state is for. And Chávez never challenged the dominant understanding on that score; he merely leveraged it to his own advantage.

The sharp spike in world oil prices since 2004 has given the petrostate a reprieve, but not a pardon. In a virtual re-run of the 1970s, a huge consumption boom is being financed with the extra money, along with a sharp spike in public sector debt. As the good times roll, Venezuelans have come to believe that Chávez made good on his promise. But it's a reprieve that will last only as long as oil prices hold. And if there's one thing we should've learned a long time ago it's that gambling your entire strategy on the hope that oil prices will never fall is a deeply foolish thing to do.

Towards a critical theory of chavismo
Posted on March 22, 2005 by Quico

Or ...

Very early attempt to build an account of chavismo on the basis of J.M. Briceño Guerrero's insights.

It is perhaps ironic that the most insightful book yet by a Venezuelan intellectual on the Chávez era was written years before Hugo Chávez rose to national prominence. J.M. Briceño's "The Labyrinth of the Three Minotaurs" presents itself as a critical theory of Latin American culture in historical perspective.

It is, however, much more than this. This is partly because the word "analysis" hardly does justice to Briceño Guerrero's sumptuous, poetic style, or to the playfulness of his intellect. This is also because Briceño Guerrero's prose, while drawing inspiration from such famously impenetrable French critical theorists as Derrida, Lacan and Foucault, has produced a curiously relevant, almost accessible text.

Critical theory will never be "light reading", but in Briceño Guerrero's hands, it can be a delight. Most impressively, in the two decades since its creation, The Labyrinth of the Three Minotaurs has gained, rather than lost, relevance – a contemporary reader will be startled again and again by the creeping sense that such analysis might well have been produced last week.

The challenge is to use Briceño Guerrero's insights as a springboard to a critical theory of chavismo, one that goes beyond the partisan posturing on either side and captures the historical specificity of the Chávez era.

Discourses at war

A starting point for a Briceño Guerrer-ista reading of the last six years is that chavismo is not a left-wing ideology. That does not mean that chavismo is a right-wing ideology. It means that the categories of left and right are ill-suited to capturing what has been happening in Venezuela since 1999. In fact, the tendency by chavistas and their opponents alike to place the experience of the last six years within familiar right vs. left terms obscures far more than it enlightens.

Briceño Guerrero interprets Latin American culture as a melding of three separate, mutually incompatible strains which, following Derrida, he refers to as "discourses." They are the Western Rationalist discourse, the Mantuano (or Hispanic colonial) discourse, and the Savage discourse.

The European rationalist discourse is "structured by instrumental reason" along with science and technology. It sees social change as driven by laws, rules, and science. It stands alongside a pre-modern European discourse, the Mantuano discourse, that owed directly to Spain's chivalric age, centered on a kind of medieval Catholicism that takes submission to hierarchy and the nobility of birth as its central values. At the other extreme, we have the salvage discourse, which emerges from the "wounds" from the conquest of pre-European cultures and the transfer of African cultures into the Americas. It is steeped in nostalgia for a non-Western way of life, and views the European rationalist discourse as foreign, strange, and representative of oppression.

For Briceño Guerrero, all of these are irreducibly incompatible, and each is eternally doomed to struggle fruitlessly for supremacy over the other two. As he explains, "it's easy to see that these three discourses penetrate one another, acting as parasites on each other, encumbering one another in a tragic combat where no victory is possible."

In Briceño Guerrero's view, both the left and the right are strains within the Western Rationalist discourse. They may be radically at odds with one another – surely they are – yet they share the same basic faith in reason, in rational analysis, as the key to understanding and changing social reality. Marx was not a savage, and neither was Adam Smith. They may disagree on almost everything, but they share a faith in instrumental rationalism as a privileged method for ascertaining reality.

Chavismo does not. Unlike both the traditional left and right, chavismo represents a rejection of western rationalism's claim to supremacy over the public sphere. In a fundamental way, chavismo cannot be placed on right-left axis without massively distorting both it and the axis. In fact, Chavismo not only falls outside that axis, it represents a rejection of the axis, a revolt of the epistemological order that sustains it.

All the way back in 1982, Briceño Guerrero had noted the "verbalist political impulse of the savage discourse." It's a devastating phrase. It gets, in just a few words, at the basic chavista determination to privilege words over reality. And by linking it to one of the deep strains in our culture, it explains not only why chavismo exists, but also why it succeeds.

Chávez's political appeal is based on the emotional bond his rhetoric creates with an audience that profoundly resents its historic marginalization. It works by echoing the deep undercurrent of rage on the part of the excluded, a rage Briceño Guerrero captures powerfully. Chávez's rhetoric is based on a deep, intuitive understanding of the un-western/anti-rational discourse in Venezuela's culture, a discourse that has been alternatively attacked, discounted and denied by generations of European-minded rulers. Chávez validates the savage discourse, reflects it, affirms it, and ultimately embodies it. He transmits to his audience a deep sense that the savage discourse can and should be something it has never been before: a discourse of power.

The magical power of words

In the Savage Discourse, Briceño Guerrero sets out a framework for understanding chavismo's otherwise baffling belief in the magical power of words, of words in isolation, that is, words abstracted from any point of contact with non-verbal reality, with anything outside discourse itself.

Looked at from a western rational point of view, this stance seems like mere superstition, if not lunacy. Because, in a sense, western rationalism is a method for ensuring that a reliable link is built between word and world. To reject this part of it is to reject the whole.

Yet this is precisely chavismo's trick. In front of a microphone, Chávez does not talk about reality, he creates it. You only start to understand the staggering, savage radicalism of chavismo when you begin to appreciate this dynamic. You only have to watch "Aló, Presidente" for 10 minutes or so to grasp this point.

But just to illustrate, consider a real world example of the chavista belief in the magic of words. There are dozens that would serve the purpose, but there's one that stands out, precisely because it drives the opposition positively batty.

Every year or so, with an expression of grave concern, President Chávez "discovers" that there's a terrible problem with unemployment in Venezuela. Every year, to much fanfare, he announces radical solutions to this problem. The employment plans he creates out of words vary in name, but not in nature. Each comes with a specific, wildly improbable, numerical target of jobs to be created. Each is announced with pride and revolutionary fervor. Each seems to consist of nothing beyond the announcement of its creation.

Twelve months later, this strange ritual repeats itself.

Now, the opposition can hardly contain its baffled anger at this game. It seems obvious to us that this is a giant scam. Not surprisingly, each year, at employment-plan-announcement time, opposition newspapers fill up with irate commentary about the rise in unemployment statistics. Bursting with principled outrage, pundits point out that nary a peep was heard about the previous year's employment plan at the announcement of the new one. They note the absence of follow-up, and they pour vitriol on the wildly unrealistic targets set.

A deep current of baffled exasperation runs through such commentary. The enlightened commentariat - the Roberto Giustis and Marta Colominas and Maxim Rosses and Teodoro Petkoffs of the world - work themselves up into a furious lather trying to force the government to establish some point of contact between the president's words and reality as it exists beyond his discourse.[8]

They insist on this. They cannot and will not countenance the possibility that, for Chávez as well as for his supporters, the announcement is its own justification.

The expression of will is reality enough, and no point of contact between it and the reality outside the discourse is needed. This is more than the opposition pundit-ocracy can handle. They cannot imagine, let alone understand, that millions of excluded Venezuelans actively want the nation's affairs to be run on the basis of a savage (non-western/anti-rational) discourse, that they crave leaders who adopt such a stance, and that they are thrilled to reward Chávez with their votes because, not despite, his rejection of rationalism, of the demand for word and world to match.

Western rationalism imagines itself to be the only valid basis of political action. Few in the opposition are willing to probe this belief, because it seems so foundational to them. Their commitment to a rationalist ethic has some costs, though, which have become increasingly obvious over time. It blinds them to the deep historical roots of the savage discourse, to its profound Venezuelan-ness, its staying power.

---

[8] Marta Colomina is a well-known Venezuelan journalist who sometimes takes shrill and, some would say, extreme positions against Chávez. Teodoro Petkoff is a former guerrilla fighter turned politician. He is the Editor-in-Chief of Caracas daily Tal Cual, and one of Quico's favorite public figures.

Armed with Briceño Guerrero's analysis, however, the verbal political impulse of chavismo can be placed within a framework of deeper cultural-historical meaning. Once you understand his framework, chavismo finds its place within the broad sweep of Latin American history. One comes to see that Chávez's political genius stems from his ability to intuit something Briceño Guerrero understands well and the opposition not at all: that the non-western/anti-rational Savage discourse is one of the fundamental building blocks of Venezuela's culture, and serves as the primary discourse for millions of poor Venezuelans.

Opposition blind spots

From a western rationalist point of view, the savage discourse looks basically like nonsense. For those schooled in the rationalist ethic, it's nearly impossible to shake this feeling, and its consequence, that nonsense must be seen very much as the ideological heart of the chavista project. That nonsense is the basis of its street credibility. That nonsense, Chávez's ideological commitment to nonsense, is the basis of his popular appeal, that chavismo cannot give up nonsense and remain chavismo.

And yet, that which looks like mere nonsense to the rationalist ethic constitutes the primary discourse for millions of Venezuelans, the basic spring-well of their identity, the heart of their understanding of Venezuelan-ness.

Briceño Guerrero's analysis helps make the rationalist reader aware of his own discursive blind spots, where they come from, why they are so hard to get around.

Consider this: how often have you heard an opposition supporter decry the fact that "none of this craziness was a problem before Chávez came to office?" How often have you seen the current government blamed for the entirety of the class resentment that now marks public life? For the sudden outbursts of anger and violence that mark the have become such a frightening aspect of public life? How often have you felt this was so?

And yet, all the anger, all that barely suppressed rejection of the west and its -isms, all that mindless *revanchismo*, all that barbaric rejection of rational ways of being and thinking, all that thirst for chaos, all that secret loathing for all that is thought and done, all that faith in magic ... all of it was out there a quarter of a century ago, visible enough to be analyzed with brilliant clarity. To his great credit, Dr. Briceño Guerrero saw it and understood it and wrote it up twenty years before it finally found its electoral vehicle in the megalomaniac from Sabaneta.

The problem is that the opposition's commitment to western rationalism prevents it, almost precludes it, from appreciating that the non-western/anti-rational aspects of chavismo are basic pillars of Venezuelans' identity.

There is a current of profound denial about the barbarous aspects of Venezuela's culture, of its people's culture, a panicked sense that to admit its existence is to surrender to it, a desperate will to suppress it. That denial is ongoing, and it is visible even now, even after six years with a non-western/anti-rational discourse entrenched in Miraflores Palace.[9]

Roberto Giusti cannot, will not accept it. Marta Colomina will go to her grave resisting it. Marcel Granier would stop being Marcel Granier if he could understand it. Much, much of the *sifrino* opposition is defined by its inability to grasp it. But it's true: resentment against privilege runs wide and deep among poor Venezuelans, and it expresses itself not just as a deep loathing for the privileged, but also as a guttural rejection of the rationalist discourse of privilege (and of the privileged.)

This rejection elevates nonsense into a cardinal political virtue. That is what Chávez knows and the rationalist opposition doesn't. That is why the last thing the opposition needs is "country consensus" plans prepared by technocrats and experts. And that is why he wins – and is likely to keep on winning.

---

[9] Miraflores Palace is the seat of government of the Presidency of Venezuela. It was built in the late XIXth Century.

The missing discourse

Absent from this discussion so far is the third part of Briceño Guerrero's overall framework: the Mantuano Discourse, inherited from colonial Spain, which "governs individual conduct and interpersonal relationships, as well as the sense of dignity, honor, grandeur and happiness." A medieval holdover conveyed to Latin America through colonization, the Mantuano discourse is the basis of the patron-client pattern of interpersonal relationships that serves as the basis for so much social interaction in Venezuela.

It's easy to see the influence of the Mantuano discourse in things like Chávez's plane, Danilo Anderson's jet-skis, Tobías Nobrega's crooked real estate deals, Francisco Carrasquero's familial clan-based recruiting, and the dozens of other seemingly counterrevolutionary outbreaks of corruption that persist within the purported revolution.

The staying power of the Mantuano discourse is startling. For 60 years after the death of Gómez, Venezuelan politicians spoke like rationalists and acted like Mantuanos – using the state's coffers the way elites always had, as a sort of petty cash box. This dissonance between discourse and behavior was one of the most jarring aspects of the pre-Chávez era. It served, in time, to build up the pervasive sense of disenchantment that eventually led to the election of Hugo Chávez.

Since 1999, the government has switched the discourse that governs public statements, jettisoning rationalism in favor of savagery. But in terms of behavior, startlingly little has changed. The sense of seigniorial entitlement over public monies remains, as does the willingness to set aside purported principles for the sake of clan-based material interests. The mantuano discourse remains. If you bracket the statements made by public officials and focus on official behavior, the last six years show surprising continuity with what came before.

And here, at last, comes a glimmer of hope. In time, Venezuelans got fed up with the evident distance between the elite's rationalist talk and its mantuano walk. In time, they could well get sick and tired of the gap between Chávez's savage talk and his government's mantuano walk.

This dissonance does not create a revolt right away, because the mantuano attitudes are deeply ingrained in all Venezuelans. Mantuano attitudes feel Venezuelan to most Venezuelans and, in a deep sense, they are. Moreover, due to the long history of dissonance between the old elite's talk and its walk, the opposition is in a very weak position to capitalize on the dissonance at the heart of chavismo. It just has very little credibility on the matter, a fact Chávez has brilliantly exploited with all his scare mongering about how the opposition only wants to turn back the clock.

It will take time to undo the damage – the damage Chávez has inflicted on rationalism, as well as the damage the rationalist opposition has inflicted on itself by systematically devaluing and attacking the discourse millions of Venezuelans primarily identify with. Even today, after six years, the opposition has yet to understand the deep cultural roots of Chávez's appeal, to see them as anything beyond a series of baffling outbursts of senselessness. Taking stock of such realities is never easy, but it is vital.

El otro carrao
Posted on September 26, 2007 by Quico

It's 11 a.m. on a dazzling Paris autumn day, and my favorite writer is telling me about his childhood in the Llanos during the Gómez dictatorship.

"I always wanted to learn how to cook. It really fascinated me, cooking. Knitting too…needle work in general. I would tell my mother to teach me, but as you can imagine, in those days, well, it was just out of the question. 'That's women's work,' she would tell me, 'you're supposed to be out on horseback, carrying a gun, getting into machete fights.' Imagine, that's what was expected of boys back then!"

It was with a mix of trepidation and bravado that I'd gone out to meet José Manuel Briceño Guerrero at his daughter's apartment in this immigrant-heavy corner of the 20eme Arrondissement, on a street named – impossible to omit this bit – Rue Lesage. He'd emailed me to say he would be spending a bit of his summer vacation there and, well, it's just a 3 hour train ride from Maastricht, so …

As I made my way there, I was terribly self-conscious of how little I really knew about the man. A journalist would get fired for turning up to an assignment this unprepared. But what can I say? There just isn't that much about him online. Worse, I've only read a couple of his books, and both of which were written decades ago. (As for the newer ones, I simply have no idea how to get them in Europe.)

The reason I felt I had to meet him was his 1981 magnum opus, The Labyrinth of the Three Minotaurs.

It's a book that shook me to the core. It split my understanding of my culture into two periods: before and after reading it. I've developed a deeply personal relationship with the book, coming to see it as a kind of road map to my own identity, a Rosetta stone capable of decoding the Venezuelan psyche. And now, here I am, clutching a glass of orange juice and sitting across from its author as he paints a portrait in words of his impossibly unlikely origins.

"This was all out in Apure," he goes on, "in a really tiny village called *Palmarito*. My mother was from there. My dad was an *andino*, from Trujillo. Gómez had sent him out there as part of his drive to 'pacify the plains.'[10] He was Civil Chief of the village then, and well, he met my mother there so that's where I was born. They wouldn't let me cook, or knit, but it was clear enough all along that I wasn't cut out to be out fighting other boys with machetes or carrying guns on horseback. The one place where I felt comfortable and where they didn't mind me spending time was my father's library. My father was a big reader, you see: he had a lot of books, so I spent my childhood surrounded by them. I loved it, really, and I've always treasured those memories.

---

[10] Juan Vicente Gómez was a brutal dictator that ruled Venezuela between 1908 and 1935.

"But it's also true that I got pigeonholed as the bookish one from very early on. In a way, I wish I'd learned more practical things. If somebody had to run an errand around the house, I was always excused because, you know, '*José Manuel está estudiando.*' So I was never the one they sent out and round up the cows, or to ride to the pharmacy or whatever. 'Studying.' That was my role. I loved it, but at the same time, well, there's so much I never learned how to do."

I chuckle at this. Venezuela's leading classicist rues not being a better cook. A man who has memorized most of The Iliad, deep down, only wishes he'd been taught to crochet.

"It was another world back then, really. I always lived in small places in the Llanos, and it was only much later I first visited a city. Until I was a teenager, I'd never seen an automobile, or a telephone, even. We just didn't have them out there. But I never felt deprived because for not having those things. On the contrary, I see kids these days tapping away on cell phone keyboards and I always feel a little sad for them. I didn't have any of that, but I never felt that as a deprivation, because I had something else, something they don't have: time."

"Many years later I went back to Palmarito. They'd called saying they wanted to have a little ceremony to honor me as an Illustrious Son of the town. I went out there and the mayor welcomed me, but then apologized profusely, saying he felt terrible that they couldn't name the one street in town after me. He explained that, unfortunately, they'd already named it, and you know after whom? After <u>El Carrao de Palmarito,</u> you know, that folk singer? Picture that, he's also from there, and he'd already had the only street in town named after him! He was there that day, I even met him, and he stepped in to tell the mayor there was no problem, that they could name one side of the street after him and the other side after me!"

It's a good story, and suddenly I feel ridiculous remembering how hard it had been to work up the gumption to contact him. I'm not the easily intellectually-intimidated type, but the idea of meeting Briceño Guerrero had filled me with dread for years.

I had been expecting…well, I don't know what, exactly. Not this certainly. Not folksy charm. His books had dripped with erudition, even his emails were liberally sprinkled with *latinazos*: nothing about his work was straightforward, everything about it was challenging, difficult. So I'd been expecting … well, a difficult man I suppose.

But here he was, bantering and cracking jokes: as easy-going and avuncular as could be.

As our conversation hit its stride, as we both overcame that initial period of reticence, I realized that his prodigious talent is no longer news to him, that he long ago stopped trying to impress it on people. However complex his oeuvre may be, however daring and iconoclastic his thought, the man himself struck me as the last thing you might expect. Deep down, he is a simple man.

"It was always the ancients that drew me," he says, when I ask him how a boy from Palmarito ended up leading a life like his. "I really loved studying Greek and Latin – and later Hebrew – and I've always loved teaching them. I've been blessed with generation after generation of great students in Mérida. It's really the most rewarding thing I've done, teaching them. So, by now I've been eligible to retire from the Universidad de Los Andes for the last 26 years, but no way, I'm not going to stop. I love this work."

A kind of mischievous grin flashes through his face. Down to the outlandish personal appearance he's crafted, Briceño Guerrero clearly relishes the anachronistic-misfit-intellectual niche he's carved out for himself. Nobody but nobody in Venezuelan academia keeps working for a quarter of a century past retirement age. This is not normal behavior. Obviously, though, he couldn't care less.

It doesn't take you long to realize what underpins his achievements is simply a prodigious, photographic memory. It's an attribute that has yet to fail him. "Somebody once asked me what book I would take with me to a desert island, and I told him 'none': the books I love I have right here," he says, tapping his forehead.

I found our meeting impossibly entertaining, but slightly awkward as well. The books that made me an instant groupie – his cultural analysis of what he calls "the Latin American failure" – are books he wrote a very long time ago indeed. It soon becomes clear that, for most of the time I've been alive, his attention has been decisively elsewhere: on poetry, on philosophy and on the classics. At times, when I try to steer the conversation towards social topics, I have the odd feeling that his writing from the 60s and 70s is considerably fresher on my mind than it is on his. I find myself laying out arguments for him that I plainly just picked out of his books.

It's not that he's forgotten them; it's that, these days – as he's the first to admit – his feelings about politics are something like a considered boredom, an annoyance at how superficial our political debates are. He accuses Chávez of "emotional vampirism" – of monopolizing the nation's attention, its emotive energy, to such an extent that he makes it nearly impossible to take a step back and consider the country's problems at a deeper level.

"Not that that's new: I remember, in previous decades, how the debates between Marxists and non-Marxists at ULA,[11] or between Adecos and Copeyanos, were similar in many ways: terribly shallow, and centered on the sense of belonging to a group more than on a genuine give-and-take of ideas."[12]

"At ULA, the faculty, which was always mostly Marxist, didn't know what to make of me at all. All they noticed is that I wasn't a Marxist and, as far as they could tell, that could only mean I was a reactionary. Personally, I never had any interest in these kinds of debates – which I always found basically sterile. My instinct, faced with confrontation, has always been to withdraw … and it still is."

---

[11] The Universidad de los Andes, in Mérida, is one of Venezuela's premier universities.

[12] AD and Copei were the two primary political parties in Venezuela during the second half of the twentieth century. People who belonged to them, or voted for them, were typically known as "adecos" and "copeyanos."

I tell him one of my blog readers (here's lookin' at you, Escualidus Arrechus) had commented recently that the measure of how screwed up our public debate is lies in the fact that the opposition would accept 80% of what Chávez says if an opposition spokesman had said it, and that most of what the opposition argues chavistas would accept if it came from their guy.

He stops, delighted with the thought, and instructs me: "please, send that reader my congratulations: I've often had that sense myself, and he managed to express it very well, very succinctly."

For all his writing on the Latin American failure, he still seems genuinely mystified about why it is that our public discourse can't seem to get out of the rut, generation after generation after generation. He looks me earnestly, right in the eye, and asks "*¿por qué será, chico?*"

And then he remembers the famous quote from Guzmán Blanco, when he was asked why he had become a conservative, and replied "we called ourselves conservatives because we saw that the others called themselves liberals. But if they had called themselves conservatives, then we would have called ourselves liberals."

"It's been over 100 years," he notes, "and that's still where we are. You have to be on one side or the other."

Against this backdrop, it's not surprising that Briceño Guerrero chose to turn his talents to other fields. Literature, and especially poetry, is what really gets his juices flowing these days. To read the ancient masters, he taught himself first ancient Greek and Latin, then Hebrew and finally, within the last couple of years, classical Chinese.

He mentions this last morsel all casual like, as though learning classical Chinese from scratch was a perfectly reasonable hobby for a septuagenarian, like canasta. I find it simply staggering. "But, but, but... why?!" I stammer, groping toward a suitably euphemistic way of hinting at the obvious: that he's far too old for that sort of thing.

"Why? The Tang Dynasty poets!" he says, "the verses they wrote are all tremendously beautiful! It's like no other kind of poetry I've encountered. I was hooked instantly. Actually I spent half of last year in China, learning the classical language. I've only learned about 1,500 characters at this point. It's a slow process: you have to learn a character and forget it and learn it again many times before it finally sticks. But even now I've managed to translate a few poems, and my Chinese teachers liked them very much."

As our meeting draws to an end I realize that, if anything, my intellectual infatuation has only grown. As I get ready to part, I feel this instinctive need to ask him for guidance, for counsel, this drive to get him to tell me what is and what is not worth doing with one's life.

"The challenge in Venezuela," he says "has always been the same: to find the space needed to reflect on a deeper level. The petty, little day-to-day quarrel in the front page of the newspapers always draws all the attention, all the energy. And these days it's worse than ever. The *pleitico* sucks away all the intellectual oxygen it takes to look deeper. But if you can find a small group of, I don't know, five or six young researchers, people competent enough and smart enough to think independently, with their own heads, and to look past the day-to-day quarrel at the forces that lay beneath the surface and drive the changes in our country...that, Francisco, is worth doing."

The forgotten trailblazer
Posted on July 22, 2008 by Juan Cristobal

Take a look at a picture of XIXth Century Venezuelan Presidents and you will be hard pressed to identify more than a handful. Few of us would be able to identify Venezuela's first popularly elected president, Manuel Felipe de Tovar.

No reason to feel bad. I had no idea who he was either until pretty recently, when I picked up a copy of Rafael Arráiz Lucca's "*Venezuela: 1830 a nuestros días.*" The book is a compendium of the major historical events of our history as a free nation, almost by necessity broad in scope and yet shallow in the treatment of most topics. It was perfect for me.

I picked it up half embarrassed, realizing the last time I put any sustained effort into learning Venezuelan history, I was a stonewashed Maracaibo teenager. Reading the book, it was remarkable how some things seemed as familiar as daylight. But I also stumbled on a few surprises.

Case in point: the man in the aforementioned picture. Manuel Felipe de Tovar was the true precursor of Venezuelan democracy, but he's now almost completely forgotten. Here's what Arráiz has to say about him:

"In accordance with the Constitution passed in 1858, elections were held in April of 1860, and the winner was Manuel Felipe de Tovar, with 35,010 votes, for the 1860-1864 constitutional period. No immediate reelection was allowed. Pedro Gual was elected Vice-president for two years, with 26,269 votes... For the first time, Venezuelans directly elected their leaders, and they did so in the midst of a cruel war that had already cost thousands of lives and was sowing the country with misery and desolation."

It's strange. Somehow my brain had assimilated the notion that we had to wait until 1948 to elect a President for the first time, a certain Romulo Gallegos. Could I have been wrong all along? Was I simply the victim of my own ignorance, or was this all an *adeco* fairy-tale, further proof of their penchant for rewriting history? Could it be that Arráiz got it wrong?

No, it's true, Tovar was the first. Sure, he was elected on the basis of a limited franchise, but then, so was Jefferson. Even the Chávez government acknowledges he was the first, which is strange since Tovar was elected as a Paecista, and we know how much Chávez loathes José Antonio Páez. (Recent reports suggest the government even desecrated Paez's grave.) [13]

I wonder how Tovar's achievement was received in Venezuela's mid-XIXth Century political circles. Being an elected, civilian President in Venezuela in those days had to be quite a handful, calling for equal measures of luck, naiveté and chutzpah. Tovar must have been a dreamer of gargantuan proportions to think he could pull it off.

Elected in the middle of a notoriously cruel civil war, Tovar faced serious military and economic challenges from day one. The government was bankrupt, so he instituted our first income tax. He freed up imports of scarce agricultural products and froze the salaries of government employees. He pardoned some political prisoners while waging war against guerrilla-style militias determined to overthrow him. The complaints about the civilian Constitution not being strong enough to deal with the rising insurgency grew louder by the day, and they eventually paved the way for the subsequent Páez dictatorship that ended Tovar's stint after only 13 months in power.

I'm no expert on Venezuelan history. I'm just a guy who read a book. But in the midst of the turbulence of the country's early years, I found a lot that's familiar.

To understand Venezuela's beginnings as a country, it's important to ponder the nature of those in charge at the time. The War of Independence was a traumatic military event. Contrary to popular myth, it was not won by a unified army with a clear line of command. Instead, it was waged and won by a semi-coordinated bunch of militias composed mostly of illiterate peasants, each led by its own caudillo. With rare exceptions, when I say "caudillo" I mean warlord.

---

[13] José Antonio Páez was a leading general of the Revolutionary War. After Venezuela broke off from Colombia in the 1820s, he became our nation's first caudillo, or strongman. He is seen by some as an antagonist to Bolívar, particularly in the latter's later years.

Immediately following the war, the caudillos and their followers found they had to submit to a government in faraway Bogotá headed by an unelected President-for-life, who went to war in Peru and left in his place an unpleasant *cachaco* named Santander. Naturally, the Venezuelans pushed to break away from Colombia. After all, they'd had to cross the Andes to go free Colombians, Peruvians and the like; it's not surprising they felt they were getting the short end of the stick having to bow to a bunch of Bogotá snobs.

In spite of their disparate interests and personalities, they joined together and fought the common cause of secession. One of the movements they started was called "La Cosiata", a derisive neologism for a group not unlike the recent *Coordinadora Democrática*.[14]

Emboldened by their hard-won military victories, and drunk from the success in achieving secession from "Gran Colombia", it's no wonder chaos ensued. During the first thirty years of our existence, Venezuela endured one failed government after another. Constitutions came and went, as did the military coups. The only intermittent periods of relative calm came when Páez reluctantly made himself dictator and managed to quiet things down a bit. When circumstances allowed, he would retreat to either his farms in the Llanos or to New York, where he eventually died.

So the nation was built by a hodgepodge of ambitious farmers-turned-generals looking to get rich quick, men who felt entitled to the spoils of war, perhaps understandably after risking their lives and their lands for the patriotic cause. Against that backdrop, it's not surprising that the few attempts to establish civilian rule, institutions and a functioning state were utter failures. But they did exist.

The early history of the republic is dominated by all things military, while the exceptions such as the civil-minded Tovar or José María Vargas lie half-forgotten in the dustbin of history. It's no

---

[14] In the first half of the 2000s, the Coordinadora Democrática was created as the opposition's first attempt at a united coalition. It did not work out and dismembered after a few years.

surprise that Tovar himself was buried in a random Paris cemetery instead of in our National Pantheon, and that instead of celebrating him in plazas or streets, we are quickly running out of boondoggles to name after psychopath-murderers-cum-half-failed caudillos.

But are we doomed to keep repeating that history again and again? Will bloggers 60 years from now be surprised to dust off a history book that informs them that Hugo Chávez was not the first popularly elected president, like their schoolteachers said?

Not at all. Because the remarkable thing about men like Vargas and Tovar is not that they failed, but that they ever had a shot. They saw disorder, yet they were bold enough to dream of a different country. That's as much a part of our heritage as the caudillo strain.

Fast-forward 180 years and picture yourself in 2013. Suppose for a minute that Chávez leaves power.

After wiping the smile off your face, think of all the people, all the groups that are going to feel entitled to the spoils of victory: businessmen, students, politicians, unions, ex-PDVSA folk, and the Plaza Altamira gang. Think of the effort it's going to take to keep everyone's interests at bay and put the nation's interests first.

It would be easy to picture this and conclude, as many swing voters do, that while Chávez may be bad, the opposition is worse. It's only natural for our fears to be confirmed by the intense tussling the opposition is currently embarked on. Is it any wonder, then, that Chávez plays on this fear with slogans like "No volverán"?

But the apparent anarchy in the opposition is not always real, nor does it necessarily imply that we are doomed to fail. Against Chavismo's ambition to "get Bolivar's dream right", maybe we should oppose a decidedly more modest goal: vindicating Tovar. The civilian current he pioneered is just as Venezuelan as *caudillismo*, and much, much more relevant in today's world. We are Doña Bárbara, but we are also Santos Luzardo.[15]

---

[15] Doña Bárbara, by Rómulo Gallegos, is widely regarded as the quintessential Venezuelan novel. It pits the struggles between civilization and barbarism, deep in the Venezuelan llanos. The character of Santos Luzardo represents the civilized world, while Doña Bárbara represents barbarism.

It's useful to keep this in mind next time we see the opposition behaving like a sack of cats with no clear goals in sight. It takes a lot of effort to be organized when *bochinche* is embedded in our DNA.[16] The thing to remember is that it's not just bochinche that's in there: the determination to do away with caudillos and bring the country together behind an elected civilian on the basis of the law is just as embedded in us, just as Venezuelan. This is why we should celebrate whenever civilians manage to talk out their differences and bring us closer to realizing that vision.

So next time you feel a vein is about to burst at the sight of Saady Bijani or other opposition losers, spare a thought for Manuel Felipe de Tovar, a man who, irony of ironies, took the oath of office one April the 12th. And if you dare to dream that yes, we can overcome our history, take comfort in the fact that greater Venezuelans have harbored the same dream when facing even longer odds than us.

The looking glass revolution
Posted on March 31, 2008 by Quico

For such a familiar object, there's something quite bizarre about a mirror, that strange device that seems to represent reality "as it really is" while quietly reversing it, making your right side your left side and your left side your right. The effect is at once familiar and, when you think about it, weirdly counterintuitive … not unlike the profoundly mystifying political contraption that now rules Venezuela by subtly, almost imperceptibly, turning left into right and right into left all the while leaving everything precisely as it was.

The Maisto Doctrine that governed US attitudes toward Venezuela until recently ("watch what he does, not what he says") makes for a good starting point as we try to understand the deep conceptual reversal chavismo operates. It primes us for the

---

[16] "Bochinche" roughly translates into "ruckus."

realization that, when it comes to chavismo, the discursive and the factual have a troubling propensity to diverge.

Back in 1999, nobody could have guessed the bizarre extremes this divergence would reach. Today, the "what he does" and the "what he says" are not merely "in tension with one another" but, rather, diametrical opposites, with the discursive rushing headlong to the left while the factual gallops triumphantly rightward.

In today's Venezuela, that split *is* the story. The smooth cohabitation between a radical left-wing discourse and a basically regressive policy posture based on *de facto* trickle-down economics is the essence of what chavismo has become.

On a discursive level – but *only* on a discursive level – chavismo really does fall squarely into the tradition of leftist totalitarianism. There's really no other word for it. The revolution's discourse is proudly, self-consciously totalizing. Chávez proposes a highly simplified explanation for the whole of social experience, the whole of political life and the whole of Latin America's history. At its core is a totalizing dualism, a clean split between pure Good (a conceptual nexus you could characterize as Chávez - emancipation - socialism - left- pueblo - solidarity - revolution) and pure Evil (Bush - empire - capitalism - right - oligarchy - greed - reaction).

What rounds out chavismo's discursive totalitarianism is that this uncompromising dualism is coupled to a Redemption Narrative, the mythic story line of the revolution, which systematizes and explains our historical experience by subsuming all events under the totalizing categories of Good and Evil.

The story is short and simple enough to summarize in just one sentence: Bolivar had a dream that was cruelly betrayed by the *mantuano* elite and lay dormant in the hearts of the *pueblo* for a long time until it re-awakened on February 27th, 1989, and was instantiated and tempered by the joint heroism of Chávez and the *pueblo* in a series of heroic trials - the coups of 1992 and 2002, the oil strike, and the ongoing imperialist-*mantuano* aggressions against the revolution.[17]

Every episode in this history is expressed in terms of a struggle of good vs. evil, and every day-to-day development is similarly characterized. Whether it's the Battle of Carabobo or the Milk Shortage, the toppling of Arbenz or a dengue outbreak in Carora, when bad things happen, evil is to blame, and when the opposite happens, good deserves the credit. Nothing escapes the totalizing perspective of chavista Manichaeism.

The State, with its growing communicative might, has been fully mobilized to support this World View. The most striking feature of Venezuelan television these days is the simultaneous proliferation of official media outlets and their soul-crushing repetitiveness. Chávez's discursive totalitarianism is now hawked aggressively, around the clock, in a whole bunch of new radio stations and TV channels, from VIVE to TVES to ANTV to Telesur to a bunch of smaller, regional channels.[18]

The station logos and anchor people are different, the typeface on the screen graphics is different, but the content itself amounts to a virtual, never-ending *cadena*. It's the same stuff, the same endless variations on the very simple themes, repeated *ad nauseam*. Watch this stuff for just a couple of hours and you can tell exactly the way each story, each agit-prop video, and each 30-second spot is going to go from the second it comes on screen.

There's a mind-deadening predictability to it. You can *taste* the producers' fear of breaking the script. Little by little, the essential, tutelage-d sameness overwhelms you until you either switch off or turn into a zombie. Nothing surprising ever happens on state TV, and won't, no matter how many new channels they air. Nothing

---

[17] "Mantuano" is a term used to describe the governing XIXth Century elites, whose fortune was made on the backs of holding large swathes of arable land. The term comes from the elegant veils, or "mantos," that elite women used to wear back then.

[18] Since this post was published, a number of previously private radio stations have joined the ranks of hawkers of government propaganda.

even remotely like a real debate, a non-choreographed exchange of views or a contrarian perspective has the faintest chance of being heard.

So we really do have all the characteristics of leftist totalitarian communications here: the dualism, the unthinking sameness, the siege mentality, the systematic demonization of opponents, the none-too-subtle denunciation of dissidents as enemies of the state and, above all, the repetition, the dreary, obdurate repetition, the drip-drip-drip of the *same* messages packaged and repackaged *again and again and again,* at *every* chance and on *every* space available.

Venezuela is witnessing every element of a communicative practice that, in other times and other places, has typically gone hand in hand with the massive use of state violence to intimidate, marginalize and, ultimately, physically eliminate dissidents.

And yet ... where are the concentration camps? The secret police torture rooms? The death marches? Where is the reality to back up all that talk? It just isn't there, and nine years into all of this, I really don't think they are coming.

When Stalin and Hitler and Pol Pot and the Interahamwe mobilized the state media to systematically demonize their opponents, the real world cost of those discursive practices was measured in millions of lives. When Chávez does it, the cost is measured in tons of bullshit, because in his hands the discursive somehow never quite bleeds through to the factual.

It's when we come to understand the dynamics of the political economy of chavismo, the real channels through which money and influence flow through society in the Chávez era that we start to grasp the scale of the disconnect between the world of meanings state TV creates and the orgy of clientelist rent-seeking the real revolution has slowly morphed into.

Again, it pays to think Maisto here. What would the revolution look like if we watched it "on mute," as it were: tuning out the discourse entirely and focusing exclusively on the way money, power and influence flows through society. What would we see then?

Well, we'd see a tiny elite, well connected to the centers of state decision-making that control petrodollar flows, exploiting its access to grow enormously rich and live extravagant lifestyles.

We'd see a much broader middle class benefiting handsomely from petrostate largesse in the form of deeply subsidized travel, imports, internet transactions and energy.

We'd notice that the truly weighty macroeconomic policies, the ones that move sums large enough to alter the overall distribution of national income, channel resources resolutely up the economic scale.

And we'd see some mass based social programs that are unsustainable, lack systematic evaluation mechanisms and are funded mostly in the run-up to elections and designed to benefit only politically docile clients, such that their portion of oil rents becomes the price they're paid for their votes.

What we'd see, in other words, is the political economy of *puntofijismo* petrostate clientelism, plain and simple.[19]

Discourse and reality are moving in opposite directions along parallel plains, never touching, never penetrating one another, and never encumbering each other in their onward march. They are as estranged as if they belonged to radically different realities rather than to a single country.

What explains this impermeability? To my mind, it's the totalitarian features of the state discourse itself that ensures that no aspect of "real" reality can ever bubble up through into the revolution's discursive awareness. Having committed completely to a discourse that automatically dismisses any critical thought as "media terrorism" or "CIA psy ops" geared at planting destabilizing "opinion matrixes", Chávez supporters effectively ban

---

[19] "Puntofijismo" refers to the political pact between the largest political parties which laid the groundwork for democracy in the late 1950s. It is usually blamed by Chávez and his acolytes as an elitist, undemocratic, imperialistic, exclusionary agreement. It is frequently held up as a symbol of what the chavista movement aspires not to be.

themselves from engaging critically with the mass of contradictions the revolution daily generates.

The revolution can't "see" the connections between the issue of Notas Estructuradas and Victor Vargas's lifestyle.[20] It can't join the dots from the operation of Cadivi to the transfer of wealth from the State to the wealthy.[21] It never notices any of these and a thousand similar anomalies because such matters are systematically blacked out from State media because the lament they carry, their implicit political message, is embarrassing to the government and therefore, *a priori*, deemed suspicious, likely part of some gringo plot to undermine the regime, of some ploy by absolute Evil to undermine absolute Good.

The cronies at the top of the *bolibourgeois* game understand this dynamic plenty clearly enough and manipulate it to their advantage, tarring anyone who seeks to hold them up to public scrutiny as agents of Evil, deploying the revolution's deeply warped discursive standards to protect their particular positions in the rent seeking game.

Locked in this watertight discursive bubble, unable to distinguish truth from fantasy any longer, the revolution has destroyed its own ability to process reality reasonably and fatally undermined its own capacity to integrate "what it says" with "what it does", to harmonize the two, or at least ensure a minimum of coherence between them.

As far as I know, there really is no precedent for what we're seeing here. Some people compare it to the Mexican PRI's brand of rhetorically incandescent clientelism but, as far as I know, no Mexican government ever approached the extremes of discursive

---

[20] The Notas Estructuradas were a scam involving government bonds that were sold to chavista cronies. Victor Vargas is the president of BOD, one of the fastest growing private banks in the Chávez era, and one of the main purchasers of Notas Estructuradas.

[21] Cadivi is the government office in charge of doling out cheap dollars to private companies, travelers, cronies, and anyone else who qualifies. The current exchange rate at which it sells is BsF. 4.3. The black market rate for the greenback is roughly BsF. 15.

totalitarianism we're seeing here. Because what we're witnessing is no garden-variety political hypocrisy, no run-of-the-mill opportunism. What we're seeing is a kind of political schizophrenia, an incapacity to integrate what is said with what is done that strikes me as closer to a mental illness than to a political ideology.

The paradoxes that this divorce engenders are almost endless. The government we have is passionately hated by the people it benefits the most, and passionately upheld by many it treats as an afterthought. Its preponderant social policies and its costliest, most far reaching and radical redistributive policies (the gas and foreign exchange subsidies) are unarguably regressive, redistributing income from its supporters to its detractors, and are almost never discussed by the official media.

Like a looking glass, the revolution has made the right into the left and the left into the right, but the effect is so subtle and the outcome come to seem so "normal" we don't quite spot it, can't quite process it, and we can't quite see just how bizarre it all is. After all, what could be more normal than a mirror?

Twenty one years ago yesterday
Posted on February 27, 2010 by Quico

As we reach the final of February's three unavoidable political anniversaries, here's a question you seldom hear raised: what was Venezuela like on February 26th, 1989?

Well, let's see. We had an economy that had stagnated for years, reversing most of the gains achieved from 1958 to 1980. The economy lumbered under massive microeconomic distortions created by an arbitrageur's wet-dream of a policy-mix: with a multiple exchange rate regime operating alongside complex price controls and selective trade protection that benefited mostly the politically connected. The whole package was administered by a massively bloated public sector more concerned with its own prerogatives than with serving the needs of the population. And we had a popular, newly elected president who had recently announced a far-reaching program to try to confront this situation.

By the following day, the country had gone over the edge.

That the orgy of anarchic looting that spread from city to city over the following days has been retroactively fitted out as a popular revolt against neoliberalism must count as chavismo's founding fib.

It's easy to forget – and, indeed, largely forgotten – that at the time the riots started, the reform program announced by Carlos Andrés Pérez hadn't been implemented yet. Aside from a rather meek hike in deeply subsidized gasoline prices, by February 26th, 1989, the *paquetazo* was little more than an announcement.

When the looting started, trade had not been liberalized, none of the hundreds upon hundreds of loss-making State-owned enterprises had been privatized, no public services had been cut, food and other essential items' prices had not risen, health and education spending had not been cut...in fact, none of the standard repertoire of left-wing bogeymen policies had been enacted at that point, save for the gasoline price hikes.

The whole story-line of 27-F as revolt-against-neoliberalism is ahistorical and silly. Unless you credit the population with preternatural powers of foresight and posit that they were somehow rioting pre-emptively, in protest against what they calculated would be the future consequences of policies announced but not-yet enacted, you have to agree that the 27-F riots were the result of mass discontent caused by the problems that CAP's reform package was seeking to solve, not by the solutions CAP had proposed for dealing with them.

Which is ideological heresy for chavismo in more ways than one, because the widespread social misery resulting from economic stagnation brought about by the layers upon layers of distortions arising from an ever more cumbersome set of economic and administrative controls enforced by an increasingly bloated, inefficient, bureaucratic state that crowds out private investment and entrepreneurship as it devotes more and more of its scarce resources to plugging the financial shortfalls generated by an ever increasing list of loss-making SOEs whose lips are virtually welded to the petro-rent teat ... well, that describes Venezuela today just as well as it described it on February 26th, 1989.

II

The daily contradictions of life in Venezuela

A blog provides the space to talk about things the mainstream media misses. A blog written from afar provides the distance one needs to ponder daily events. It helps us compare them to how they are elsewhere, to how they should be in an ideal world.

Whether it is standing in line to get a Venezuelan driver's license, visiting a school in a slum, or going to a fancy wedding, the stories about the real Venezuela are right there, waiting to be written about.

Most of these stories are not a direct by-product of chavista foolishness, although some undoubtedly are. But inasmuch as chavismo is itself a consequence of our Venezuelan-ness – could Hugo Chávez have possibly happened anywhere else? – in the end, the study of Hugo Chávez is a study of Venezuelan culture. After all, one could argue Chávez's inability to impose his authoritarian views completely is a direct result of our own propensity to chaos, incivility, conformity, and fun.

Don't mess with my nuggets!
Posted on June 29, 2007 by Juan Cristobal

"Our first speaker today is Dr. Eva Golinger, who will lecture us about the ills of neoliberalism."

Imagine being in a conference room and hearing those words.

Listening to a talk by "the bride of the revolution", the unabashedly fanatical Chavista apologist Golinger, was going to be a serious test of my tolerance.[22] Luckily, Eva's presence did not materialize, but it did not make my experience any less painful.

See, I spent much of Monday sitting in a well-lit, air conditioned conference room overlooking the Caracas valley, surrounded by video screens and state-of-the-art sound equipment, watching the Gulf Streams of the revolution's kleptocrats land in the middle of this traffic-congested city.

The purpose? I wanted to get a first-hand experience of the revolution's indoctrination and the effect it is causing. Yet painful as it was, what I learned was surprising and I was happy Quico practically forced me to go.

The story began the previous week with an email from my old friend Roger. Roger works for a government institute affiliated with the Venezuelan Navy. After finishing his studies abroad, Roger applied for this job and got it by virtue of his excellent qualifications and, most of all, because he never signed any petition against President Chávez.

Roger asked me last week if I wanted to tag along to this event. It was called "The Third Engine of the Revolution: Morals and Enlightenment."[23] It consisted of a seminar on socialist

---

[22] Eva Golinger is a Venezuelan-American attorney who has become very adept at defending the Revolution in international forums. Her most well-known contribution to this task is a book, The Chávez Code, unread by me, which aims to show how the U.S. was involved in the coup against Chávez.

[23] In Spanish, "Moral y Luces", part of a famous quote of Simon Bolivar's, identifying them as the country's primary necessities.

indoctrination held by the government - at taxpayer expense, of course.

Attendance was mandatory for the entire office. Roger's bosses made sure the building where they work was locked up, lest anyone think of going to the office for work instead. Not knowing what to expect, I decided to tag along.

The event was held at UNEFA, formerly PDVSA of Chuao.[24] UNEFA stands for the National Experimental University of the Armed Forces, and by the look of it, it is a regular university with regular civilian students, only here all students have to wear a uniform with the seal of the university. Thankfully the uniform is white and blue, not red, but I was still impressed with the sui generis ways of chavista universities. Can you imagine the reaction of US students at, say, Berkeley, if they were forced to wear a uniform to class?

The crowd included hundreds of employees from Roger's office, from the maintenance staff to uniformed naval officers. The head captains of each and every Venezuelan port were seated in the first few rows, having flown to Caracas especially for the occasion - I had to wonder who was minding our ports if all the port captains were here.

The first talk was from a man named Haiman El-Troudi. As I later found out, Mr. El-Troudi is an old communist workhorse from Barinas, the President's home state, which has surely helped him rise high in the rankings of chavista "intellectual" *nomenklatur*. The talk was basically a retread of old Marxist principles I heard many times during my studies in public universities, where the nefarious "IVth Republic" gave these Marxists plenty of freedom to spread their ideas. But a few things sounded new to me.

For example, Mr. El-Troudi outlined why XXIst Century Socialism was different from the XXth Century version, as practiced in the Soviet Union and its satellites. He said Pres. Chávez's project was different because it was:

---

[24] Chuao, a central Caracas business district, was the starting point for the march on April 11th, 2002, demanding Hugo Chávez resign.

a) Not based on State capitalism;

b) Not averse to popular participation and to putting the people in a starring role;

c) Not totalitarian, nor a believer in excessive democratic centralism;

d) Not populist, not messianic and not paternalistic;

e) Not based on building up armament;

f) Not atheist;

g) Not a single-party system;

h) Not a believer in extrapolating or exporting models.

The laundry list of everything the Revolution supposedly "isn't" but so clearly "is" made me chuckle.

He also riffed on the new forms of private property, one being a brand-new "revolutionary" notion they like to call "Social Production Companies." These companies are supposed to function as cooperatives supported by the government, but their design is still hazy because, according to Mr. El-Troudi, the employees participate in the decision-making process and their capitalist values lead them to think they are the owners or that they are the government's partners, which they are clearly not. The speaker said this came up in negotiations with *Sidor*, a company partly owned by the workers. They are addressing this issue with the President, fine-tuning the system so that workers' capitalist vices cannot find a way of expressing themselves.

An intermission for a "beverage" was animated by a *tambora* group, which, as Roger explained to me, was typical in Chavista seminars, always including some form of "cultural expression." The dancers were quite skilled, and very provocative. Their movements, their attire - which left little to the imagination - and the beating of their drums reminded me of long-gone weekend nights in Choroní, but as you can imagine, the whole thing did not seem appropriate for a seminar on political indoctrination in a University. This, however, didn't prevent some of the participants from joining them in the ruckus.

More talk followed, this time about education. The speaker, a mild-mannered professor of Education at Simón Rodríguez Experimental University, bored us to tears with tales of Rodriguez and how the Revolution's educational project resembles his ideals of inclusion and racial diversity in the schools. He mentioned that Rodríguez died in poverty, surrounded by his books, which made me question his concept of poverty since books must have cost a fortune in the XIXth Century.

Although less controversial than the previous talks, the speaker's tone made it perfectly clear that underneath his navy-blue sweater vest beat the heart of a true Marxist. Through it all, he did not bother to speak about increasing educational coverage, or the quality of the nation's teachers, or the infrastructure of our public schools, or the lack of technology, just to mention a few of the pressing issues that make our current educational system a failed one.

We were about to leave when the question-and-answer session began.

Only one person stood up. He identified himself as Marcos, a small-scale fishing entrepreneur from Apure. Marcos was in his late forties, and his European looks had been darkened over the years by the unforgiving sunlight of the Llanos.

Marcos said, in a typical *llanero* accent, that he was a follower of the process and a believer in the President. He then proceeded to ask why it is that they were being lectured on giving up wealth and letting go of capitalist ambitions when there were so many important figures in the Revolution buying expensive cars, traveling all over the world and hiding behind tinted-glass windows "so the people won't see them."

The speaker asked Marcos to finish his question quickly, to which he replied that he was forced to sit there for five hours, and that his time deserved respect and he was going to say his piece without being rushed. He spoke about how there are many environmental problems in the rivers of Apure, how the only infrastructure for fishermen was built by Carlos Andres Pérez and how he thinks that, no, it's not heresy to acknowledge that and throw CAP a bone.

In his straight-forward manner, he said he believed in the process and that he thought we should all let go of the capitalist values that made us, for example, want to go eat at McDonald's or Tropi-Burger.

At that moment, people started groaning, with one woman behind me saying *"con McDonalds no te metas! Ve que me gustan los nuggets"* - roughly translated into "don't mess with McDonalds, I like my nuggets!"

Marcos finished his speech asking how a revolutionary like himself can reconcile the need to let go of his goods while the revolution's big-shots enjoy an excess of sudden wealth. Spontaneous applause broke out in the crowd, and my squalid jaw hit the floor.

The speaker's answer was that people succumb to the temptations of luxury goods because they have been programmed by capitalism for too many years - see, it's not the crooks' fault; it's capitalism that made them do it. Ergo, the only way to get rid of corruption is to get rid of capitalism. In the meantime, he said that the only way to counter this is by enforcing "social control" or *"contraloría social"*, a catch-all phrase of imprecise meaning used by chavistas when they want to convince the people they are empowered in situations where they clearly aren't.

I didn't want to attend this forum. Quite frankly, I was a bit scared to go there, not knowing what I would find or even if I would be allowed in the building. I fully expected to go home in a state of depression and anxiety. With all the friends I have in Caracas, why waste precious time immersed in revolutionary rhetoric?

Imagine my surprise when I left feeling a renewed sense of optimism. See, the forum convinced me that chavismo's internal contradictions are slowly coming to the surface.

I spoke to other participants. One woman said she liked the talk, but she didn't like the part about education because she didn't want her kids exposed to a single doctrine. Another woman rolled her eyes when I asked her about the seminar, and told me she wouldn't be there if they hadn't forced her to go.

Slowly but surely, chavistas are beginning to resent the manipulation. Being taught to forget about comfort and consumption by people who drive around in Hummers is, quite simply, a farce, and people know it.

The people in the forum were mostly lower-level employees from a particular public office. They may or may not be representative, and while most of them do not have much formal education, they can sense the danger in the government's Marxist rhetoric and values.

They see the hypocrisy in being told about the benefits of letting go of material things by a Navy yes-man who enjoys the many perks of his position (and then some) by virtue of having been the skipper who finally moved the Pilín León tanker.[25] They see the contradiction in being lectured about the ills of capitalism from people taking bribes for the necessary permits to move ships in and out of Venezuelan ports.

Venezuelans from every spectrum like to earn money and enjoy spending it, just like everybody else. They want to work and build a better future for themselves and their kids, just like everybody else. And yes, sometimes they like going out and buying themselves some McNuggets. The time will come when the madness of the Revolution will wake them up from their slumber, and they will realize their lives are changing for the worse and that liberty is worth fighting for. Who knows, they may even use "Don't mess with my nuggets" as a rallying cry.

---

[25] During the oil strike of 2002, an oil tanker belonging to PDVSA, the Pilín León, lay idle in Maracaibo bay as a sign of protest.

Sinamaica Chronicles
Posted on February 26, 2008 by Juan Cristobal

"That one over there, that's my mother's house. The house next to it also belongs to my mother, but she's loaned it to make a *Barrio Adentro* module. That's where the Cuban doctors work and live."

With these words, Rolando, our boat driver in the Sinamaica lagoon, hinted that he was a hardcore chavista. He is an Añú, one of the several indigenous groups from the Guajira peninsula shared by Venezuela and Colombia.[26]

I took a deep breath and asked Rolando how he had voted on the December 2nd referendum. He said that, after thinking about it, he'd voted "No". While President Chávez had done a lot for his community, he felt what they needed now were jobs, a hospital and better security. He thought the reform would not help accomplish these goals.

I didn't believe him. I was sure he was saying what I wanted to hear. Yes, Zulia tends to lean against Chávez: it has one of two opposition governors in the country and the "No" won in the state by a large margin. But Chávez has an immense lead in rural areas, especially indigenous ones. I knew I was in red country.

Sinamaica is a unique place. Right in the middle of the Limón river delta's mangrove lagoon, you find a town of 5,000, with most of its inhabitants living in huts built on stilts in the water. The town is poor and jobs are hard to come by, but the mystique of the place remains: it was these houses that Américo Vespucci was looking at when he first blurted out "little Venice!", or, in Genoese dialect, "Venezuela"!

I was visiting relatives in Maracaibo last week, along with a Chilean friend. When I told them we were planning to take our friend to Sinamaica, they warned against it. They said we'd get kidnapped, that the lagoon was dry, that the boats couldn't navigate and that there was a dengue fever epidemic. My relatives hadn't

---

[26] Sinamaica Lagoon lies about an hour north of Maracaibo, Zulia State.

ventured to Sinamaica in quite some time, so their warnings were based on hearsay. With a wee bit of hesitation, we decided to go and headed north.

The day was as cool and crisp as Zulia can get - picture a mild summer day in the Northern hemisphere. The boats were there just like they had been the last time I visited this place, twenty years ago. They all had life-vests and a rustic yet functional canvas canopy to shield us from the searing midday sun.

We set off upriver and the beauty of the place started to sink in. While some things had barely changed, others were noticeably different. There is a new hostel in town, next to a brand new school that, according to Rolando, is teaching the Añú about their heritage and their language. The huts have had electricity for as long as I can remember, but now some have Direct TV satellite dishes too.

While a few of the huts had "No" scribbled in graffiti on their walls, I saw a lot of "Si - con Chávez" signs. And while I managed to see a couple of health-care facilities run by the state government, Chávez's presence was overwhelming.

"See," I thought to myself, "this is Chávez territory."

When I got home, though, I was surprised. The place is more complicated than I'd thought. It turns out that the No won in Sinamaica last December, 52 to 48, a larger ratio than in the nation as a whole. Maybe Rolando was telling the truth.

Twenty years had passed since my last visit, and the place now looked better, not worse. Schools, doctors, Añú language classes...surely the good burghers of Sinamaica were grateful to the President for all that, right?

Yet there were many signs that suggested something wasn't right. Take, for instance, the road trip.

On our way there we passed at least ten military checkpoints. I thought this was usual, but for the people of Sinamaica that has to be uncomfortable.

Not only does the military drive away the tourists, they also hamper the lucrative smuggling business that some of these communities have long thrived on. The National Guard is notorious in Venezuela for muscling in on the trade, so rather than stemming the flow of cheap gasoline across the border, they divert some of the funds away from the community and into their own pockets.

At the same time, the region is notorious for its FARC presence. Some of the people here are large cattle and goat-herders, and small fortunes have been made from this trade. Yet the military presence has done precious little to turn the tide on the many problems safety poses for legitimate businesses such as these.

On our drive up there, we noticed dozens of brand new cars parked along the road with serial numbers painted on their windshields. We didn't know what this all meant, but it made us uneasy. I thought it could be some sort method whereby stolen cars held for ransom are returned to their owners.

Not to be. This is what is called *"tripletear"*, a common way to make money out of the thousands of inefficiencies in Chávez's Venezuela.

Due to foreign exchange controls, it now takes about six months on a waiting list to buy a new car in Venezuela. Some people in the Guajira who manage to score one have figured out a way to cash in on the distortion. They raffle the new car away by posting serial numbers on the windshield on the side of the road. The numbers are a subset of the possible winning numbers of that week's state lottery - if you buy a ticket from the car's owner and the lottery draws that number, you win the car.

When the only local industry that is booming is a makeshift pyramid scheme, people won't be happy. Guajiros want jobs and security just like anyone else and the *Barrio Adentro* module is old news.

Rural Venezuela is more complex than I'd assumed, plus it's changing. The government is still very strong, but in the eyes of many, Chávez has turned a corner. And while first impressions can make you think that, yes, things are better now, the few improvements you see are things the locals see as either old news or just unfinished.

It all brings me back to the importance of November's state and local elections. A lot of Chávez's votes from rural areas come because the opposition simply has no presence in these out of the way places. Some towns have probably not seen an opposition politician in years, and it's hard to make credible promises when you've been shut out of local government for decades. In light of the positive impact an opposition local government can have, it seems clear to me that boycotting the elections four years ago was a huge mistake. It's a view all but the most extreme slivers of the opposition now seem to share.

When we were getting off the boat, I asked Rolando how to say "thank you" in the Añú language. He was embarrassed to say he didn't know, but added that they're trying to recover their language and their culture with the government's help.

"At least that is what the government has been saying all these years," he said.

He couldn't say "thank you" in his ancestor's tongue, but the disappointment in his tone said enough.

Love Chávez; Hate the government
Posted on January 23, 2012 by Quico

Some friends invited me to the *Comuna Cacique Tiuna*, the big new housing development behind the Poliedro, in Caracas' southwest corner. I tagged along hoping for some insight on low-income housing in Chávez's Venezuela, and on the people who benefit (and suffer) from it.

Our contact at *Cacique Tiuna* was the head of the Communal Council there, a lovely, very friendly lady who also happened to be a hyper-partisan chavista. We asked her to introduce us to some recently resettled families, so she took us to meet the Spokeswoman for one of the new buildings, handed out to 50 families brought up from the shelter in the *La Rinconada* stands in the last few weeks.

Before we'd really managed to ask the first question, the building spokeswoman was off on a rant about how useless the government was.

"They told us we'd get to coordinate with the national government to decide who got which apartments, but it wasn't like that at all. They just forgot all about the Popular Power (poder popular) and started handing out the apartments to whoever they wanted … plus they don't really coordinate with each other, so you have two ministries plus the vice-presidency, plus another foundation – all handing out apartments here. Nobody asks for our opinion."

I found this bizarre. I'd expected that maybe some disgruntled chavistas might take me aside and, under their breath, mumble their frustration about the government out of their handlers' earshot.

But this wasn't like that at all. The spokeswoman was ranting right in front of her communal council head, a woman with the power to throw her out of her apartment if she wanted to. As her chavista neighbors came in and out of the building, they'd stop by and join the little circle all casual like.

Clearly, Pyongyang it ain't.

The rest of the visit was all like that: bitching and moaning about shoddy building work, bad urban planning leading to sewers that overflow, deteriorated rainwater collection leaving the area prone to flash floods, and the looming fear these recently homeless people felt that the buildings were so rickety that as soon as a hard rainy season comes they could be made homeless all over again.

Maybe a few years ago chavistas bitched about the government under their breath, but that was then. These days, there's no taboo about it anymore.

Of course, the story is entirely different when you ask about president Chávez himself. Genuine gratitude and real warmth shine through whenever people talked about him. There wasn't anything coerced about it, as far as I could tell: people seemed genuinely delighted to look up to him as their leader.

But the disconnect between the way they saw him and how they viewed his government struck me as … weird.

In fact, if I let myself tune out the sporadic incantations of personal loyalty to Chávez that would pepper their rants, I could easily forget myself altogether, losing sight that I was in one of the flagship projects of the *Gran Misión Vivienda* deep in chavista Caracas, and imagine I was listening to a gaggle of ranting *escuálidos.*[27]

This gap between people's perceptions of the government and their perception of Chávez isn't new. Chávez's personal popularity has outstripped his government's approval for most of the last decade. But the gap seems to be widening, in ways that have important political consequences.

What you see in *Cacique Tiuna* is a new discursive standard at work, a set of ground rules about what is say-able and what is un-say-able in polite company.

Just as you would tune out anyone who said, "Personally, I hate all niggers, but…" people in *Cacique Tiuna* are not willing to engage in conversation with someone who launches a head-on attack on the president.

It takes a real effort of the *escuálido* imagination to picture just how socially unacceptable that is in the social universe they inhabit. To East Side ears, María Leon's speech during Chávez's *Memoria y Cuenta* might have seemed insanely extreme, but in *Cacique Tiuna* her outraged response to any direct attack on Chávez is just common sense.[28]

---

[27] "Escuálidos," or "squalid ones," is a common derogatory term used by Hugo Chávez to denigrate his political opponents. The term has become so popularized, sometimes even opposition people refer to themselves as "escuálidos."

[28] María León, a deputy in the National Assembly, was positively horrified when fellow deputy Maria Corina Machado attacked the President – to his face - for his policy of expropriations.

Faced with this kind of knee-jerk solidarity with the president, it's easy for opposition minded people to throw in the towel, picturing chavistas as an unthinking horde. Of course, when we do that, we fall directly into the rhetorical trap Chávez has set for us, and we shut ourselves off from the possibility of engaging a broad swathe of middle-of-the road Venezuelans who love Chávez and hate his government.

Chavistas are not an unthinking horde. You can engage them, critically, seriously, about shortcomings in the central government (shortcomings that they're very lucid about) ... but only as long as you leave Chávez out of it.

That, ultimately, is the price of entry into the conversation.

Perhaps you think that's too high a price to pay. But it's important to be clear-eyed about what that means. You need to grasp that in demanding that opposition leaders "take the fight to Chávez", you're demanding that they engage the 15-20% of the country in classes A, B and C at the cost of a fatal rift with the bulk of the 75-80% of the country in classes D and E.

The real fault-line running through the February 12th primary campaign, I think, has been between the three candidates willing to pay that price (Capriles, Pérez and López) – and those not willing to (Machado, Arria, and Medina).

And that's one thing we can be grateful for: after 13 years struggling to settle this question, the opposition is on the verge of putting this debate to bed. February 12th is, after all, just around the corner.

The Hard-up Elite
Posted on January 23, 2010 by Quico

This is a story about two friends of mine: Carola and Andrea.

Carola is doing pretty well for herself. Born to a reasonably well-off Caracas family, she nevertheless enjoyed a free university education in *La Cuarta* and ended up taking a prestigious, even glamorous job at a prominent private firm you've certainly heard of.[29] She enjoys her job, and it pays her reasonably well: certainly better than the outsized majority of people in the country. At cocktail parties – Carola is the kind of person who gets invited to cocktail parties now and then – she gets a lot of attention: her job fascinates people. A knowledge worker, she often works on projects with foreign partners, which has allowed her to develop a wide international network. All in all, Carola's pretty well thriving. Certainly, she's a member of the elite.

Then there's Andrea. She also got herself a free education financed by *La Cuarta*, and went on to get a professional job, but life's a struggle. Her small apartment in a not-particularly-fashionable part of Caracas is in a 50 year old building that hasn't received any maintenance in about as long. Most of her furniture consists of hand-me-downs from relatives. Maintaining a middle class lifestyle on the $600 a month she makes is a hard slog. Some of the choices she regularly has to make would shock most U.S. Americans. Sometimes, when you call her on her home phone, the thing's just not connected: it's hard to keep up with the bills, and sometimes her service just gets cut off while she catches up with them. Going out to catch a movie at the theater is a pretty special luxury: the kind of thing that she really has to plan for carefully because it will throw her finances all out of whack for who-knows-how-long. Andrea's terrified to carry a balance on her credit card, but sometimes it just can't be helped. In the U.S., somebody in her position would certainly be considered working poor. And her whole lifestyle, precarious as it is, gets more and more difficult to sustain with each passing year, because her pay rises just aren't keeping pace with surging inflation.

Carola and Andrea are the same person. She's just one of many of my friends who occupy a strangely contradictory social space I like to think of as the Hard-Up Elite: high-status professionals living off their salaries who are vastly better off than the average Venezuelan but struggle hard to afford the kind of lifestyle a truck

---

[29] La Cuarta is short for the IVth Republic, the term Hugo Chávez uses to refer to the governments that existed in Venezuela prior to his election.

driver in Madrid or a school lunch lady in Columbus, Ohio take for granted.

In Venezuela, this Hard-Up Elite is usually glossed as "the Middle Class" but, when you think about it, that's a tag that obscures much more than it reveals. There's nothing "middle" about them: they're not in the "middle" of the income distribution, they're decidedly towards the top end. Their lifestyles aren't "average" in any meaningful sense: they have a level of economic and personal security most Venezuelans could only dream of. At the same time, they're constantly on the brink – one pink-slip away from drastic hardship. Certainly, they are decidedly not middle class in any way that would make sense to somebody in a developed country. Nine-times-out-of-ten their mobile phones are pre-paid, and out of credit.

The Hard-Up Elite is at the same time the core of the anti-Chávez movement and the most misunderstood class in the country.

Much more than the Moneyed Elite – which is just too small to be electorally relevant – it's the Hard-Up Elite that's made up the backbone of that 40% of the vote that's always been the hard-core of the anti-chavista vote. Much more than the popular classes, who are better positioned to capture the government's spurts of spending, it feels its future threatened by the government's lunacy. Much more than any other group in the country, its social status and aspirations are fundamentally out of sync with its living standards.

Official discourse totally ignores this group. The dichotomous way Chávez carves up the country lumps everyone on the upper half of the income distribution into one big, undifferentiated mass of the rich, treating the Hard-Up Elite as identical to the Moneyed Elite. Culturally, this is almost comprehensible: both of them finished high school and went to college. Both work indoors, typically behind desks, for multiples of the minimum wage. Both live in formally built housing, and both are much more likely to have names like Carola or Andrea than Yuleidi or Yajaira.

So how can you tell them apart?

Easy: the Moneyed Elite has credit on its cell phone, the Hard-Up Elite doesn't.

One thing that's always struck me as particular is the way the Hard-Up Elite scrambles first world people's categories and understandings about Latin America, to the point where they really can't see them. This, in a way, is a testament to the effectiveness of chavista propaganda abroad. The image of the Venezuelan opposition as a bunch of fat cats is now so deeply ingrained in foreigners' understanding of the Chávez era – even when the foreigners in question are largely opposed to the government – that the Hard-Up Elite fades almost completely out of view.

Try to explain to your average European or North American that the vast majority of people who vote against the Venezuelan government are much, much poorer than they are, and all you get are blank stares back. "But, but…they're lawyers and accountants, engineers and small business owners!" they'll say.

And that's absolutely true. But they can't necessarily afford more than one pair of new shoes a year. And that, also, is absolutely true.

Lonely planet, petro-state style
Posted on August 14, 2007 by Juan Cristobal

Pick up a Lonely Planet Venezuela and it'll tell you that one of the highlights of the country's Eastern shore is the seaside village of San Juan de las Galdonas, set on a remote inlet on Sucre state'e breathtaking Paria Peninsula. Sandwiched between a picture perfect Caribbean beach and a rainforest mountain, it's just a special place, unspoiled by mass tourism.

More than a few foreigners settled there in the last thirty years, convinced they had found a slice of paradise. It's no wonder - Christopher Columbus stumbled across this stretch of coastline 500 years ago and came to the same conclusion.

Having heard all this, my friend Roger decided to drive out there for his vacation this year. The other day he wrote in to tell me about it.

He said that, though it sure looks pretty, the mood in San Juan de las Galdonas has changed rather drastically since Lonely Planet last dropped in for a visit. The place might look like it was purpose-built for tourism, but these days, the townies treat visitors more as a nuisance than an opportunity.

To hear him tell it, it doesn't take long before you start noticing something isn't quite normal about San Juan de las Galdonas.

The town is overrun with very expensive cars. People behave aggressively toward tourists. A deafening, thumping *reggaeton* pours out of every car, house and business. Parts of the once pristine vegetation around the town have been squatted on and crime has shot up.

What the hell is going on here?

Asking around, Roger found out: the town has become a magnet for smugglers and drug traffickers.

One of the more profitable ventures apparently involves the town's only gas station. It's being used as a port of departure for gasoline smugglers, who ship it off to nearby Trinidad and sell it at multiples of its regulated price. Rent-seekers that we all are, it looks like a lot of people in town have decided that arbitraging gas in Trinidad is a much more attractive way to make a living than making piña coladas for tourists.

I guess this is what Petrocaribe is all about, right?

Obviously, PDVSA and the National Guard are in on this scam. Roger tells me that several gas trucks have to go to San Juan every day to refill the gas station's deposit. Any marginally awake bureaucrat would have found it odd by now that San Juan "consumes" as much gasoline as Maturín. The National Guard is, in fact, supervising the whole operation.

As for tourists, the town folk are doing what they can to keep them away. People like Roger, who only came looking for a parasol and a cold Polarcita to keep him company on the beach, get in the way of their little operation, and a mean-spirited campaign is underway to drive out the foreigners who run the beachside guest houses (posadas).

Roger spoke at length to the owner of the "posada" he stayed at. She's an older Swiss lady, who came to this place looking for a bit of tropical heaven and built her guest house from of scratch. She has genuine affection for the people, for the country and the overwhelming nature that surrounds her. Her affection does not extend, however, to the squatters who took over the lush, green patch of mountainside directly in front of the entrance to her business. What used to be a wall of green is now a shantytown, and the unending *reggaeton* serves as a constant reminder that she would be better off leaving.

Ever the Swiss, she ventured all the way to the state capital, Cumaná, to speak with the Sucre government's tourism commission about her problem. The official there said he couldn't help her, but that if - cough-cough - she decided to call it a day, he could find a buyer for her guest house in two days.

Roger tells me his vacation left him depressed, as if the general lawlessness that is gripping the country has reached even its purest, most picturesque places. At this rate, it won't be long until we see the walls of Angel Falls covered with graffiti glorifying the revolution.

On his way out of town, he saw a couple of teen-agers hitch-hiking and decided to give them a lift to Carúpano. They were awfully nice, as kids tend to be in that part of the country, but they sadly reported that the whole town is being spoiled. In the town's only high-school, the girls' main aspiration is to bed one of the *narcos* running the show. It's easy to spot them, she said, they're the only ones who can afford the flashy cell phones and showy motorbikes.

There's a book, based on a soap opera, making the rounds in Venezuela and Colombia: Sin tetas no hay paraíso - literally, "No tits, no paradise," set in the Colombian city of Pereira. It's a dramatic take on how the main aspiration of poor girls in Pereira's slums is to get a boob-job and land a nice narco-"Goodfella" to whisk them away from the barrio life.

Just as the lure of easy drug money is proving too much for any prudish Pereira girl to resist, the lure of a 300% return rate for siphoning gasoline is too much for the good people of San Juan de las Galdonas.

Sin tetas no hay paraíso, y sin rentas no hay revolución.

Gone to the dogs
Posted on June 21, 2009 by Quico

The sun was setting by the time he got to the farm gate, so it wasn't immediately evident to Kenneth that the guys loitering there were soldiers. Sure, they were toting assault rifles, but they were wearing plain olive-green t-shirts over their camouflaged pants. No uniforms, no insignia, nothing like that.

"Stop!" one of them said as Kenneth approached, raising his rifle. "Identify yourself!"

"Ummmm..." trying to piece together whether he was about to get robbed at gunpoint, Kenneth struggled for a way to say the next few words without sounding entirely preposterous, "es que...we, uh, made reservations."

Blank stares.

Turns out the flunkies who'd been sent to expropriate this particular farm had no idea that, alongside their agricultural business, the old owners ran a *posada* - a kind of farm lodge for tourists.

"Reservations?!" the soldier barked back, "¿cómo es la vaina!?"

"Bueno, officer, you know, because normal hotels won't take this many dogs, so..."

Even blanker stares.

Of course, if the soldier didn't know about the *posada*, he certainly didn't realize that its location - just outside Valencia - made it a favorite lodging place for dog breeders, owners and handlers heading to last weekend's big Pedigree Dog Show there.

Kenneth had been driving for hours and hours by this time, having toured Caracas to pick up the dogs and then taken on the massive traffic jam in *Tazón* before hitting the highway with 22 - that's right, twenty-two - dogs in kennels piled in the back of his van.

He was tired, and just wasn't prepared for any of this. Five minutes earlier, his mind had been entirely occupied with worries about last minute grooming and such ahead of the big show the next day.

"Dogs?"

The soldier didn't look much older than 18, and this stuff about dogs this took things from weird to downright surreal. "What dogs nor what *coño*?!"

"Sí, sí, you know, for the big dog show in town...we usually stay in this posada cuz they don't mind about the dogs..."

At this, the kids at the gate realized they needed to take this to their higher-ups, and one of them headed into the farm. A few of minutes later, a fat army officer came out to Kenneth's van to figure out what this was all about.

"*Bueno*, we took control of this farm yesterday, *ya sabes, para la nación*. Now, what's this about dogs?"

Kenneth explained what was going on. He said he had no idea the farm was about to get expropriated. He showed the officer his printed out reservation. Finally, he showed him the dogs.

"*...ud. no lo va a creer, pero hay escuelas de perros, y les dan educación...*"

"Officer, um, what can I say? How were we supposed to know about this invasi...erm, expropriation? We've been driving since this morning and the show's tomorrow and *de pana que* you gotta let us spend the night here!...there's just nowhere else we can stay in Valencia with twenty two dogs at this time of night."

The officer looked over the reservation papers, looked over the dogs, thought about it for a second and then, to Kenneth's astonishment, waved them in.

As the van rolled into the farm, Kenneth noticed the soldiers still following it with their rifle barrels...

Kenneth's friend, who turned up a few hours later, had a rather rougher time of it. When he turned up, the soldiers had left the gate unguarded. A regular at that *posada*, he just jumped out of his truck and started trying to open the gate to the farm himself, like he'd done many times in previous years.

Seeing this, the soldiers freaked out, ran over, and started screaming at him to stand back, at one point holding their Kalashnikovs up to his nine year old daughter's head as they shouted questions at him.

It was not a pretty picture.

"*Coño*, nobody told us they were running a posada here," the officer said over beers with Kenneth later that night, almost apologetically.

"All we knew was that they were planting sugar cane on the farm, and you know, sugar cane's no good. I mean, for the revolution, it's just not a priority. Ecologically, too. That stuff fucks up the top soil. So we took it over, for the pueblo."

Kenneth looked at the fields all around, though, and something wasn't quite jiving for him.

"Ummmm," he said, a little hesitantly, "well, y'know, I'm no farmer, but that stuff looks like corn to me."

"*Sí claro*," the officer shot back, "the owners got wind that we were evaluating a takeover a while back so, sure, this year, those *vagabundos* planted corn. Y'know, just to take the heat off. But last year and the year before that, and for a long time, they were always planting sugar cane."

"Ah, gotcha, understood," Kenneth said, letting it slide.

What he didn't say, for obvious reasons, was what he was really thinking, which ran more along the lines of "holy fucking shit! these guys got expropriated because, years ago, they used to plant stuff the government later decided it didn't like!!"

Followed closely by "what the hell does this guy mean sugar-cane isn't a priority?!!? hasn't he ever heard of CAAEZ?! of rum!???"

Staggered, Kenneth got back to tending his dogs.

At the show venue, the usual community of dog freaks from all over the country had come together to show off their mutts. Kenneth's story made for something of an amusing anecdote backstage.

Not that he'd want to make too much of it, though. This is a dog show, after all. Non dog-related talk is strictly frowned upon at these things.

"Well, that's The Process for you...hey did you see that beagle from Maturín?! What a beaut..."

Kenneth, along with his 22 dogs, spent two nights total at the posada.

The last day, as he got ready to pack up his dogs and head back to Caracas, he couldn't help but notice that the revolution-ization of the farm had started.

The first thing the soldiers had been ordered to do was to take the whitewashed façade of the main farm-house, paint it bright red, and stencil a silhouette of Che Guevara onto it.

When unity becomes a wedge issue
Posted on July 20, 201By Quico

Look at any picture of *La Vinotinto*.[30] Can you tell the chavistas apart from the *escuálidos*?

The lazy point to make about *La Vinotinto*'s exhilarating run at the *Copa América* this year is that it's a rare, exciting moment of National Unity – football as the one last bastion of non-polarization in a politically fractured nation.

But there's an odd paradox surrounding that line: celebrating the "unity" La Vinotinto has brought about has become a partisan talking point. Only the opposition goes there, the government never does!

It isn't that surprising. When you've built so much of your political *raison d'etre* around the notion that some Venezuelans are good and others are bad, and the government is about boosting the good ones and keeping the bad ones under control, any social event that tends to flatten those differences is a threat to you. There's nothing more menacing to chavismo than having Venezuelans cheer viscerally, from the gut, and as one, over something meaningless but fun.

There's a spark of mass tribal self-identification implicit in all that where class differences recede and political narratives of division seem viscerally out-of-place. Unity is our thing – the government knows it, and fears it.

Tonight, as the whole nation sits down to cheer on *La Vinotinto*, the very non-partisanship of the whole affair will quietly undermine the entire narrative structure the regime has spent 12 years trying to build. That alone is reason enough to watch and cheer our boys, even if you don't give a toss about the match.

---

[30] La Vinotinto refers to Venezuela's national soccer (football) team. Until recently, Venezuela had long been the worst performing soccer team in South America, so the team enjoyed little popular support. As the team began winning, its popularity grew. The team's uniform is colored burgundy, hence the nickname.

The emerald city
September 25. 2008 by Juan Cristobal

One of the biggest challenges in writing this blog is bridging the disconnect between our perception of Venezuelan politics and the day-to-day reality on the ground. While I firmly believe that distance isn't an impediment to staying well informed (in fact, it's a huge plus), I realize it tends to deaden our feel for the ironies and contradictions of life in revolutionary times.

Sure, distance allows us to provide a different perspective, but what if we end up becoming a bunch of curmudgeons? What if the Revolution is, deep down, just another *cague de risa*? What if our focus on the trees that are the day-to-day outrages prevents us from seeing the farcical forest that is Chávez's Venezuela?

A few weeks ago I was in Caracas for the wedding of a college buddy of mine. The wedding was held at La Esmeralda, the flagship of the prestigious Agencia Mar, Venezuela's top provider of quality, conspicuous, over-the-top, unabashedly in-your-face-expensive entertainment. La Esmeralda had long been the premium spot for Caracas social life and a fixture in big events for the past twenty years, but I somehow assumed it was past its prime.

I remember my first wedding at La Esmeralda. It was back in 1989, in the weeks following El Caracazo. You could sense the country was changing, but here I was, a college sophomore, fresh out of Maracaibo, with my date, in a lavish ballroom, being treated like a king. The canapés were succulent, and they just kept coming. The Scotch was 12-year-old Black Label, of course, and the champagne was French, obviously. The live orchestra was on fire, and I remember we danced 'til 5 in the morning. It was, for lack of a better word, memorable.

But there was also an eerie feel to the proceedings, as if we were waltzing in the Titanic oblivious to the icebergs all around us. I wasn't aware of it then, but I can't help recalling those days without a certain sense of dread. It's as if 37-year-old me wanted to go back in time and warn 18-year-old me about how fake it all was, how it was all going to go up in smoke.

I didn't know what to expect this time around. I hadn't been to La Esmeralda in years. In the interim, fortunes have been made and lost (and remade and re-lost) and the Revolution plows through, taking no prisoners. I was expecting it to be the decadent reminder of better times, a lonely ballroom waiting to be nationalized.

Silly me, I found myself in the middle of a swank party unlike any I'd ever seen: a *bonche* worthy of the dizzying petro-boom we're having.

There was champagne like the last time, only it kept flowing until 5 in the morning. The band was on fire as well, only it, too, played until the wee hours. There was a sushi bar, a Chinese chef, and a dessert bar to kill for, with thousands of individual chocolate-and-cream concoctions I don't even have names for. I left at close to 6 in the morning, and there was enough food left over to feed a small orphanage for days.

As I was soaking it all in, having a great time, I suddenly remembered: wait, wasn't this supposed to be a Revolution? Don't these people read the newspapers? In which chapter of *Das Kapital* is the bit about the sushi bars? I haven't had this much fun in years!

The dissonance, she is strong. Somehow, nine years into the Cuban revolution, I don't think Fidel's opponents were throwing bashes where the towels in the bathroom were monogrammed with the initials of the bride and groom. And I just have a strong feeling that, by 1927, anti-Bolsheviks in Russia were not getting married in mansions that gave away baskets upon baskets of cosmetics, sewing kits, hair accessories and glossy magazines in the ladies' room.

I told my friends how impressed I was with the lavish attention and how cool the party was, but also how weird it felt to be there when this was supposed to be a socialist revolution. They smiled back at me, saying that I hadn't seen nothin': one time they went to a *boliburgués* wedding in La Esmeralda where the bride's mother had demanded furniture to be flown in from France to enhance the art-deco motif they were gunning for.

The more things change, the better they get. Chávez may throw out the American Ambassador, milk may be hard to come by, crime may reach unheard-of heights and war with Colombia may be imminent..."*pero como se goza*...!"[31]

As long as the gush of petrodollars keeps swamping the country, a good time can be had by...a few.

Roger and out
Posted on June 12, 2009 by Juan Cristobal

My friend Roger used to be my mole in the government. A committed *escuálido* working undercover deep inside chavista bureaucracy, he somehow managed to tolerate the mind-numbing paper-pushing and the constant backstabbing from colleagues and underlings alike, to say nothing of the forced participation in chavista rallies.

But over the last year, Roger also got a crash course on the true nature of chavista bureaucrats, people for whom corruption, inefficiency and amateur Machiavellianism are the norm.

Unwilling to play along, Roger got fired last month.

Roger is a classic example of the underpaid overachiever. After getting his law degree in Venezuela, he went to Switzerland on a scholarship and got his doctorate. There, he specialized in an obscure area of international law that, luckily, is also incredibly relevant for Venezuela.

As it happens, he never got around to signing the recall petition against Chávez so he's not in the Tascón or Maisanta Lists. Long story short, that meant he could get a job in the government institute that handles the exact area of his expertise, doing the things he was actually trained to do. His legal knowledge and his ability in three languages became important assets and helped him stand out in the many international conferences he went to.

"Deep inside," he fesses up, "I kidded myself with the idea that I was giving something back."

---

[31] This roughly translates into "a good time can be had by all!"

These days, Roger whiles away his afternoons in his apartment in La Urbina, where he lives alone with his computers, his books and his view of Petare. He hasn't worked in weeks and is living hand to mouth.

And yet, he's at peace with himself. When I ask him the story behind his firing, he is almost wistful, disconcertingly zen about the whole thing.

He says the beginning of the end of his public service career came when his institute got a new chairman a few months back, his fourth new boss in as many years.

"This last guy took part in the 4-F military coup," he says. "The fact that he was dispatched to a relatively obscure technical outpost of chavista bureaucracy as compensation speaks volumes about his performance that day."

From day one, the chairman decided he didn't like Roger one bit. His language skills, the depth of his knowledge and his personal demeanor all rubbed him the wrong way.

"The problem is that you don't fit in with the culture," one of his assistants told Roger.

How so? he asked.

"Well," she said, "you don't socialize, all you do is come in, do your work and you're out. You don't joke around with everyone, and you don't seem to like us. You're very Swiss that way."

Roger spent six months trying to get a meeting with the chairman, trying to get him to read his reports. In six months, he got nothing.

Well, not quite. He did get a lot of work on weekends.

In the months leading up to last November's State and Local Elections, Roger got dragged to election meeting after meeting and rally after rally. On several occasions, he was part of special PSUV cleanup operations in the squares and plazas of Caracas.

The demands on public employees before elections became difficult to put up with. Right before February's referendum, Roger was forced to sell BsF. 1,000 worth of raffle tickets to raise funds for the PSUV's campaign. Needless to say, Roger couldn't think of anyone who would want to buy his tickets, so he had to pay for them out of pocket.

"Did you at least win anything in the raffle?" I ask, all hopeful.

Hardly. As it happens, the raffle tickets were fake. The real ones were supposed to have a serial number and a bank account where the funds should be deposited. Roger's had none of that. The *chavistas* in the office forcing him to sell them had given him *tickets chimbos*.

Under the new chairman, office life soon took a turn to the bizarre. One Saturday, the guy decided to stage his own little backyard version of "Aló, Presidente." He made all senior and middle management go to work and sit in a conference room, from 8 to 4, hearing him talk about whatever was on his mind.

His secretary, who is actually his mistress as well as the niece of one of Chávez's ministers, was in charge of filming. During the proceedings, she would point the camera and focus on managers who looked bored, were staring at the ceiling or sending text messages. The chairman would review the tape and reprimand managers who weren't devoting 100% of their attention to the boss.

The level of paranoid control just kept getting ratcheted up. During regular weekdays, all managers had to text message the chairman every time they left the office. The Saturday *séances* soon became compulsory, with attendance strictly enforced. One Saturday, Roger arrived an hour late and was asked to provide the reasons why he was late ... in writing. Needless to say, he had to suck it up and say it wouldn't happen again, just like ministers do on *Aló, Presidente* when the big guy humiliates them.

In the Chávez administration, imitation has gone from highest form of flattery to outright obsession.

One of the problems Roger faced was the lack of personnel. Even though he was technically a manager, he never got an assistant or a secretary, so all his department's work fell on his lap.

Conveniently, the 28-year old daughter of his longtime nanny was looking for a job. Thanks to her mother's hard work, Judith had received a technical degree and had just arrived from a stint living in London.

Since she was bilingual, qualified and available, Roger pushed hard to hire her as his secretary. After many interviews and even after sucking up to all the right people, he was told they couldn't hire her because she was in the Tascón List. Roger was forced to apologize, saying he didn't know and simply forgot to check. Had he known, he said, he never would have insisted.

Judith is still unemployed.

In the weeks leading up to his firing, Roger got assigned an "advisor." Edgar, a PSUV *apparatchik*, had a simple job: sit across from Roger's desk every day and make his life miserable. While Roger tried to focus on his work, Edgar would talk on his cell phone non-stop, only pausing to bark at Roger demanding he finish his reports so he could take them up to the chairman and pass them off as his own. Roger later found out Edgar was making twice as much as he was.

The day Roger was fired - by Edgar, of all people - he received several anonymous text messages. "The institute is rejoicing," one read, "so much for your fancy degrees and your languages. Go eat shit, you show-off."

I ask him what the source of so much animosity is. It turns out that, with Roger being in charge of international legal analysis, his office was responsible for most of the trips abroad. The decision of who to send in each delegation frequently fell on Roger, and he obviously preferred sending the few qualified people available.

This, of course, did not sit well with the rest of the sprawling bureaucracy. Thanks to *Misión Cadivi*, going to one of these international trips was a quick and easy way of landing some hard currency in the form of juicy per diems, which everyone simply kept and later sold in the black market. Plus, you could have a good time abroad too. Roger recalls one particular conference in South

Africa where the head of the delegation simply did not show up for the meetings, preferring to go on safari with his mistress instead.

I ask Roger about the laws Chávez has passed, banning the firing of employees. He tells me he really isn't an employee. Since the institute is relatively new, they have not established the positions and their role in the larger picture of the government's bureaucracy.

This is on purpose. Done this way, everyone is under contract and can be fired at any time. Plus, this allows the institute bigwigs to bypass regular budget laws and just hire all their friends, giving them cushy jobs as payback for political favors.

These days, Roger is reinvigorated. Leaving all those negative vibes behind, he says, he's starting to enjoy life again. He'd gotten to the point where he was spending most of his energy thinking up ways to out scheme the schemers out to get him. Now, he says, he's glad to have the time off, getting in touch with his friends again, teaching.

"It's funny," he says, "but the more I think about it, the more it makes sense. Of course the government doesn't work. My former boss is an ex-con, a convicted felon, an anonymous military man whose sole claim to fame was to break the very oath he had taken and violate the democracy he had sworn to defend. Of course they don't believe in building institutions! Their only talent, the thing they spent years planning, is how to do away with them. What was I supposed to expect - decency?"

My sense is that Roger is going to be OK. He may have lost his job, and may well end up having to live abroad, but he is well on his way to getting his life back.

No hay material
Posted on March 27, 2008 by Quico

Ask anyone at all and they'll tell you: hands down, the three most feared words in Venezuela's bureaucratic vocabulary are "there's no material."

It's a kind of code phrase, meaning something like "no, seriously, there's no use trying to bribe me: I genuinely can't help you." The cargo gods have not come through. For whatever reason, the tenuous link with the fairy country that manufactures the little physical booklets that, provided a photo and a battery of official stamps, become passports, has been severed.

For what reason? For how long? These are questions no sane Venezuelan ever asks.

I ran into the dreaded phrase at El Llanito's INTTT Inspectoría, Venezuela's DMV, as I went to get my driver's license renewed.

"No, mi amor, es que no hay material."

Oh, shit. Well, *"y ¿cómo hago?"* I say in a gambit to see if there's some back channel way to get that coveted bit of laminated plastic.

Amazingly, uncharacteristically, it works...for some baffling reason, she takes a shine to me and decides to confide.

"Mira," she says, "word on the street is that they'll have material tomorrow in Los Chaguaramos. Otherwise, you can try again here next week."

I can't believe my luck. I have a tip, an actual *dato*, straight from the bureaucrat's mouth, good as gold.

"Muchas gracias, amiga," I say and rush out smiling, actually happy, as though I haven't just wasted a trip that cost me an hour and a half in traffic.

The next day I go to the bank to pay my fee and then rush off to the *Inspectoría* in *Los Chaguaramos*, getting there at about 9:00 a.m.

Or, rather, I get to the metal fence setting off the *Inspectoría* from the sidewalk. A little hubbub of maybe 20 or 25 people are crowding in on the gate, as one single guy – a security guard – holds off the barbarian masses, trying to give out information one case at a time.

I kind of jostle my way up to the front and eventually get to ask him, "*amigo*, to renew my license?" as I show him my documents.

"Yeah, ok, we have 30 spots, and it's first come first serve, so you better get in line right there."

He points to a spot just outside the gate, on the sidewalk. I'm amazed, there are just a handful of people in line there. "This is going to be a piece of cake," I think to myself.

"*Disculpe*, is this the line for license renewals?" I ask the guys in line. They nod.

"And do you know what time they'll let us in?"

"At 1:30," one of them says.

"What?!"

"Yeah, 1:30...this is the line for the afternoon spots...the morning people already went in."

Oh Christ.

"Ay *coño*," I say, and add... "pero, sí hay material, ¿verdad?"

They all nod, a little too eagerly for my taste, as though they're trying to convince themselves.

"That's what they said...30 *plásticos* this afternoon."

Bueno...nothing to be done. Just hunker down for four and a half hours on a sidewalk in Los Chaguaramos breathing exhaust fumes and passing the time who knows how.

Damn it, I should've had breakfast.

The vexation on my face must've been pretty clear, cuz one of the guys looks at me and says "c'mon, *chamo*, don't make such a face: just think, this *señor* here's been doing this for a whole week."

I look at the round faced man just ahead of me in line.

"Really?"

He smiles, beatifically, obviously way past getting exasperated by this kind of thing anymore.

"You have no idea what they've put me through this week..." he pauses, thinking through the memories. "I spent all day queuing at El Llanito on Monday just to be told at the end that they'd run out of *plásticos*...on Tuesday they said they had no more material and didn't know when any more would be coming in. Lost day. Wednesday a friend told me to head out to Los Teques and try there so I had to shell out for transport to get all the way out there, but it was a bust there as well. They told me to come here...and yesterday it was just like today, they said they had 30 *plásticos*, and I was number 23 in line, but right as I got up to the front, after 8, count them, eight hours standing here taking the sun like a roof tile, they said no, '*es que se acabó el material*' and sent me home."

He pauses, savoring the string of disasters.

"Bueno, the good thing is that at this point I'm immunized against frustration," he says, shrugging the whole thing off. "Today I came even earlier and now I'm fifth in line. If they turn me away again I'll toss a Molotov cocktail in there."

It's the kind of story to put my own problems in perspective.

"Thing is, I'm a *transportista*, a bus driver," he continues, "so every day without a license is a day I can't work, and a day I don't work is a day I don't bring home anything to my family."

A bit of a circle is forming around the guy's story. Everybody's nodding. Pretty soon one of the other guys pipes in as well.

"That's where I'm at too. The guy who owns the *microbus* I drive won't let me go out without a license. The bribes we have to pay the cops if we get caught are so high they'd wipe out two weeks' worth of work. But in the meantime...hell, you know how it is, we're contractors, if we don't work we don't earn."

"¿Oh yeah?" one-week-running-after-a-license-man says, "¿what part of town do you cover?"

Pretty soon, it's social hour at the license renewal line. Everybody knows we're in for a long wait and conversation seems like as good a way to pass the time as any.

I find Venezuelans remarkably good humored in situations like this. I'm surrounded by people suffering real economic hardship because the damn government can't get it together to source enough drivers' license cards, but nobody really bitches. They crack jokes, trade stories, share anecdotes about being held up during work, and soon a pretty strong esprit de corps is arising in our group.

In my little sector of the line we have three bus drivers, a taxi driver, a guy who runs an ice delivery truck, a housewife who needs her license to drive her kids to school, and a guy doing a PhD in political science in Europe. It strikes me that standing in line waiting to be humiliated by the bureaucracy is one of the few spaces for genuine social equality in Venezuela. Right here, right now, there are no social distinctions: we really are all the same.

One thing is clear, though: nobody brings up politics. We're strangers. More than likely some of us are chavistas and some are anti-. Bringing it up could only bust the vibe we've developed. It's not a risk worth taking.

Just to keep things from getting too chaotic, somebody pulls out a pen and a note pad and starts making little numbered slips so we each know what our exact place in line is. The move makes the gate guard nervous. He comes over and warns us in no uncertain terms that the *Inspectoría* will not recognize those numbers, and that come 1:30 it'll still be first come, first serve. His tone is that of a dad warning a 6 year old kid.

We grin and bear it: however squalid his little quota of power may be, right here, right now, he is the one guy we can't afford to piss off. We reassure him we're just doing it to keep track of who is where among ourselves. But, actually, by this point, it's kind of superfluous...we've spent 2 hours in this line already, talking, hanging out, and by now everybody knows who's in what spot in line. The chances of someone cutting and getting away with it are nil.

Come to think of it, if the gate guard wasn't treating us like shit, would we be bonding the way we are? I kind of doubt it...when you get right down to it, the only thing bringing us together is the disdain of officialdom.

Still, we're antsy...we kind of feel better with an actual number in hand, whether Power chooses to recognize it or not.

At about 11:30 I fall into a one-on-one conversation with Nelson, one of the bus drivers. After asking me a few questions about public transport in Holland (yes, a bus ride really does cost Bs.7,000 there; no, you don't get a Welcome Drink for that kind of money) he decides to confide.

"Really I'm an accountant," he tells me, "I got my degree from INCE, but you know how the *vaina* is, I couldn't get a job so...now I drive a bus."

I ask him about his work. He lives up in *El Junquito* and drives down into downtown Caracas a couple of times per morning. He tells me about the intricacies of timing his runs just right to maximize his take. Go too early and there aren't any passengers. Go too late, and there's too much traffic. You only make money when you're loading passengers, and you can't load passengers if you're stuck in a traffic jam.

The best, he reckons, is to set off at about 5 a.m., that's pretty much the sweet spot when good passenger numbers meet relatively unclogged streets. Then he gets back to *El Junquito* by about 6:30 and has a nice, leisurely breakfast just long enough to miss the student-heavy time slot; another variable in his little optimization problem.

"Students? Why do you go out of your way to avoid them? Are they really that raucous?"

"Nah," he says, "it's the student ticket thing."

He explains that they're not allowed to charge students full fare. Technically, the government is supposed to make up the difference but, surprise, refunds are invariably late.

"Right now, the delay in getting paid is about three months," he says, "and hell, I studied accounting, so I know exactly what that's called: a forced loan. Interest free, to boot."

With inflation running as high as it is, the bolivars they get paid three months late can be worth a good 8% less than the bolivars they were originally forced to loan the government, he explains. It's just not good business, driving during time slots when half your customers are going to be students, he explains. Not surprisingly, kids have a hell of a tough time finding a bus to get on to get to school in the morning...just one more downside to schooling, one more prod to drop out.

Just then, we see a military vehicle pull up to the *Inspectoría* gates. Three, four, five army guys in uniform make their way inside. The line goes from sociable to restless.

"*¡Que arrechera, chamo!*" one of the guys says, "man that pisses me off! Each one of those guys going in is one less *plástico* for us."

We've been standing out there for three and a half hours, now. It's noon, it's hot, some of us haven't had breakfast. Nobody dares make too much of a fuss, though. Those guys are army, y'know.

Within five minutes, the gate guard comes out to announce that, mysteriously, there are now just 25 *plásticos* to hand out today. The back of the line (which, in effect, has just been told that *no hay material*) is more deflated than furious. They slink off, muttering cuss words but resigned to come again the next day.

It's the DMV, after all: it's not like you can go to the competition if they give you shitty service.

As 1:30 draws near, a palpable sense of expectation builds in the line. Soon, the carefully differentiated lines for license renewals, first-time licenses, and car registrations that had remained neatly separate all morning all clump together into a mass around the door.

The gate guard definitely can't cope. Soon, he's pretty much forced to rely on the little scribbled numbers he's already told us he wouldn't accept. People shove and push and yell and you can't really tell if people are cutting in line in front of you or if they're just from one of the other lines that have gotten all mushed up into one big melee. The people from "my" line try to help each other out, as far as possible, but frankly that's not very far. It's pretty much chaos as the gate guard gets into a series of increasingly testy exchanges with the hordes clamoring to get inside.

"*Lo que pasa*," he yells at us in exasperation, "is that you people aren't properly organized! You need to get organized, otherwise look at the chaos we're left with!"

In time, a Tránsito Terrestre official comes out to look over this mess. He sees the gate guard arguing with the users, shakes his head, and reprimands him, saying – loud enough for all of us to hear – "why do you waste your time talking to them? Don't talk to them, man...*no hables con ellos.*"

In his own, haplessly testy way, the gate guard was treating us like human beings. Rookie mistake, obviously.

In the end, I manage to sneak in somehow and hand in my documents:

One cédula copy – check.

One bank payment slip – check.

One certificado médico – check.

One renewal form – check.

Now we wait inside the gate, finally sitting in proper chairs and under a bit of shade, it feels like relative luxury as we finish the conversations we'd started earlier. A half hour later, a *Tránsito Terrestre* official comes out and starts calling out names, handing out our 25 renewed licenses. I tremble in anticipation when he calls out Toro...

Then, just as suddenly as it had formed, our little community disappears.

As I stroke my still warm plastic, I can't help but muse on how thoroughly pointless the whole exercise is. Nothing I did, no part of the bureaucratic nightmare at all had even the slightest, most oblique bearing on my ability to drive a car. There were no tests, practical or theoretical, no checks of accident records, no part of the procedure has anything to do with driving at all...and yet, if you want to drive a vehicle in Venezuela, you have to subject yourself to this baffling set of low level humiliations once every ten years, just because.

For me, normally stuck away in a Dutch provincial town, the whole thing was a bit of a curiosity, almost worth it just for the chance to talk at leisure with an accountant *buseta* driver. But for these other guys, the hours or days spent dealing with all this idiocy are days of real economic hardship, days of wages foregone for people living a hand-to-mouth existence.

Their good cheer baffled and charmed me, yes, but seemed to me also just a case of learned helplessness, of a deeply justified intuition that it's just always been like this and it's just never going to get better so what's the point of getting upset?

As I left the *Inspectoría* with my *plástico* burning a hole in my pocket, I noticed a sign gracing the inside of the gate. In big, propagandistic blue letters it belted out,

"Now getting your license is easier!"

Heh. Quite.

Bureaucracy as it should be
Posted onJuly 20, 2009 by Quico

A little over a year ago, I wrote this epic post about going to get my driver's license in Caracas. In this blog's seven year history, it's one of the posts I'm proudest of: I just think it captured something special about both the glories and the miseries of Venezuelan-ness.

Alas, last week I had to go trade in that hard-earned Venezuelan license for a new one so I can drive here in Quebec, so I thought the time was ripe for a bit of compare and contrast. Because the contrast really couldn't be more complete: Quebec's provincial bureaucracy operates with simple, bone-chilling efficiency, minimizing both your aggravation and the chance to make real human connections with the people you share the experience with.

The first thing you have to do here is make an appointment with the SAAQ, the *Société de l'assurance automobile du Québec*, which is a kind of hybrid DMV/public insurance company. See, everyone knows Canadians get socialized medicine, but I guess not that many people realize that Québec just had to one-up the RoC (Rest of Canada) by socializing their damn car insurance, too.

When you call, there's usually a couple of weeks' wait for an appointment. Mine was set for last Wednesday, at 1:40 p.m. I turned up at 1:40 on the nose, but of course the 1:40 p.m. appointment people still hadn't been let through. A guard at the door pointed us to a waiting room off to the side of the entrance lobby where we had to wait for the call, which came, by my watch ... at 1:42 p.m.

We went through to the reception where you present an ID. The receptionist crosses your name off of a printed out appointments sheet, asks you what you're there for, and gives you a little printed-out number. Then you're told to go to a larger waiting room inside, where about 8 different computerized lines move along in parallel to each other, with numbers called out by the computerized system.

Anyway, I had about a 20 minute wait there. The crowd was seriously mixed. Maybe 70% of us were obviously immigrants - Arabs and black Africans and Brazilian oligarchs and lots of Chinese families with kids in toe. The other 30% were Quebeckers - basically teenagers there with their parents to get their learner's permits, most of them nervously paging through their heavily dog-eared Driver's Handbook just before their tests. At 2:03 p.m., by my watch, my number came up.

I sat down in semi-private booth with a SAAQ official and explained my case, which was slightly unusual in that I'm a new immigrant, but I also have an old SAAQ dossier from when I lived here with my parents back in 1997-98. He listened carefully, asked me for all the documents required, looked me up on the computer, meticulously updated my file, and within 20 minutes, was charging me the $78 it costs to issue a replacement license. He left me with a handshake and a smile. By 2:30 p.m., I was cycling back to my house.

Obviously, the contrast with what happened to me in *Los Chaguaramos* couldn't have been more complete. On the one hand, the entire procedure was freakishly devoid of aggravation. On the other, nobody in the SAAQ waiting room would've dreamed of trying to strike up a conversation with anybody else in that line. We sat, silently, anonymously, safe - in the expectation that the state would fulfill its minimum duty to us to treat us with professional courtesy, and not to waste more of our time than is necessary.

In the SAAQ waiting room, we were dehumanized, but we were equal. Nobody could skip ahead of anybody else in that line - there's no way to bribe the computerized queue-management system. In fact, our dehumanization was the guarantee of our equality: it's precisely *because* the computer treated us all as numbers that we could be certain nobody would get special treatment.

And that, in the end, is what bureaucracy does.

In Venezuela, bureaucracy is, of course, a dirty word, but it really shouldn't be. Real bureaucracy - rational bureaucracy of the kind that Canadians are so damn good at, and Venezuelans so catastrophically hopeless at - is the truest guarantor of equality. In the SAAQ's hands, you temporarily trade in your individuality in return for equality, because in the SAAQ's eyes, you are not a person, you are an abstraction - an object that pre-determined rules are simply applied to.

If you're so inclined, you could see that as a terrible affront to your dignity. But believe you me, I've been through both, and I would infinitely prefer to get a driver's license in Montréal than in Caracas.

Sukhois over Petare
Posted on February 3, 2012 by Juan Cristobal

"I'm glad you're here," says Carmen. "I don't know if you know this, but a few weeks ago, the guy who delivers the school lunches witnessed four people getting gunned down at seven in the morning – right here, just as the kids were coming to class. Now he doesn't want to come anymore. He's afraid he's next."

Welcome to Escuela Ebel Pastor Oropeza, a municipal school for special-needs children in the heart of Petare, Caracas' biggest, meanest slum.

Carmen, one of the teachers at the school, matter-of-factly recites these grievances to the authorities accompanying me, while at the same time giving us a slice of birthday cake for another teacher. Life and death, it's all in a day's work here, she says.

I'm visiting the school with the people from the Sucre city hall, part of the greater Caracas municipal government. Sucre is in charge of Escuela Oropeza, along with fifty other schools in highly vulnerable areas.

This is my first time in Petare's hills. You drive up through an impossibly-sloped hill, surrounded by brick houses, garbage, motorcycles, and people – people everywhere. The higher you go, the narrower the street gets. The feeling of claustrophobia and fear is hard to shake, even more so when we realize ... we are lost.

My friends from the Sucre municipality wanted to take me to another school, but in the cerro's winding streets, we lose our way. No problem – a National Guard informs us that Escuela Oropeza is right up the hill, and Lucio, Sucre's Education Secretary, tells me we should go there instead. "*Es una de las nuestras.*"

Escuela Oropeza treats at-risk children from the entire barrio. Kids with hyper-activity, Asperger's, ADD, and various learning disabilities find a sanctuary from the chaos of the shantytown in the school's tidy, narrow classrooms.

The teachers at the school are modern Venezuelan heroes – it's as simple as that. Faced with impossible circumstances and few resources, they provide a caring and safe environment for their kids, to the best of their abilities.

I ask them where they live. One of them lives in Guatire, east of Caracas, an hour or two commute each way. Another lives in the 23 de Enero, in the other side of town. The one with the shortest – but possibly most hazardous -commute lives fifty meters below, in the barrio. She takes the stairs to come to work every day.

I ask Yosemi, the sixth-grade teacher, if her kids are on Ritalin. She looks at me as if I was from another planet. The school doesn't have running water. They haven't had an onsite psychologist in months. She tells me the more severe cases have been evaluated, but they never get the results back. You can't treat what is not diagnosed, she says.

She does what she can to help them, but the problems are overwhelming: physical and sexual abuse, self-esteem issues, and abandonment are par for the course. A twelve-year old recently knocked on their door to enroll on his own initiative. His junkie mom had never bothered enrolling him, he was illiterate and had heard this was a school for kids like him.

I poke my head into the fifth-grade classroom. I ask the kids to guess where I'm from. When they hear I'm from Maracaibo – Venezuela's second-largest city – I ask them if they know what state it's in.

None of them know. I am later told most of them are barely learning to read and write.

I ask Susana, the fourth-grade teacher, about textbooks. She says the mayor's office gave them textbooks last year, but this year they gave them half of the amount. The Mayor's Education Secretary, on tour with me, makes a note, and talks about how the national government has cut the opposition municipality's budget. He promises to do what he can.

The school teaches basic job skills such as electricity, woodwork, sewing, and cooking. I ask Suleima, the cooking teacher, about some of her success stories. She tells me, with obvious pride, about a couple of her students who recently got stable jobs. One works at a bakery, the other at Domino's Pizza.

I ask her for a picture, and she says no. First, she says, I need to put on my uniform.

All over the school, you see signs about basic values: companionship; respect; responsibility; work ethic. One sign reminds kids that your job is only important if you do it well. In the kitchen, another reminds them that the table is where a person's true culture reveals itself, and that they should treat the dinner table with respect.

Public schools are voting centers in Venezuela. When there is an election, the military takes over the school for a few days before, and a few days after.

Maydelin, another of the teachers, tells me that after the last election, they came to work to find that somebody had stolen the entire computer lab. They have yet to raise the money to replace it.

I have a hard time hearing her. Directly above us, eight recently-purchased Sukhoi war planes are practicing for a military parade.

We wonder, in silence, how much the parade is going to cost.

III

The Economy

Since both Quico and I know a thing or two about economics, we feel pretty comfortable discussing the topic, and some of our posts on this subject were, specifically designed to challenge our readers' conventional wisdom. Looking back at this chapter's selection, I think our relative comfort allowed us to branch out and be bold, explaining things that seemed clear to us in a way that – hopefully – made sense for our readers.

Venezuela is a country where few economic decisions make sense, so there is always something worth discussing. At the end of the day, ours is an economy in permanent state of malaise. Double digit inflation is the norm, more than half of the population works in the informal sector, and there are serious issues of poverty, crime, inequality, and lack of quality education.

Our social and economic ills are mostly related to oil dependency, and the vices it creates. Breaking the vicious cycle the petro-state creates is a task for a generation or two. Hopefully, we've played our part in explaining the issues in an accessible way, tilting the public sphere just a tiny bit toward sanity.

Petro-states for beginners
December 15, 2008 by Quico

It's not easy being a progressive Venezuelan opposed to the Chávez Regime. A lot of my leftie friends in the US look south and see a fresh, irreverent if slightly over-the-top leader sticking it to the man and fighting for Latin America's poor. Understandably, they can't help but wonder if I haven't gone all "Wall Street Journal" on them when I voice my rejection of his regime.

"But I heard the poor are doing much better than they were before, and they really love him," they'll say to me, struggling to grasp how an apparently sane person could fail to grasp the romance, the heady excitement of seeing a popularly elected leader fighting back against the years of Washington Consensus crap imposed on Latin America by the neoliberal elite.

I've been down this road many times before, and I know the conversation that follows won't be easy, because the misunderstandings about Venezuela are deep.

For one thing, most Americans remain under the impression that Venezuela is, basically, a Latin American country. It isn't. We are, first and foremost, a petrostate - a place where the government gets to pump massive amounts of money more or less directly out of the ground.

Nothing about Venezuela makes sense until you've worked out the deep implications of that one, basic fact. Deep down, Venezuela has much more in common with Algeria, Iran, or Russia than with Colombia, Brazil or Cuba.

For starters, we experience the oil cycle upside down.

Take the 1970s. Folks in the US remember them as the bad times: gas shortages, inflation, unemployment and the general, society-wide funk that came to be known as the age of malaise. Your oil crisis, though, was our oil boom: we remember the 70s as the time we hit the jackpot, an age when a huge amount of free money suddenly flooded the country, setting off a collective spasm of high-intensity shopping the likes of which Venezuelans had never seen before.

Needless to say, our president was intensely popular back then, too!

The flip side came in the 90s, when Americans enjoyed an economic boom made possible, among other things, by dirt cheap energy, which, on our end, led to a string of bank failures and a decade-long recession that left the country in the mood for radical change.

At the start of this decade, the pendulum swung again, bringing yet another oil boom which you'll recall mostly in the form of the murderous prices you were paying at the pump last summer. From our end, though, the last five years have been a time when the gods of global energy decided to smile upon Venezuela again, sending the government on a breathless spending spree, and setting off yet another country-wide consumption boom, with unemployment falling, wages rising, and smiles all around.

The twist is that, this time, the oil bonanza happened with a self-described Marxist revolutionary in power, a guy who claims to be locked in a mortal fight with global capitalism but leads a state run by a gaggle of platinum-card toting socialists.

This has contributed immeasurably to the weird sense of dislocation of Venezuela in the last few years, an era of revolutionary slogans painted on the sides of massive new shopping malls. This is a country where the people whose job it is to administer the Revolutionary Bolivarian Socialist state think nothing of plunking down a couple of thousand dollars for a plasma-screen TV before heading off for a bit of lunch in an LA-style sushi bar, where obscenely overpriced bits of fish flown in from the other side of the globe get washed down with $4 bottles of Corona.

It's this oil-fueled spending boom that accounts for the popularity of the Chávez regime, and there's nothing progressive about it.

All the boom-time spending ended up sloshing all around the Venezuelan economy, where it set off a dynamic the world had surely never seen before: a kind of Marxist Trickle-Down Economics. In the end, for all the rambling ideological speeches, the Chávez boom is just a tweaked rerun of the 70s for us, with vastly different ideological *muzak* but social and political consequences that are pretty much the same.

The irrelevance of Chávez's ideology to his popularity comes into sharpest relief when seen in international context. In fact, just about every petro-state has seen its government's popularity spike over the last five years, whether those governments are Marxist (like ours), nationalist (as in Russia), Islamic (think Iran) or, even, genocidal (Sudan). The political economy of petro-spending binges doesn't actually hinge on the ideological label a government prefers to slap on its own lapel. In the end, oil goes out, money comes in, stuff gets imported, jobs are created, people get happy, and leaders get popular.

It is a fact that Chávez has been far less repressive than his hyper-radical rhetoric might lead you to fear. To me, though, the measure of Chávez's tolerance has been the scale of the oil revenue stream.

Chávez grasped all along that there was no point in jailing masses of people, censoring newspapers and generally playing the highly damaging role of repressive ogre when he had enough cash on hand to co-opt the coopt-able and bankrupt the rest. It's a trick the Chávez regime has mastered with chilling speed, and one that has allowed it to avoid the reputation costs of repression without really having to compromise its increasingly tight grip on society.

Now, though, the credit has crunched and the oil market's gone off a cliff. Venezuelan oil, which was selling for $129 a barrel just five months ago, fetched just $31 at the end of last week. The revolutionary elite are facing wrenching spending choices. Suddenly, not every labor union's wage demands can be met, not every interest group's aspirations can be underwritten, and the feel-good factor the oil boom once generated is dissipating with alarming speed.

For years now, what traditional autocrats achieved with the gun and the gallows, Chávez has been achieving with his bulging pocketbook. That's not going to be possible for much longer.

The quiescent society of the Marxist trickle-down era risks being replaced with something much more fractious. It risks being replaced with a society where interest groups fight one another for their share of a shrinking resource pie and none of the shortcuts for batting down dissent are available. It's a situation Chávez has never had to face, and the temptation to maintain control through force will be strong.

Will Chávez resist it? Stay tuned...

The fjords of Macuro
Posted on June 25, 2008 by Juan Cristobal

The most developed nation on Earth.

The most peaceful country on Earth.

Insanely high life expectancy.

The second-highest GDP per capita in the world.

A near-absence of poverty and income inequality.

These are some of the honors bestowed on a little country, with just over 4.4 million people, perched on a bunch of cliffs in the top of the world: Norway.

Thinking through Venezuela's problems is depressing enough, so holding ourselves up to a place like *that* would only add to our misery. The urge to find a role model to copy is understandable. But, surely, Norway can't be that benchmark.

There are no fjords in Macuro. As much as he may like to think otherwise, the guy in Miraflores is no king, just a fat man surrounded by yes-men. And while we have plenty of blondes, let's just say they're not quite Scandinavian.

But face it: we're hard up for a good benchmark. Comparisons with Latin American countries border on useless. Venezuela has more in common with Iran, Algeria and Nigeria than with Guatemala, Peru or Uruguay. Thing is, instead of offering hope, the experiences of our fellow oil exporters serve up a deep well of despair.

It's no wonder that people resort to near-apocalyptic terms to describe our economy. Some talk about "the devil's excrement." A Google Academic count on "resource curse" came up with a whopping 36,900 articles. Many of them mention Venezuela.

Thinking through this stuff, it's easy to end up mired in a self-flagellatory funk over our screwed-up national psyche. The conclusion seems inexorable: easy oil money has a lot to answer for. Successive petro-booms have only served up our society to one predatory, authoritarian regime after another, from Gómez to Pérez Jiménez to CAP to Chávez.

But is it is really that simple? Aren't we forgetting that many modern economies, such as Canada, Australia, and Norway, have been built on the back of natural resources? Isn't there something lazy about this blanket denunciation of the petrostate, as though we could just pass the buck to the black stuff under our feet and turn the page?

Oil wealth isn't necessarily a curse. Norway, in particular, is an example of a petrostate that works.

Norway is the world's third-largest oil exporter, a bigger exporter than Venezuela. It is also the world's third-largest gas exporter. In spite of this, Norway's "curse" is nearing its end: its oil and gas reserves are very small compared to other countries, and production is expected to decrease dramatically in the coming years.

So Norwegians, in spite of having lots of oil, have managed to make a nice little country for themselves. What has worked?

A lot of things come to mind: their European mindset, their weather, their history. Yet while some of this may have played a role, it would be a mistake to believe a country's development path is so deterministic. After all, few people fifty years ago would have looked at the mindset, weather, and history of Singapore and predicted it was going to become the powerhouse that it is today. It's not all in the genes, and under-development is not an inescapable trap.

What has made the difference in Norway - the reason it's no Nigeria - is that it Norwegians have not fallen into the traps of petro-states.

Thanks to mechanisms put in place to isolate the country from sudden oil windfalls, the country is an exporter of diverse goods and services. Contrary to expectations, Norwegians managed to avoid the disease that plagued their Dutch neighbors and was so pervasive that it created its own little economic malaise.

How did Norway do it? One explanation frequently espoused has to do with timing. In particular, countries in which a boom in commodity exporting coincided with the formation of the modern state now exhibit bloated bureaucracies and an inefficient state apparatus, one that makes ad-hoc, arbitrary decisions on economic policy and usually gets it wrong. Norway was the opposite.

Norway discovered its oil in 1962, relatively late in its development. By then, it was an established monarchical democracy. This, however, did not prevent Norwegian politicians from spending the dough.

As documented by Stanford political scientist Terry Lynn Karl in her magnum opus, *The Paradox of Plenty*, public expenditure in Norway rose just as fast as income from oil exports. Norwegians went on a spending spree in the late 70s and early 80s that rivaled that of the Venezuelan *ta'baratos*.[32]

---

[32] In the 70s, Venezuelan tourists in Miami were known as the "ta'baratos." Due to the strength of the bolívar those days, they would often be seen in Miami shopping malls saying "ta'barato, dame dos," meaning "that's cheap; I'll take two of them."

Inevitably, the Norwegian economy hit the wall, just like that of other oil exporters. However, that is where the similarities end. As Karl puts it,

"Unlike all other exporters, it (the Norwegian state) established substantial control over petroleum policy on the basis of consensus, protected against the worst excesses of petrolization, and permitted voluntary and relatively rapid adjustment. In effect, its highly institutionalized state structures provided a type of "creative resistance" to the overwhelming impact of the bonanza that was simply unavailable to the developing countries.

The contrast to other exporters from the point of departure – that is, from the discovery of oil on the North Sea shelf – is telling. The structures that "received" Norway's boom could hardly have been more different from those of the developing countries. Oil companies, especially eager to exploit resources outside OPEC's dominion, did not encounter a poor country, a weak state, undeveloped social forces, or a predatory, authoritarian ruler… The state in Norway was, in Olsen's words, a "typical civil servants' state," which came remarkably close to what Weber labeled an ideal bureaucracy operating under rational legal authority."

Karl lists several key features of the Norwegian state structure that allowed it to absorb the oil shock in a sane, rational manner. Recruitment was based solely by merit. Civil servants were unusually insulated from and impervious to influence peddling. Advancement depended on nominations from other (higher-ranking) civil servants. The attempts by political parties and interest organizations to influence the State were frowned upon. Corruption is virtually nonexistent. As Karl depressingly puts it, "this "civil-service state" was the complete antithesis of Venezuela and the other politicized states examined previously."

In other petro-states, the beginning of oil booms found oil companies negotiating with a rapacious, unequipped, underdeveloped bureaucracy, whose main goal was to establish a tax base. Norway's bureaucracy had no interest in this. Their emphasis was on regulating the industry correctly, using sophisticated financial planning techniques and tools that maximized collective welfare.

One of these tools is Norway's Petroleum Fund. This Fund is a mechanism ruled by clear guidelines through which the Norwegian state saves the money coming from extraordinary oil funds for the pensions of future generations. Very literally, it is a way for current generations to use their extraordinary good luck in order to free future ones from the burden of trying to support them.

The Fund's shadow over Norway's economy looms large. In 2006, Norway had a budget surplus of a whopping 25.9 percent of GPD. Venezuela, on the contrary, ran a budget deficit that year. That same year, the net assets of the general government were 1.5 times the size of the entire Norwegian economy. To put this number in context, it would be equivalent to the Venezuelan government having savings worth $270 billion instead of the roughly $40 billion it has.

The rules of the Fund are simple. Most of the revenue from oil goes into the Fund, which invests the money abroad. The key rule sets the non-oil structural budget deficit of the central government to the fund's long-term real return, 4 percent.

In other words, it sets spending limits on the government by setting a maximum amount that the government can withdraw from the fund each year, capping them to the "interest" that the Fund earns. That way, the long-term value of the fund is preserved. Money goes in the Fund only when the oil market is doing well, and it goes out of it when the market tanks.

Although it may be tempting to simply copy and paste, it's important to keep in mind that the particular form that these rules adopt is not what is key. Some rules are designed so that the long-term value of the Fund is maximized while short-term cash disbursements are sacrificed. Other rules are more flexible as to the amount of windfall you can spend in the short run. And the rules in Norway are not always complied with to their fullest.

The important thing is that Norway's fund, like the ones in Alaska or in Chile, is borne out of a consensus among the political classes and civil society as to the economy's medium- and long-term goals and prospects. Countries that successfully cope with resource windfalls (or shortfalls) are those with stable rules that meet some minimum requirements. It's important to keep this in mind and to understand that consensus and stability are more important than the rules themselves.

The Norwegian example shows us that sudden oil wealth is not the root cause of a country's problems. Oil is not a curse, it's a blessing - it's what we as a society choose to do with it that makes a difference. And much of this boils down to a series of institutional arrangements and political consensus that should be the main goal of any political party.

Norwegians are not a special race. They live in a remote country that is inaccessible in many places and, while rich in natural resources, is poor in population.

Yet through clever institutional design and a little bit of luck, they have managed to do right for themselves. There's no reason why Norway can't serve as a guideline to future policy decisions.

So before giving up hope, thinking that we will never be like Norway and that there will never be fjords in Macuro, let's think about what is within our grasp. We would be well served to use the Norwegian benchmark and try and adapt to our own country the principles and setups that have worked for theirs.

Using Norway as a benchmark may sound crazy, but it's better than our current role-model. While the road to hell is paved with good intentions, the road to success is usually built on plans that may appear to some as impossible pipe dreams.

Let's face it - we can't do much worse than we've already done, so what have we got to lose?

Margot & Maria Luisa
Posted on March 21, 2006 by Juan Cristobal

".....Particularmente es un síndrome que es endémico en nuestro manicomio: la histeria. Estudiando lo escrito sobre esta enfermedad -que solemos achacarle, injustamente, sólo a lo femenino-, he encontrado que la histeria viene a ser la antítesis de la historia, por consistir en una condición que bloquea la posibilidad de entender el sentido y las lecciones de nuestros fracasos y limitaciones. Dice un historiador que la histeria es como una plataforma donde rebota todo lo que nos acontece, impidiendo que lo vivido pueda transformarse en experiencia. Esto hace que nos quedemos continuamente en la superficie, sin llegar jamás a profundizar, sin llegar a tener una visión interior, sin unir nuestro pasado a la historia del hombre sobre La Tierra. Tenemos pues que Venezuela es un país histérico sometido a una repetición infernal. Nuestra mayor pobreza es carecer de una verdadera historia de nuestro empobrecimiento..."

Federico Vegas, "Falke" [33]

Maria Luisa

Maria Luisa lives in a comfortable house in Prados del Este. A staunch anti-chavista, she prides herself for having gone to dozens of marches. She figures in the Lista Tascón as, in her words, a "hopeless squalid one." [34]

Maria Luisa works for a law firm that has seen better days. In spite of her diminishing productivity, she is proud of being a self-made woman. She is the single mother of Claudia, a student at the UCV School of Dentistry. She hopes her daughter goes to the U.S. to earn a Master's degree after graduating, and wishes she stayed in

---

[33] "Falke" is a historical novel about a botched attempt to topple a dictator. The quote above refers to Venezuelans' seeming inability to process our experiences into something meaningful, something that prevents us from repeating the same mistakes again. The author says that we have no "history," but rather "hysteria."

[34] Prados del Este is an upscale neighborhood in Caracas. However, it is not where the most lavish homes are.

the U.S. to start a new life there because, she claims, "there is no future in this country."

She enjoys travelling to Florida with her daughter once every couple of years, to "decompress from this country run by chavistas." She is more than happy to use the profits from the sale of her Cadivi dollars to help pay for her trip.

Maria Luisa says she lives in a "ghetto," which is her way of calling the area between Plaza Venezuela and Petare where all the "oligarchs" live. And she adds, "I only include Plaza Venezuela because my daughter has to go there and study every day." She drives a three-year old Ford Explorer, which she bought after she had to give her daughter her seven-year old Toyota Corolla so she could get to class.

When asked about the *Misiones*, Maria Luisa dismisses them as "Chávez's vote-buying schemes." Maria Luisa agrees that some people are probably made better off by the Misiones, but in general she opposes them because, so she claims, for every *bolívar* that makes its way to the poor, three make its way to the pockets of some corrupt general. She tells me about her former neighbor, a general, who left Prados del Este after buying a house in Cerro Verde for his family, demolishing it and building a brand new one in its place.

Maria Luisa seems proud to say that, because she figures in Lista Tascón, she does not benefit from "this government run by Cubans." She earns her own paycheck and makes do. She claims she does not indulge, but she is proud of all she has earned, and she does not owe the government or anyone else a single "locha."

Margot

Margot lives very close to Maria Luisa as the crow flies, in a brick house in Barrio Las Minas. Margot and her 19-year old daughter, Nayareth, wake up at 5 AM every day to catch a jeep that will bring them to the entrance of the barrio. From there, she takes a bus to Chacaíto where Margot works as a short-order cook at a small "cafetería." Nayareth shares a street-stall in Sabana Grande with three friends, where they sell ladies' undergarments imported from Colombia. Margot feels lucky to be working relatively close to Nayareth, and she gets to share the two-hour bus rides each way, every day, with her.

Margot and Nayareth are devoted followers of Pres. Chávez. Thanks to the President's social programs, Margot has enrolled in Misión Ribas, where she is working toward getting her high-school diploma. She and Nayareth were able to get their ID cards for the first time thanks to Misión Identidad, and this allowed them to vote for Chávez in the Recall Referendum "and in every election since."

Margot and Nayareth have been eating well lately, thanks to the opening of Mercal in their barrio. They were not able to afford meat before, but now they enjoy a steak once in a while. Although she hopes someday Mercal will sell products with uniform quality, "like those you find in the supermarkets of the rich," she claims the meat and the produce in Mercal are "excellent." Just last week, she had asparagus for the first time in her life.

Margot suffers from occasional back spasms, a side effect of being on her feet all day, so she visits Barrio Adentro frequently for treatment. Nayareth also goes once a month for pain medication for a bad hip.

Nayareth has a high-school degree, but she would like to continue her studies. She says she has looked at Misión Sucre, but feels she is not ready to leave her job for a career that will probably have uncertain job prospects.

Margot and Nayareth believe what their President tells them. "The oligarchs want to take away the *Misiones*," she says, and she is willing to do anything to protect "mi Comandante." She clearly feels empowered for the first time in her life, and she claims Chávez has done more for the poor than anybody ever has, "or ever will."

Breaking down their gifts

Margot earns 200 thousand *bolívars* a month at the *"cafetería."* Nayareth's income averages about 200 thousand bolívars per month. Margot also earns 200 thousand *bolívars* per year as a Christmas bonus. Margot also receives a *"Misión Ribas"* scholarship of 160 thousand bolívars a month. Their total income for the year amounts to 6.92 million bolívars, or roughly US$2,768 at the market rate of 2500 Bs/USD.

Margot and Nayareth pay 100 thousand bolívars per month as rent. They spend the remainder at Mercal. From a cursory comparison of the prices at Mercal relative to the prices at Excelsior Gama, an upscale supermarket, one could assume that the market prices of goods are about 133% higher than prices at Mercal.

Margot's total spending at Mercal each year amounts to 5.72 million bolívars. The market value of the goods she buys is roughly 13 million, 50% of which is probably attributable to import costs. Since imports are subsidized through Cadivi, the "international" market value of Margot's shopping is 14 million bolívars. The implicit Mercal subsidy Margot and Nayareth receive is the difference – roughly 8.28 million bolívars a year.

Last year, Nayareth went to Barrio Adentro 12 times. Margot goes to Barrio Adentro about 28 times per year, or 2-3 times a month. One could assume that the market price of each trip to Barrio Adentro is about 40.000 bolívars per visit, including medication and treatment. The value of the Barrio Adentro subsidy for Margot and Nayareth would then amount to 1.6 million bolívars per year.

Finally, one would have to include the cash value of Margot's Misión Ribas scholarship. This amounts to 1.92 million bolívars.

The total implicit and explicit subsidies Margot and Nayareth enjoy amount to 11.8 million bolívars, or roughly US$4,720.

Maria Luisa and Claudia enjoy a subsidy from the government stemming from the lower price of gasoline. We can assume a market price equivalent to U.S. market prices, which is 18 times the price in Venezuela. I assume that Claudia and Maria Luisa currently spend about 30.000 Bs. per month on gasoline. This implies the total subsidy they receive from the government's cheap gasoline is 6.12 million bolívars per year.

Claudia studies at UCV for free. If she were to go to law school at UCAB, she would have to pay 3 million bolívars per year. Dentistry is a more expensive degree than law, but only public universities are allowed to offer health-care degrees in Venezuela. I conservatively use the UCAB estimate as the market price for Claudia's studies.

Maria Luisa earns 3 million bolívars per month. She also gets a Christmas bonus of 5 million bolívars. Her yearly earnings are therefore 41 million bolívars. She spends 85% of her salary on different goods and services, which carry an imported component. I assume that 50% of Maria Luisa's consumption is imported at the official rate of Bs. 2150 per US$. Therefore, when Maria Luisa and Claudia consume in Venezuela, they are indirectly paying less for goods and services than they would be if imports were allowed in at the market rate. The total amount of this implicit subsidy is 2.836 million bolívars.

Maria Luisa and Claudia each are allowed US$4,000 at the official rate for spending abroad. They are also each allowed US $2,500 at the official rate for Internet purchases, and a separate US $400 for ATM withdrawals abroad. If they were to buy these amounts at the market rate, they would have to pay 34.5 million bolívars. Instead, thanks to Cadivi, they only have to pay 29.67 million. The implicit Cadivi subsidy is therefore 4.83 million bolívars.

The value of total subsidies enjoyed by Maria Luisa and Claudia are therefore 16.786 million bolívars, or roughly US$6,714.

Maria Luisa can't wait to see the end of the revolution that she claims is destroying her country. In a few years, both Maria Luisa and Claudia will move to the U.S., where Claudia will use the education she has received for free from the Venezuelan government to join an established dental practice in Bethesda. None of Maria Luisa's descendants will ever live in Venezuela again.

Margot and Nayareth will stay in Venezuela, as will their many descendants. It is unlikely any of them will get to live in Prados del Este.

Each year, the Chávez government increases its net public debt by roughly US$3 billion. Future generations of Venezuelans, which includes Margot's descendants but not Maria Luisa's, will have to carry this burden on their shoulders.

Margot and Maria Luisa will never meet.

Adventures in Petro-caudillism
Posted on April 27, 2012 by Quico

In order to understand the current state of Venezuela's economy, you, dear reader, need a tiny bit of background to understand what petro-caudillism is.

As far back as I can remember there have been three ways the oil industry can transfer money to the Venezuelan state:

It pays a percentage of its *profits* in income tax, just like everyone else -this happened even before nationalization in 1975.

On top of that, it pays a percentage of the *gross value* of oil taken out of the ground in the form of royalties because the state owns the stuff – this also pre-dates nationalization.

Finally, since 1975, the state has been PDVSA's only shareholder, so it also gets dividends from the oil industry.

That's the *zanahoria* stuff. Before Chávez, all three mechanisms transferred oil rents into a single pot – the National Treasury – and all three were well established, transparent, and unquestionably legal.

Then, Chávez happened.

Slowly at first, strange new ways of shifting petro-dollars into state coffers came to be used. As time passed, PDVSA came up with new ways to bypass the National Treasury finance state programs directly.

Now, the difference between this kind of direct spending and the *Zanahoria* Fiscal Contribution might seem arcane, but it's profound. By spending money directly instead of handing it to the National Treasury, PDVSA abrogates a privilege the constitution reserves to elected members of Venezuela's National Assembly. In picking and choosing government programs and handing them cash discretionally, PDVSA becomes – what was that phrase, again? – a State within the State; utterly beyond the reach of democratic oversight and accountability.

You'll search high and low in Venezuela's 1999 constitution for PDVSA's right to spend money this way. In the polite fictions of Bolivarian constitutional doctrine, Venezuela operates under the principle of the *"Unidad del Tesoro"* – all funds paid to the state are meant to go into a single pot. Once there, representatives elected by the people to the National Assembly must give explicit permission, through a budget law or other lending laws, before the government is allowed to spend any of it.

That obviously can't happen if PDVSA skips the whole parliamentary rigmarole and starts spending money on whatever the president orders that day. This, more and more, is what actually happens.

PDVSA's Direct Spending (a.k.a. the Hanky-Panky Budget) started out as a marginal sliver of Venezuela's fiscal math. In 2001, it was $34 million, in 2002, just $14 million. Soon enough, though, that particular frog was boiled all the way through, and the Hanky-Panky stuff started to balloon. With the single exception of 2009 – the closest thing we've had to a non-election year in that time, since the only vote happened in February that year – PDVSA's Hanky-Panky Budget has grown every single year since 2002.

The thing is that PDVSA's *Zanahoria* fiscal contribution is no longer keeping up. While from 2005 to 2008, its fiscal and para-fiscal contributions grew in tandem, over the last three years it's starting to look like Hanky-Panky spending is replacing PDVSA's *Zanahoria* Fiscal Contribution.

Witness the contrast between 2008 and last year. The total amount PDVSA dished out to the state didn't change that much: $55.4 billion in 2008, vs. 58.6 billion last year. But while in 2008, twice as much of that was spent legally than illegally, by last year those proportions had been reversed.

This allows us to have a look at our Petro-caudillism Index in historical context. Again, we're dealing with a simple ratio here: the amount of money PDVSA spends illegally divided by the amount it spends legally.

As recently as 2009, just 24 petro-cents were spent without legislative approval for every petrodollar spent under legislative oversight. Last year, that proportion jumped to 2.08 to 1. Therefore, I can say, with scientific precision, that today we are 8.7 times more Petro-caudillistic than we were three years ago.[35]

Parapara-nomics 101
Posted on February 9, 2012 by Juan Cristobal

Venezuela's main opposition candidates seem to spend 80% of their time talking about social policy – better schools, functioning hospitals, and more police. It's a focus born out of political necessity, I get that. But when they come to power, they'll soon discover a social agenda is not enough. You can't get people out of poverty permanently without serious economic reform, and there's no point pretending otherwise.

Parapara is a case in point.[36] The great thing about the town was how easy it was to talk to the people, since many of them lull away their mornings in the town's sidewalks and plazas, eager to strike up a chat with any Tom, Dick or Quico who drops by.

---

[35] All the Data for this post came from PDVSA's "Informe de Gestión Anual 2011", pages 158 (for the Hanky Panky stuff) and 214 (for the carrot juice), with additional data from the 2009 Report (page 200.)

[36] Parapara is a small town in the state of Guárico. It has been the subject of quite a few of our posts, coming to represent the challenges in Venezuela's countryside. Quico and I visited the place in 2012. In the next chapter, we talk about our trip to Parapara in more detail.

But let's not kid ourselves – this may seem quaint, but it points to an economy in serious disrepair. After all, shouldn't able-bodied middle-aged men and women be out ... working? What are they doing talking to *forasteros* in a plaza at 11 AM on a Tuesday morning?

"Sure, there used to be day labor to go work in the fields, picking peppers, or lemons. But there's little of that anymore," says one recently made chavista friend.

The ways chavista public policy has conspired to keep Paraparans idle are visible even as you drive into town. The main road, a potholed, unmarked mess, suddenly widens into a veritable 6-lane highway – sans dividers or lane markings, but smooth and massive – but only for a stretch of about ten kilometers.

Then it narrows back to a death-defying mess.

We ask them about that.

"Yeah," they say disheartened, "there has been some work on that. But most of the jobs go to people from other towns, those who are better connected."

What about the railroads we keep hearing about?

"There are two railroads being built," they explain. "One is the North-South line that links to Cagua. Two Italian companies are in charge of that one, but the work has been stopped for well over a year. There is another one being built by the Chinese, but most of the workers there are Chinese. Every day people knock on their door asking for work, but only a few get hired."

"*Menos mal*," one Consejo Comunal guy says, "that we have the Consejos Comunales. Thanks to them we get to build some houses for *Misión Vivienda*. But the bureaucracy makes things go slow."

Notice a thread here? Every avenue in these guys' economic outlook – the *misión*, the railroad, the city hall, the ambulatorio, the road works – everything is state-owned. Formal, private sector jobs are as elusive as a unicorn out here.

As some authors have argued, Venezuela's steady decline tracks back to a collapse in productivity, and this has a direct link to the numerous distortions set in place by a succession of governments intent on strangling what remains of the private sector. (See Bello, Blyde, and Restuccia for a recent take on this.)

In Parapara, agriculture is a bust. This is a direct consequence of government policies both at the macro and micro levels: unrealistic price controls, chaotic land grabs, and an over-valued exchange rate that makes it cheaper to import peppers and lemons than to grow them there. At the micro level, the once functioning agricultural input and credit sector has collapsed under the heady cocktail of mismanagement and corruption of the Loyo era.[37]

It's also a consequence of the government's failure to do the things it should be doing. If you look at Google maps, you will see that there is only one paved road that goes through town, linking it from North and South. There are no east-west roads for miles on end. Irrigation infrastructure hasn't gotten serious investment in years. Electricity is hit or miss. And the infrastructure spending that does reach the region is wildly misspent on pharaoh-like railroad projects rather than unsexy – but high return – projects like simple roads.

The basic enabling environment for a functioning rural economy just isn't there. No amount of love for the land can survive profitably under those conditions.

But hearing opposition candidates and the economists that are advising them, you'd think building schools and paying teachers higher wages is going to address Parapara's underlying productivity problem.

Maybe the lessons of 1989 have been over-learned. Back then, a narrow focus on a technocratic register of concerns together with appalling tone-deafness to the social impact of reform made the country basically ungovernable.

---

[37] Juan Carlos Loyo, chavista bureaucrat who, for a while, was in charge of land grabs throughout the country. He has recently been re-appointed to his old job as minister.

But these days the pendulum has swung far too far in the other direction, to the point where expressing concern over the rudiments of the macro economy – whether it's the competitiveness of the exchange rate, the balance of payments, fiscal stability or productivity – are strictly verboten, and even micro-economic reform is approached hesitantly.

The danger is that this new orthodoxy hamstring any effort to address the whole set of supply side issues keeping Parapara unable to support its own without an ongoing influx of petrodollars from Caracas (or San Juan de los Morros.)

It's as though we've come full circle, from the impenetrable macroeconomic-focus of Miguel Rodríguez's *paquete* to an opposition technocracy whose mindset is Misiones…on steroids.

We need to keep some perspective: nobody is advocating a return to the socially maladaptive cluelessness of late-80s reform. But even the best social policy won't do away with the distortions keeping the people of Parapara in their plazas.

On its own, investment in Human Capital cannot create the jobs that people need to overcome poverty on a sustainable basis. What good is a quality education if the only employer in town is the government?

What's needed is a sense of balance: focusing on Social Policy to the exclusion of the nuts and bolts of economic governance carries risks. Unless the government addresses the serious distortions holding Parapara back, we won't be on the long-term path to prosperity.

The opposition's focus on gradualism is surely welcome, so long as gradualism doesn't become a pretext for inaction. It's a tough balancing act they face. But then, *nadie dijo que iba a ser fácil.*

Getting out while you can
Posted on May 14, 2007 by Juan Cristobal

"I think what everyone is hoping is that they'll get expropriated." Manuel's words surprised me, to say the least.

"Why would you say that?" I ask.

He sighs. "Juan, the way things are going here, it's really the best thing that can happen to your business," he says. "When they expropriate you, the government pays for your company in hard cash, and at a price that is probably higher than anything you'll be able to get a year or two from now, when the economy is fully socialized."

Manuel is a close friend of mine from college. After graduating, he took his hard-earned Venezuelan degree and got into an elite MBA program in the US. He went back home a few years ago and now manages a mid-sized company that manufactures health-care products.

To talk to him these days is to stare into a deep well of frustration. After all those years studying strategy, finance, marketing and things of the sort, he realizes his job is not so much to manage the company as to implement the decisions the government makes.

"The government decides at what price I can sell my products, who competes with me, and how much my raw materials cost," he explained. "I can only buy raw materials when they say, at the price they say. They decide how many people I can have working on my factory floor, and what I can pay them. And all of this is done at their whim so you don't even get to have any input into their decisions."

He sounds like he's at his wit's end.

"Actually," he goes on, "if you don't get expropriated your second best option is to move all your production overseas and just import finished goods. After all, the government lets you import stuff at the official exchange rate, and once you import, inflation means the stuff you sell fetches a higher price each month. Then, at the end of the year, the government lets you repatriate your earnings at the same exchange rate you used to import. So if you're an importer, they basically subsidize your profits! It's a steal."

He pauses.

"It's just too frustrating to work like this."

In his words, you can gauge the immediate dangers facing the Venezuelan economy. Nobody can deny that the past few years, Venezuela has been growing at a frenetic pace. But can it last?

Not if the mood around the private sector mirrors Manuel's. And all signs show that, like him, the business community is casting around frantically for ways to salvage some capital as they get out.

The economy is awash in petro-dollars, but the parallel exchange rate has shot up and foreign reserves have begun to dwindle. Just today, the International Energy Agency is reporting that oil production fell once again. And oil prices don't seem to be going up anytime soon.

What does that tell you? That Chávez's drive for full nationalization of the economy has the business community beyond jittery, and that's starting to show in the national accounts. Businesses are operating at full capacity, but with the threat of nationalization hanging over them and all those heavy-handed controls, few are willing to invest to expand. In fact, Venezuela was one of the few Latin American countries to have had negative foreign direct investment last year, according to ECLAC.

All the signs point to capital flight. Until relatively recently, businesses seemed happy to use their subsidized dollars to buy imported goods or raw materials to satisfy swelling demand. But now, as inflation eats away the margins for price-controlled products, demand is not being satisfied - scarcity is rampant, with basic food stuffs like grain, beef, chicken, eggs, black beans and cooking oil missing from the shelves. This is not limited to East-side Caracas grocery stores - a friend of mine tells me that Mercal's market share has fallen dramatically and is now at the level it was in 2003.

That tells you that, even with the enormous inflow of petro-dollars, the government just doesn't have enough to import all the goods people want to buy and buy up private industry and supply the demand caused by capital flight. This suggests we will see a devaluation of the currency soon, possibly before the year is done. Unless the Gods of the oil market smile on Chávez again, the government is going to have no choice but to turn the same number of dollars into more bolivars just to make ends meet on its own budget.

This will inevitably cause prices to go up even more quickly (inflation is already flirting with the 20% mark, and rising, in spite of price controls). Depending on what happens to the price of oil - and we know how unpredictable that is - it's not far-fetched to think that a year from now, Venezuela could be on the brink of recession.

As another friend of mine put it yesterday, the nub of it is that "it's not enough for oil prices to stabilize; Chávez needs constantly growing oil revenues just to make ends meet." And if oil prices fall, well, let's just say it won't take a big drop for the bottom to fall out. After all, when we had our first capital-flight-induced devaluation back on Black Friday, back in 1983, the price of oil was a comfortably high $30 per barrel.

Let's just hope all the Manuels out there get safely expropriated before the government runs out of cash.

Oil, econophobia, and the staggering intellectual bankruptcy of chavismo
Posted on January 21, 2007 by Quico

Miguel points to this lovely Chávez quote...

"A President shouldn't listen to economists."

A fine sentiment, no doubt, as long as you can get away with it. If 100,000,000 dollars just happen to gush out of the ground beneath you every day, say. Yes, I agree, economists are pretty superfluous then.

I've been thinking more and more about the lack of intellectual seriousness in chavismo, about its active hostility to specialist knowledge in general, and to economic knowledge in particular.

I think econophobia is at the heart of chavismo and of its popular appeal, its arrogance, its basic anti-rationalism and also its tendency to authoritarianism. Chávez holds specialist knowledge in deep, deep contempt - and the more power he amasses, the more contemptuous he gets.

And here, again, oil is a curse. Chávez can get away with it only because money is kind enough to ooze out of the ground in Venezuela. The basic resource constraints that end up persuading a Lula that, y'know, maybe it's not such a bad idea to talk to an economist now and then just don't come up in Venezuela...well, not during an oil boom, anyway.

Thanks to the petro-dollar flood, chavismo can just skirt the questions that dog any normal, earthly government - left, right or center - on any normal day: how do we ensure we have a good enough revenue stream to fund public services? How can we sustain a decent living for our people? How can we generate more wealth using the limited resources at our disposal?

Nobody cares. Nobody has to.

Oil is our magical elixir...the solution to all economic conundrums, the guarantee of the irrelevance of economists and their dreary, dense theories and dehumanizing categories and soul-sapping concern with work. Who would want any of that? The money's free...

It's easy to forget it now, but socialists used to have serious answers to the problems posed by economic life in industrial society. They were the wrong answers, sure, but they were serious.

Nationalization was supposed to reduce wasteful duplication of investments, lead to economies of scale, and cut out the bourgeois dead-wood from the production process. This would enable living standards to rise more quickly than was possible under capitalism. It didn't quite work out that way, but the proposals were the outcome of detailed analysis on the basis of meticulous reasoning.

20th century socialism never shied away from intellectual engagement in economic debates. Socialists from Clement Atlee to Joseph Stalin understood that socialism had to outperform capitalism in solving the basic problems of economic life. When Khrushchev banged his shoe on the podium at the UN, saying "we will bury you!" he meant that the superior Soviet economy would so decisively out-produce the West that capitalism would wither and die. That was supposed to be the whole point, the reason socialism was supposed to be better than capitalism as a way of organizing society. If it was to take its own claims seriously, 20th century socialism had to have the better solution to the problem of production.

What I find remarkable, unprecedented really, is the way 21st century socialism simply dispenses with any kind of economic reasoning whatsoever. Nationalizations are announced without reference to any kind of abstract discourse setting out the logical links between means (nationalization) and ends (higher productivity, or lower costs, or better service, or anything really.)

It's not even that chavistas are wrong in the causal claims they make. It's that they don't feel the need to put forward causal arguments at all. In their place, we get denunciations of greed and glorifications of solidarity - gut-level appeals to raw emotion - as the sole basis for economic policy-making. Public good, private bad.

Collective good, individual bad. That's as sophisticated as Chavonomic reasoning gets.

In the end, 21st Century Socialism is just the hollowed out husk of 20th Century Socialism. The headline grabbing moves - Nationalization! - haven't changed, but they've been completely stripped of the reasoning that once made them meaningful.

The suicidal dream of becoming an immense parasite that feeds off of our Oil
Posted on October 3, 2008 by Quico

Esta gran proporción de riqueza de origen destructivo crecerá sin duda alguna el día en que los impuestos mineros se hagan más justos y remunerativos, hasta acercarse al sueño suicida de algunos ingenuos que ven como el ideal de la hacienda venezolana llegar a pagar la totalidad del Presupuesto con la sola renta de minas, lo que habría de traducir más simplemente así: llegar a hacer de Venezuela un país improductivo y ocioso, un inmenso parásito del petróleo, nadando en una abundancia momentánea y corruptora.

-Arturo Uslar Pietri, 1936 [38]

Sembrar el petróleo - "sowing our oil" - is the central cliché of Venezuelan public life. Used, misused and abused by governments of the left, right and center virtually since the day it was penned, the phrase has been progressively drained of its content, slowly coming to mean pretty much the opposite of what Uslar Pietri had in mind in those heady days right after Gómez's death.

It takes going back and reading the chillingly prophetic essay the phrase originally came from - an exercise all Venezuelan public figures should be required by law to undertake at least once a year -

---

[38] Arturo Uslar Pietri was the leading Venezuelan intellectual of the XXth Century, and the first to discuss the need to shift away from oil dependency into other areas of the economy in a more or less serious manner. His mantra, sembrar el petróleo, or sowing oil, has remained in the public consciousness since being uttered more than 70 years ago.

to quite grasp that *"sembrar el petróleo"* is more a statement about morals than economics!

For Uslar Pietri, the real issue wasn't what oil dependence would do to our wallets; it was what it would do to our souls. Diversifying our economy was a means to the end of inoculating our society's moral fiber against the fecklessness and depravity that comes from unhinging consumption from hard work.

The great portion of our wealth of non-renewable origins shall doubtlessly grow once our mining taxes become fairer, and bring us closer to the suicidal dream of some ingénues who hope one day to pay for the whole of the national budget with mining rents alone. We could restate this more or less as: to one day make Venezuela an idle and unproductive country, an immense parasite feeding off of our oil, swimming in a momentary and corrupting abundance.

It's in this passage that it comes through most clearly, but the entire piece is only superficially about economics. Dig down just a bit and you see that Uslar's real game is to use economic categories to illuminate questions of morality. (Indeed, he turned out to be far more competent as a moralist than as an economist: the relevant metric for petro-dependence turned out to be oil's share of exports, not of government revenue.)

Uslar's essay stands as a stark warning about the corrosive influence of the petro-state: a buzzword that hadn't yet been coined for a condition we hadn't yet experienced, but that Uslar Pietri could see clearly just over the horizon.

It's interesting to speculate what might have been if *"el sueño suicida de convertirnos en un inmenso parasito del petróleo"* had become the take-away cliché from that piece, instead of that other one.

Because for much of the following 72 years, Venezuelan governments have taken turns missing Uslar's central point. One after the other, they've interpreted the call to sow the oil as a justification for dumping oil money into a succession of boondoggles requiring a never-ending infusion of petrodollars to stay afloat, a practice that entrenches the corrupting petro-dependence Uslar wanted to protect us from.

The results were clear from the start: a society where values like thrift, industry, and prudence come to seem quaintly out-of-place, the schoolmarms' admonitions of prudes who haven't the faintest clue how the copper is really beaten around here.

What's sad is how the grand old man's *bon mot* ended up being turned in against itself, used to give a patina of respectability precisely to the kinds of parasitic accommodations he was so keen to forestall. The irony is that now we have realized the suicidal dream of becoming an enormous parasite that feeds off of our oil, and we've done it under the banner of sowing the oil.

For eight decades, we've done little but plumb the depths of Uslar Pietri's greatest fear: not that oil would make us poorer, but that it would make us worse.

The Exporter
Posted on June 23, 2009 by Quico

"Así estarán las vainas que ... when we manage to get the National Guard to show up at our factory, we celebrate," The Exporter says, savoring how counter-intuitive his sentence sounds.

"Huh?"

"Well, sure. They make you jump through so many hoops before they'll even send an inspection team over to certify your shipment, it's a bit of a victory just having them there."

Bewildered? So was I.

Welcome to the world of The Exporter: a topsy-turvy universe where businesses positively relish the chance to get shaken down by some fat *Guardia Nacional* bloke who's holding their business plan hostage.

"Check it out, by the time the National Guard deigns to send an inspection team over, that means we've already gotten the Cadivi permits, the certificate saying that the internal market is already fully supplied, and we've finished the crazy little Treasure Hunt through the Caracas offices of the *Ministerios* to get all the various permits: health ministry, tax office, labor ministry, the works. The export certificate has to have nine official stamps on it by the time you're finished and - credit where credit is due - that's actually the new, streamlined procedure because until a couple of years ago you needed seventeen!"

"Even nine, though, is a mighty struggle, especially because it turns out the last stamp has to be signed by the same MILCO official who signed the first one. Not the same agency, mind you, the same official. So if the guy is out sick, or on vacation, or just didn't feel like coming in that day...you're out of luck. The guy knows he can hold up your entire shipment so...as you'd expect, wheels have to be greased. Biggest racket in the world, that one..."

"So yeah, by the time that nightmare's over and you finally have all the papers you need to get the Guardia to come over to the plant, you're de fiesta."

Yowza. "Y ¿entonces?" I ask.

"Well then these guys come into the plant and they go through your shipment box by box, crate by crate, pallet by pallet, actually physically inspecting each one before putting a big plastic sheet over the pallets and an official Guardia Nacional seal on them."

I'm a bit puzzled by this.

"To make sure you're not over-invoicing, I guess?" I add tentatively.

"Well, in part," The Exporter says, "but mostly to make sure there aren't any drugs hidden away in the shipment. And that part, of course, you can understand. The Guardia doesn't want any competition, y'know? If any cocaine is moving through the country, they want a cut..."

"Anyway," The Exporter, who's in full swing now, goes on "you'd think now that your package is fully permisologized, inspected, signed and sealed, that's the end of it, right? *No, mi amor.* Not a bit of it, because then you have to put it on a truck and ship it off to a port where, the second it gets there, it gets stopped by...wait for it...La Guardia Nacional. That's right, a second set of Guardias take off the old Guardia seal, undo all the plastic and inspect it all over again, box by box, crate by crate, pallet by pallet. And when they're done they put a new plastic on it, and another seal on it, which, actually, looks just like the first."

"It's a nuthouse, Quico," he says, laughing, "and the really insane part is that, on average, a shipment takes 4 to 6 weeks to move out of the ports in La Guaira or Puerto Cabello. But the Guardia seals expire in three days! So every three days you have to suck up to them to get them to come back, take old seals off and put new seals on...and, of course, every three days you gotta pay someone off to do that!"

I'm staggered already, but it gets worse.

"But let's say somehow you manage to jump through all the hoops and you put your stuff on a ship, send it abroad and sell it...guess what? At the start of the entire process, you had to tell Cadivi you were going to export this stuff, so you're forced, as a matter of law, to take no less than 90% of the dollars you get paid and give them to the Central Bank, at which point they'll turn around and give you the princely sum of two bolivars and fifteen cents for each dollar worth of exports!"

"That's what?" I say, "maybe a third of what a dollar is worth, in purchasing power terms?"

"Right," The Exporter replies, "But since they've been inspecting you inside and out for weeks, they know exactly how much you exported and there's just no getting around it. If you don't hand over the dollars to BCV, you'll never get another export permit again."

"The way it works, basically, is that you have to go through that whole sprawling, steaming mass of hassles just for the privilege of having Chávez confiscate two out of every three dollars you earn. Or, to put it more delicately, tax your export revenues - your gross export revenues - at something like a 60% or 70% rate. Because that's the implied tax when they force you to hand over a dollar worth Bs.6 or 7 and they pay you just Bs.2.15 for it."

"Que bolas," I say.

"Nice, huh?" He's smiling this big masochist smile of his. "*Es que* not even PDVSA buys bolivars at the official rate anymore - or did we forget all about Rosemont already? It's basically occasional confused gringo tourists and us - those are the only *pendejos* left who'll fork over one full dollar for Bs.2.15."

It takes some time to digest The Exporter's story.

When you take it all in, it's no wonder that Venezuelan non-oil exports have collapsed to historic lows this year. The real wonder is that anything at all continues to be exported in these circumstances. Basically, the only firms that export are firms that have absolutely no other choice because there's no market for their products at home, or because they need to keep a presence in foreign markets if they're to have any hope of becoming competitive again someday in the future.

On this blog, we used to have some debate, now and again, on what an appropriate, progressive development policy for Venezuela might look like. But seen against the light of the utterly insane reality The Exporter describes, those kinds of debates look so incredibly misplaced it's embarrassing.

Needless to say, these kinds of stories are the ones that first-world researchers miss by a mile. Somewhere, in an ivy-covered computer lab, a twenty-six year-old trade economist is running a regression and concluding that Venezuela suffers from a terrible case of Dutch Disease, a technical term that helps explain why oil-exporting countries export little else.

But it's not just Dutch Disease. It's not the over-valuation of the currency that is the main factor holding our non-oil exports back. It's the fact that the entire apparatus of the State is mobilized to stop you from exporting.

A change in perspective is in order. Any export regime that isn't certifiably bonkers would be a massive improvement over what we have now.

A layperson's guide to Venezuela's long recession
Posted on November 17, 2010 by Juan Cristobal

Yesterday, the Central Bank of Venezuela published its quarterly report on economic activity, covering the third quarter of 2010.

Since these documents are close to impenetrable for a lot of people, I thought it would be a good idea to spell out the few things you can take away from it.

1. Venezuela continues to be walloped by a recession most of our neighbors have escaped from. GDP is – roughly - a measure of the value of the total goods and services produced in a country. In other words, you add up the value of what each and every person, company, or government office produces in a particular period of time (a year, a quarter), and you get the country's GDP.

When GDP goes up, we are producing more, and presumably, we are earning more – because when we produce stuff and sell it, the proceeds eventually go to somebody inside the country.

There is a close link between GDP and a country's income, and GDP per capita is frequently interpreted to represent the average income earned by a country's inhabitants. That is why GDP per capita is sometimes used to measure how developed different countries are.

You hear a lot in the news about recessions. Technically, a country is in recession when its GDP contracts for two consecutive quarters. In other words, you measure GDP in a quarter and compare it to what you were producing in the same quarter a year before, and if you are producing less, then your quarterly GDP is falling. If that trend continues in the next quarter, you are in a recession.

Venezuela has been in a recession for several quarters now, and the GDP figures that came out yesterday confirm that we are not yet out in the clear. While other countries in South America are posting very healthy growth rates, we are mired in the mud. In fact, some people say we are the worst performing economy in the continent. But of course, the BCV being part of the government, the press release spins this away by saying that our fall is not as deep as it used to be.

Cold comfort that is.

2. Perhaps producing less oil may explain why we are in such a rut. You may think that the recession is caused by less production of everything. As it turns out, most of the fall in private output happened a year ago, so when you compare this quarter with the same quarter in 2009, you come out with private economic activity being roughly even.

The real drag on GDP is "oil activity." In other words, we are producing 2.1% less of the stuff included in "oil activity" than we were a year ago.

But it's not like oil is all that important to Venezuela's economy. Just one of many numbers, right?

3. This and that – some are better, some are not. Non-oil GDP is down 0.2%, a slight fall. This does not mean that every non-oil activity is roughly even with a year ago. Hidden underneath that 0.2% drop is a wildly heterogeneous picture. When you count the goods and services produced in an economy, some sectors of the economy are going to show up as growing, while others are going to appear to be shrinking.

In Venezuela, the breakdown suggests the weakest sectors are mining, electricity, banking, and commerce.

This is crucial, because it helps explain the overall drag in the economy. In Venezuela, if commerce, banking, and electricity (not to mention oil) are shrinking, that tells you right there your economy is in trouble. It's not the same as finding out that the local production of iPods was plummeting.

But not all is gloom and doom. There are economic activities that are growing: communications, government services, and transportation.

In other words, we are texting a whole lot more than last year, the government is ever expanding, and there's a lot more trucking activity going on – presumably thanks to the restitution of trade with Colombia and the general uptick in imports, which we discuss next.

In a nutshell, our economy is evolving. We mine less, produce less electricity, and shop less. But we are texting more, government is growing, and we are importing lots of trinkets.

I call that "drifting to a veritable sea of happiness."

4. Manufacturing can barely get it up. One of the few bright spots is that manufacturing activity seems to have increased slightly, 1.8% to be exact.

What exactly are we manufacturing more of? Food, drinks, chemicals, electrical appliances, clothing. What are we manufacturing less of? Well, a lot of things, but in particular, metal, furniture and machinery production are plummeting.

5. Paging Bob the Builder. Construction is a big part of these reports for two reasons. First of all, construction is a pro-cyclical indicator of economic activity. What this means is that when the economy is doing well, construction activity usually shows up as booming, and when it is not, it usually shrinks. In that sense, construction is a good "thermometer" for the economy.

The other reason is that the construction industry employs a lot of people, so a fall in this sector is particularly painful to a lot of folks, and typically shows up in unemployment figures.

Well, according to the BCV, we're simply not building stuff. The government is building less than a year ago – 3.8% less, to be exact. But the private sector is building way less than a year ago, 13.9% less.

I have no idea why this could be... and yes, I'm being snarky.

6. We may be producing less, but we're importing a lot more. The BCV's report also includes numbers on the evolution of the supply of goods in the economy. The supply of goods is different than GDP because GDP measures what was produced in Venezuela, while the supply measures what is actually available in the country, including stuff we did not produce ourselves.

As it turns out, the supply of goods is growing by 1.5%. Now, we know GDP is shrinking, so it's not like supply is growing because we're making more stuff. No, supply is growing because we are importing more than a year ago, 6.3% more to be exact.

So there you have it. We're producing less oil, texting more, earning less, growing government more, building less, producing more drinks and less heavy machinery, and importing a whole bunch of stuff.

The BCV calls it an economic report. I call it the economic reality of 21st-Century Socialism.

Development is a state of mind
Posted on March 25, 2011 by Juan Cristobal

"In this country, GDP per capita could hit $20,000 per year, and people would still think like backwards Latin American assholes."

The words from my Chilean friend shocked me.

We were in the middle of a sophisticated, expensive meal in one of Santiago's many hip new eateries, a Peruvian-fusion joint in the city's poshest district. The conversations in the tables around me would have been unthinkable thirty years ago. They all touched, in one way or another, on Chile's remarkable transformation – people were discussing their latest car, the latest merger or acquisition, their recent summer skiing tryst at Whistler, or the beach house they had just bought.

The entire milieu gave me hope that perhaps, thirty years from now, I could be having a similar conversation in a prosperous, normal, post-Chávez Caracas. And here came my friend, bringing us all back to Earth with his bummer.

But did he have a point? What is development, exactly?

When I tell my Venezuelan *panas* about my move from the US back to Chile, I unanimously receive heaps of admiration. The general tone of the comments is along the lines of "Chile is doing really well, right?...", "it's amazing that Chile is going to be the first country in Latin America to develop...", and "those Chileans know what they're doing."

That's true to some extent. But it's also wildly off base. If this move has taught me anything, it's that development is much more than GDP per capita, growth rates, shiny infrastructure, and export statistics.

Development is a state of mind, one that the IMF has trouble quantifying.

I first visited Chile in 1998. Back then, the country was coming off a period of China-like growth rates, and yet the memories of poverty and dictatorship were still fresh. Everyone was still in awe of what had been accomplished, and the future held much promise. They were all drunk on heightened expectations, and the vertiginous change helped one overlook the obvious flaws in the system. Everything was so recent – you couldn't expect things to change overnight, could you?

Chile has continued in its path to development in recent years, but the same nagging problems persist. The general sense of possibility has been replaced by one of doubt. While the country's GDP is likely to continue growing, the question remains: will it be enough?

I thought about this recently when learning of the latest scandal involving Chile's uber-empowered, unaccountable elite class.

Cencosud is one of the nation's largest retailers. Its owner is one of Chile's richest men, and as many powerful men before him, he likes to build big things. He is currently putting the finishing touches on Latin America's tallest skyscraper.

As it happens, Cencosud also forces its workers to labor under some unusual – some will say cruel – conditions.

A Chilean TV show recently uncovered a shocking truth. Night workers at Cencosud's Santa Isabel supermarkets are routinely locked up inside the supermarket in order to prevent theft. They were even locked inside and unable to get out during last year's massive earthquake and they were in danger of drowning when the tsunami hit their store. They were only let out when looters came to visit the supermarket. One of the managers drowned trying to get another group out.

The company's response? It vows it follows the laws fully. Even Chile's right-wing Labor Minister – if there can be such a thing – is shocked.

Of course, all developed nations go through scandals like this one. No country is perfect, and one of the things that distinguish good societies from bad ones is not the absence of scandals, but the ability to self-correct. So it's still possible that this will not fall by the wayside, that the people responsible will be held accountable.

But when you realize the government's front-runner for the 2014 Presidential Election, Mining Minister Laurence Golborne, is a former manager of Cencosud, the cynic in you gets worked up.

Regardless, the fact that these things still happen – that companies think they can still get away with this *fundo* mentality – is a sign of how far society has to go.

When we first moved to Chile in 2003, one of the things you would read in the paper coming from the mouths of the *mojoneada* elite class was that Chile really shouldn't compare itself to Latin America anymore, but to small, developed, natural-resource- or agriculture-intensive countries such as Denmark and New Zealand.

And while their hubris was admirable, I kept thinking how out-of-place the beggars or the jugglers in the street corners would look in the streets of Auckland or Copenhagen.

So yes, you can walk into a Starbucks and pay with your credit card, but good luck finding exactly what you want. The schools for your children are good and expensive, but your daughters' school planners come shockingly packed with advertising for sweets and TV shows. People think nothing of jetting off to Cancún for the long weekend, but customer service everywhere is the pits.

This massive reality check makes me think that even if we get everything right in Venezuela, even if we were to magically fix our politics and our economics, we will still be dealing with the same human capital. The many cultural traits that hold us back, the generations of Venezuelans raised in a malnourished, under-developed, disenfranchised environment – well, they (us?) and their (our?) way of thinking will still be there.

This will not go away no matter how much we grow, no matter how high the price of oil.

The change in mindset required for economic and social development to really grab hold – well, that takes generations to accomplish. The most we can aspire to in our lifetimes is to lay the groundwork.

Torres in Bethlehem
Posted on July 17, 2007 by Quico

Everybody knows Jesus of Nazareth wasn't from Nazareth at all: he was born in a barn in Bethlehem. But what on Earth was Mary doing gallivanting around Galilee nine-months pregnant? Luke's Gospel explains the Romans had ordered everyone back to their hometown for a census, so Joseph had to go back to Bethlehem to register.

It's a detail I've always found extraordinary: a census in the ancient world? Can you imagine the logistical challenge? Why on earth would they go to all that trouble?

The answer, when you think about it, is not at all surprising: for tax, of course!

The Roman Empire ran on taxes. The Romans understood that if you're going to tax people, you need to know who lives where and how much money you can take from whom. There was no way to keep track of all that information without writing it all down. So the ancient census was really more like a huge tax assessment drive - a technological solution to a pressing political and administrative problem.

And it wasn't just Rome: all over the ancient world, empires came to realize that if they were going to levy taxes, they would need records of people and their property. The Persians held a tax census as far back as 500 BC, the ancient Indians starting from 288 BC, and the Chinese from at least 140 AD. Japan had its first tax census in 670 AD; England's Norman conquerors set about raising a census almost as soon as they'd defeated the natives in 1066. I guess it seemed obvious that if you're going to call yourself a conqueror, this is one of the first things you have to do.

The tax census was, in that sense, one of the fundamental institutions of civilization.

Through the census, relationships of subjection and tribute that had always lived "out in the open air of the spoken word" came to be embodied in paper, set down formally for the first time. In this way the written word came to mediate that most basic sphere of the individual's relationship with the state: his monetary obligation to it.

If you accept the image of state making as organized crime - the idea that the mafia don is the best contemporary analogy for the earliest stages of state building - then the tax census marks a step-change in the nature of the State. Because writing down a tax obligation, implicitly or explicitly, builds a safeguard into the individual's relationship with authority. Once Joseph's property had been registered in Bethlehem, once he'd "done his taxes," it became much harder to come back and try to charge him more arbitrarily. His obligations had, after all, been set down, affixed for posterity through writing, that artificial expansion of memory.

Census taking, though designed to extract money from people, had deeply subversive implications for the way a state and its subjects would henceforth interact. The tax census ensnared the state and the individual in ties of mutual obligation that couldn't have existed in an earlier era stage, when tribute was set by people rather than paper, and looked more like protection money than tax.

That citizen-state relationship would come to be dominated more and more thoroughly by the written word, the odd embodiment of authority in shards of dried tree pulp. As Briceño Guerrero puts it, that relationship would grow exponentially, coming to envelop more and more aspects of each citizen's life until, by the twentieth century, it had metastasized into a tangle of:

ID cards, contracts, property titles, diplomas, protocols, mortgages, appointments, wills, dismissals, permissions, receipts, bills, decrees, resolutions, authorizations, sentences, letters, safe-conducts, credentials, resumes, work records, court briefs, payrolls, black lists, bank cards, credit cards, military cards, hanging folders, memos, forms, applications, notices, citations, agreements, bulletin boards, orders (of payment, arrest, eviction) certificates (of birth, marriage, death.)

At the root of it all, though, was the tax nexus: that primordial point of contact between power and the individual, as codified in the tax census: that original blueprint for all subsequent mechanisms of routine bureaucratic control.

Nothing fascinates and mystifies me more than the gaping chasm we see in Venezuela between the laws as written and the society they are supposed to regulate. My documentary, Law of the Land was really an extended meditation on the subject, as is much of what I've written over the years.

It's a feeling that's both hard to explain and impossible to miss if you spend any length of time in the country. We have layers and layers of laws and regulation, and then we have reality - never the twain shall meet. I've been asking myself why that is for a long time.

More and more, I think it has to do with the tax nexus. Or, rather, with the way oil distorts it, and along with it, the whole principle of authority-embodied-in-text.

See, for the ancient Romans and Indians, for the Chinese and the Normans, making written authority work was a necessity. They didn't make a census out of sociological curiosity: they saw it as a pragmatic solution to a pressing problem. They had to do it if their empires were to operate at all - that's where the money came from!

The written word had to have authority - not on some abstract level, but in the nitty-gritty business of regulating each individual's obligation to the state. It wasn't enough for power to flow through paper notionally - making the system work was a fiscal necessity.

Fast forward a couple of thousand years to Venezuela's contemporary history and you realize that making sure power flows through paper has never been a necessity here. Not counting the rump state-let we had in the 19th century (which was rarely able to extend authority effectively beyond Caracas itself) the rise of the Venezuelan state coincides quite precisely with the onset of massive oil revenue. When we talk about the petro-state in the Venezuelan context, we're not talking about the transformation of a pre-existing state: we're really talking about the only state we've ever had.

For the last 90 years or so, for as long as we've had a state worthy of the name, we've had a state that didn't really have to tax us to sustain itself. Making authority flow through paper has never been a matter of state survival, codifying authority's relationship with individuals has always been an ideal fondly to be wished for, never a need. When politically expedient, the Venezuelan state has always been quite comfortable letting laws and realities drift happily apart.

Now, in a sense, there's nothing new about this argument: Terry Lynn Karl has spent a distinguished career discussing the way oil pries apart the taxation nexus in rentier economies and de-links the state from society. But I'm trying to get at something slightly different here. While Karl focuses on the macro-social, high-politics of the petrostate's alienation from society, what grips me is the microlevel, the way the petrostate patterns each Venezuelan's individual relationship with authority.

In a normal country, citizens are keenly aware that the wealth the state spends is wealth they created. The hackneyed gringo letter-to-the-editor writer's catchphrase, "as a tax-payer, I..." captures it nicely. Citizens feel they own the state for the same reason they feel they own their toothbrush: they paid for it.

The petrostate turns this symbolic nexus on its head. The state doesn't depend on the citizen for money; the citizen depends on the state for money. The state has no prod, no pressing need to formalize and codify its relationship with citizens: why go to all that trouble, when you can just pump cash out of the ground?

I think this fact explains much of the mystery of the gap between the world of "papel sellado" and real life in Venezuela. The citizen is perpetually placed in the role of supplicant, continually conscious that he needs the state much more than it needs him. Seen in this light, it's not at all surprising that the state comes to see written authority as superfluous. Why bother?

The question, then, is what can be done about it? And here is where having extremely persistent commenters comes in really handy: those of you who read the comments section know that Torres has been pushing the solution to this morass for ages.[39]

His idea is disarmingly simple: Take all the oil revenue, divide it by 26 million, and hand it out to people. That's it. Torres sees this as a poverty-alleviation scheme, and there's no doubt that many, many Venezuelans would be lifted out of poverty if his idea was implemented.

Now, the main objection to Torres's plan is also pretty straightforward: you can't just deprive the state of all that oil revenue because the state needs that money to pay teachers, and road builders, and everything else the state does. The fiscal hole you would create would be far too dire for any politician to seriously entertain the idea. Indeed, when Manuel Rosales proposed a version of the plan, he didn't dare promise to distribute more than 20% of our oil revenue. I mean, you'd have to be crazy to go any higher than that, right?

---

[39] Torres, who also goes by "extorres," is a long-time commenter on the blog. His idea is shared by many in Venezuela's academic circles. For example, it has recently been pushed by IESA's Francisco Monaldi, Jose Ramón Morales, and Pedro Rodríguez, and has been cited by, among other places, the Wall Street Journal.

It seems like a knock-out blow, at first - but like most good ideas, the apparent simplicity of Torres's plan conceals layers of possibility.

Certainly, if his idea was implemented, the state would find itself seriously short of cash in the short run. One way or another, the state would have to make up the shortfall simply to guarantee the minimal level of service its constituents have grown used to: people wouldn't stand for mass hospital closures and the like.

But where could the state possibly find the money to make up a shortfall on that scale?

In the same place every normal state in the world finds it: in its citizens' pockets!

This, I think, is the concealed genius of Torres' idea.

Yes, the state would need to claw back much of the oil money it gives out in the form of new taxes. But that, to my mind, is not a drawback: just the opposite, it's the idea's biggest selling point.

Distributing the nation's oil money and then clawing back a portion of it in tax would completely reverse the direction of dependence in the state-individual relationship. It would turn Venezuela into a normal country.

Suddenly, you would see tax become what it has never been in Venezuela - a major political issue. People would become keenly aware that the money that funds the state is money that comes out of their pocket. In one fell swoop, individuals would be transformed from supplicants into citizens. Demands for accountability would soar. The idea would drive a wooden stake through the heart of the petro-state model.

In time, the proposal could help mend the traditional chasm between the world of official paper and real life that has marred Venezuelan public life for so long. Forced to get serious about codifying its relationship with its citizens once and for all, the cavalier attitude of the state elite towards the authority of the written word would have to yield.

I don't think the process would be fast or dramatic - cultural change never is - but within two or three generations the habits of mind of petrostate dependency could be substantially weakened and something like the rule of law could start to take hold for the first time ever in our country.

I sat on the fence on Torres's idea for a long time, but I can't really think of another way of achieving these kinds of results. No amount of speechifying, no system of education, no volume of grassroots activism could achieve a fundamental shift in the individual's attitude to the state (and the state's attitude to the individual) so long as money and power in our society continues to flow in pretty much the same pattern as they did in the Gómez era. The template for state-individual relationships needs a violent shake-up. And Torres's idea, well, it would certainly do that.

How strategic is "strategic"?
Posted on April 16, 2012 by Juan Cristobal

We had a big discussion over in the comments section regarding Henrique Capriles' astonishing admission that he believes the State should own all public utilities because...they're "strategic."

Some of you, particularly those who live in socialist nirvanas, seem to think there is absolutely no problem with that. I respect that, and understand where you're coming from. Clearly, capitalism is no panacea, and I'm on the record for dumping on inefficient private companies.

However, economists and politicians long ago discovered that public utilities don't have to be owned by the government through and through in order to work. As the OECD stresses, many public utilities combine a non-competitive element with segments that are potentially competitive. For instance, while railroad tracks and signaling equipment are by nature non-competitive, trains themselves compete with aircraft, cars and buses. And while high-voltage power transmission, grid operation and power-delivery to homes aren't really competitive sectors, power generation, retailing and marketing activities can be. The key is to separate out the non-competitive segments from the potentially competitive chunks of the utility's activity: there's plenty of international precedent for that kind of approach.

Introducing a little entrepreneurship, a little competition, and a little bit of the free market into the competitive chunks of public utilities can do a ton of good, as long as it is done carefully.

What benefits does it bring? Not only does competition foster innovation and, in theory, lower prices, but it also privatizes losses. State-owned companies that provide a public service need to keep operating even if they can't make a profit. However, you can also force private providers to keep operating in the midst of losses, and the shareholders pick up the tab.

Take, for example, the case of highways here in Chile. In a move that would give Montrealers the heebie-jeebies, the Socialist governments that preceded Sebastián Piñera implemented a model of private highways. Private companies came in and built highways, and they charge tolls to whoever uses the roads.

What happens if they don't plan well and few people use the highway? Well, they lose money, because they can't recover the cost of building it in the right amount of time. Only in this case, the white elephant is on the shareholders' tab, not the taxpayers'.

In Venezuela, instead, you have the CANTV subsidizing God knows how many things, over-employing thousands of people, and providing dumpy service (ABA anyone?), all paid for by the taxpayer. Because of this mistaken idea of "strategic" things that only the government can do well, you end up with loss-making companies that are actually a danger to society.

Of course, Beelzebub is in the details. There is no point to privatizing if you don't regulate the industry. The free market on its own will now transmit electricity to the people of Parapara, for example. And there are a number of cases of privatized public utilities that have not performed well.

But one thing is public regulation, quite another is public ownership that turns PDVSA into the ultimate paymaster cleaning up the mess left behind by every criminally mismanaged state-owned utility.

In Venezuela we should know by now that state-owned companies are simply the pits, an unending source of corruption, inefficiency, and waste. Unless, that is, they happen to operate in a market selling something that costs $7 to produce for $110 a pop.

This whole idea of "strategic" public services in economics is so vague and ill-defined, so old fashioned, it would almost sound quaint if it wasn't coming out of the mouth of a serious contender for the Presidency.

You can't put optimal oil policy on a bumper sticker
Posted on July 29, 2011 by Quico

...well, not a sensible bumper sticker, anyway.

Oil policy in a context like Venezuela's is irreducibly complex. You could say you want to maximize the cash flow to the public purse, but it only takes a moment's reflection to realize that's a non-answer, because the question becomes – when?

The policy that will maximize the tax take next year – invest nothing, hand every penny to the treasury – will be a disaster two years from now, when underinvestment causes wells to run dry en masse.

But the other extreme – invest everything, pay nothing out now – is fiscally untenable and politically impossible.

What we are faced with is a good, old-fashioned inter-temporal optimization problem. What we need to find is a solution that spreads oil rents equitably over time. But what "equitably" means in this context isn't at all straightforward. It hinges crucially on how well you think people will live in the future.

If the economy grows sustainably over the next 20 years, Venezuelans a generation from now will be far wealthier than they are today. In that case, equity demands that we front-load the bulk of the take, because the current generation needs the money more than its children will.

But if the economy continues to languish into the 2030s, then equity demands that we invest relatively more and spend relatively less, because the next generation's going to be just as hard up as the current one.

The detail, of course, is that we don't have any idea if the next generation is going to be richer or poorer than we are, so uncertainty floods any attempt to really give a definite answer to the question.

And notice that we haven't even gotten to the whole vexed issue of market power: whether Venezuela might cause the global oil market to tank by ramping up production too far too fast. We haven't stopped to ponder the unknowable mystery of what demand for crude oil is likely to be over the next 20 years. And we're not touching with a 10-foot-pole such wildcards as whether physicists might finally crack Cold Fusion, putting everyone into electric cars and rendering the whole issue moot.

In fact, there's a virtually endless line of other questions, each one surrounded by the kind of deep uncertainty that reduces us to mere speculation.

Let's be clear: in the medium run – say, the next five years – nobody seriously disputes Venezuela needs to invest in much expanded production capacity. Not even PDVSA.

Whether it's actually possible to raise the financing needed to achieve it given current institutional constraints is up in the air, but that the goal is desirable is one of the few points of consensus left in the political world. On the margin, Venezuela is a price taker, so ramping up production to take advantage of high oil prices is a slam-dunk.

Beyond that, though, we're into wild guessing-game territory.

Leopoldo López's stated goal of turning Venezuela into the world's top oil-producing country would require more than quadrupling our production to the neighborhood of 11 million barrels a day.[40] That would amount to a 10% increase in global oil production.

It's simply impossible to overstate the sheer titanium-testicled ambition of the call. It's for statements like this that the word "hubris" was invented for.

Whether Venezuela can ever find the international credibility and domestic institutional arrangements it would take to attract the gargantuan levels of investments required to make that happen is doubtful. Whether there's even enough capital in the world economy willing to go into oil extraction to make it happen is questionable. Whether the massive deferral of consumption involved makes sense is an open question. Whether the Venezuelan economy would have a prayer of overcoming the titanic case of Dutch Disease this would bring on is unsure. And whether we may not find ourselves devoting a decade worth of dislocation to finance enormous investment just in time to be overtaken by new technologies is up for grabs too.

Raising production capacity gradually in tune with the oil market? By all means.

Pharaoh-like decade-long vanity projects? *Me bajo en la parada, por favor...*

---

[40] Leopoldo López is an opposition politician, founder and leader of the center-left Voluntad Popular political party.

Venezuela's useless elites
Posted on January 24, 2012 by Juan Cristobal

"That thing you just said," he growls, pointing right at me, "that Cadivi is a subsidy for the rich ... that is FALSE!"

My dad's friend is a smart, well-respected *maracucho* lawyer, someone I looked up to when I was growing up. He's fired up at my comment, his voice raised in anger, but also trying to overcome the deafening sound of the AC.

"You don't live here, so you don't know the number of poor and middle class people that benefit from Cadivi. Just the other day, I helped my secretary fill out her paper work so she could go to Aruba and use her cupo."

And then it hits me: I'm not 12 anymore. I can be barked into a corner, but I don't have to take it. I raise my voice even more, and fight back.

"No, tío, you're the one who doesn't understand," I say, my face flushing. "Whether or not a policy is a subsidy for the rich doesn't depend on the number of anecdotes you can collect. This is a technical issue, and from all we know, the vast majority of the dollars that are sold in Cadivi are not sold to people like your secretary, but sold to the bankers, the military, and the well-connected, to the people claiming they need $100 million when in fact they need $20 million, all so they can pocket $80 million at below-market price. That is free money, and it is coming from the pockets of Venezuela's poor, from the people paying IVA at the bodega."

I calm down, and it hits me. Venezuela is full of back-asswards policies that supposedly favor the poor but, in fact, favor the rich. Cadivi is just the tip of a mammoth iceberg that includes the gasoline subsidy, the free tuition for Universities, the toll-less roads system, the subsidized electricity prices, y *pare usted de contar*.

It's always going to be a challenge to explain these things to the poor. How can you make someone with a fifth-grade education understand that letting the price of gasoline go up … actually benefits them? It's not easy.

But this is not el pueblo acting thick, failing to see the basics of social costs and benefits of stupid, corruption-inducing policies.

With few exceptions, these are the elite: the wealthy, the educated, and the fat cats who have lived through El Gran Viraje, and Recadi, and the Otac. These are the people that saw the failure of La Gran Venezuela, and Corpomercadeo, and the CVG. These people … we still have to convince them that rentism simply doesn't work? That money the government gives to these guys is money that is not available for this kid? That Metro systems that don't work are a huge waste of money, even if a few poor people use it?

How hard is it to understand that when the rich get perks, this only makes us poorer?

Because, rest assured, the elites will be the first ones lining up when a new government – if such a thing ever materializes – tries to untangle the chavista mess.

If we can't even count on the elites to back us up, if they will be the first one trying to stab reform in the back, then what hope is there?

IV

The Opposition

Nothing riles our readers more than when we discuss the opposition movement and its strategies. In preparing this book, we realized that a lot of our more interesting posts dealt with discussing the opposition's characters. Whether it's Manuel Rosales, Henrique Capriles, the student movement, or even (gasp) Er Conde Del Guácharo, we tried to provide a fresh perspective by focusing on the main players, their faults, and their strengths. Sometimes we got things right, other times we got things horribly wrong.

As for the opposition as a whole, it remains a work in progress. Whether it's dealing with the challenge of gaining the support of rural Venezuelans, or managing the unfulfilled expectations of the beneficiaries of chavista largesse, we tried to shed a light on the most pressing issue of Venezuela's democratic forces: how to build, and sustain, a governing majority in a country where chavismo has taken hold.

Winning in Petare, shooting for Parapara
Posted on December 10, 2007 by Juan Cristobal

"All politics is local"

- Former US Speaker of the House Tip O'Neill.

Many things changed in the last election: chavistas stayed home or otherwise voted No; opposition people stayed home; the CNE declared an opposition win. Yet one of the few constants was the sharp disconnect between rural and urban Venezuela's voting patterns.[41]

The victory of the No was concentrated in wealthier, mostly urban states such as Zulia, Miranda and Carabobo. Surprisingly, the No even won in places like *Petare*, thanks to the efforts of the student movement and local politicians who have been trekking those *cerros* for years now.

However, Chávez won in the rural Llanos and in places like Monagas and Bolívar, where the presence of the state looms larger than average. These results highlight how important local knowledge is in turning out the vote, and they also point to the obvious next step for the opposition.

Let's look at a concrete example. The state of Guárico overwhelmingly approved of the Constitutional Reform, 58% to 42%. However, neighboring Anzoátegui favored the No by 54% to 46%. Does this mean that somehow Guariqueños are more prone to communism than Anzoateguienses?

Hardly. The difference is probably due to the fact that the opposition retains some presence in Anzoátegui, whereas they are practically nonexistent in Guárico. In fact, most people in Guárico probably did not even find out there was an opposition in this election. Since Guárico has few elected officials that do not belong

---

[41] The Consejo Nacional Electoral, or CNE, is Venezuela's main electoral authority. It is usually packed with chavista sympathizers. During the Chávez era, it has been mired in controversy for making Venezuela's elections system completely automatized, creating doubts in the minds of some on the veracity and secrecy of the vote.

to chavismo, there is no student movement to speak of and Globovisión probably does not reach many homes in Calabozo, the government has a virtual monopoly on the state.

Even within Guárico the divide is clear. While in San Juan de los Morros, the capital, the "Si" option won by a hair (50.4% to 49.5%), the government won overwhelmingly in places such as Parapara, trouncing the opposition 70% to 30%.

The issues in rural Venezuela are different than in the cities. People in rural areas don't care much about high-brow concepts such as "freedom", "democracy" and "Cuba", but more about basic things like health care, education, land reform and patronage from the state.

Without a permanent presence in rural Venezuela, it's simply no contest for the government. People in Parapara don't watch *Globovisión,* and they haven't the foggiest idea who opposition politicians such as Manuel Rosales or Yon Goicoechea are.[42]

In both rural and urban Venezuela, turning out the vote is crucial, and the most effective way of accomplishing that is by having local authorities on the ground. Local politicians make the difference. They know their neighbors, they can quickly scan voting centers, they can rally volunteers, and yes, they can establish patronage linkages - after all, this is Venezuela we're talking about.

Our victory was a narrow one, one that can be quickly overturned. We must build on it by staging another one, and continue to prepare for more important battles down the road. Regional elections scheduled for October 2008 are the perfect way of building on that - we can't do worse than how we did in the last ones, and we have plenty of time to get organized, build coalitions and sustain our momentum.

---

[42] Manuel Rosales was the losing presidential candidate in 2006. He was governor of Zulia and Mayor of Maracaibo, before he fled the country after being accused of corruption. Yon Goicoechea was the most visible leader of the student movement that contributed in the opposition's victory in the December 2007 Constitutional Referendum.

Furthermore, political parties have suffered from not having a way of channeling the efforts their faithful have made into something else. After all, people join political parties (in theory, at least) because they want to participate in public policy and effect a change in the country. Parties that cannot deliver on these goods suffer after a while. They are channels for making a change, but if we keep relying on a mainly volunteer force that cannot make changes and where the volunteers cannot actually *work* in public life, parties will wither down and die, and with them democracy.

To me, regional elections are the way to go. If we want to get ready for further battles, we need to start casting our net a little more widely. Elected local politicians can help us accomplish this more easily. Everything else is a distraction.

Shooting for Parapara
Posted on February 6, 2012 by Quico

Two parallel streets coming off the main road from San Juan de los Morros to Calabozo, each six or seven blocks long, with a Plaza Bolívar at the end.

That's pretty much all there is to Parapara, a town of maybe 1,000 people in a parish of some 3,500, located thirty kilometers south of Guarico's capital, where the coastal mountains finally give way to Venezuela's vast central plains.

Arrive in Parapara on a Tuesday morning and the place is oddly idyllic: doors open and people chatting in a Plaza Bolívar that really works like a Plaza Bolívar is supposed to – as an open-air community center where folk of all ages and political views come together.

Depending on which numbers you believe, 12-20% of Venezuelans live in towns like this – easily more than live in Caracas. Yet they seldom get polled, or talked about, or listened to, or strategized over in political circles. And while a day spent chatting up folks up and down the main plaza in a single town does not a comprehensive study make, given the almost complete lack of political debate about rural areas in Venezuela's public sphere, we thought it was important to give it a go.

"Crime?" says one of a group of high school kids we stop to chat with, "no man, that's in San Juan. Here, listen, you could leave a stack of bills lying on that park bench there in the morning, walk off, come back in the evening and find it waiting for you. *Aquí todo el mundo se conoce*, that kind of thing doesn't happen."

I shoot Juan a staggered look that says, "Toto, we're not in Kansas anymore."

Up and down the town's two streets you see "Hay Un Camino" signboards and stenciled Pablo Pérez murals. We ask the kids who put those up.

"I guess people from San Juan came down," says one, to general nods. The opposition is certainly visible here, but the kids can't think of a single activist in town.

We ask the kids about their high school and they're all into it. One of them wants to be a doctor, another wants to go to technical school. All but one, whose family farms, want to get the hell out of Dodge when they graduate: most of them to San Juan or Calabozo, one or two to Caracas. They have dreams, projects, and aspirations. Just one of them is old enough to vote, and she's not quite sure if she'll participate in the primary.

"That Capriles seems ok," she says, but then remembers "of course all my family is chavista." She's 18; politics is not high in her list of priorities.

None of her friends recoil in horror at the thought of her supporting Capriles. "Yeah," one of the boys says "he seemed ok, Capriles. He even went to San Juan de los Morros and they brought a bus here to take people up to see him. I guess a few people from town went up, not many. I'm with Capriles."

Then they go back to flirting with each other, but not without getting Juan's name so they can add him on Facebook. Every kid there is on Facebook, they tell us. They really wish they had broadband, though.

fOn the other side of the Plaza is the ancestral home of Joaquin Crespo. It lies in ruins, covered in Pablo Pérez *pintas*. Crespo was also wise enough to get out of town, going on to build a bigger, better house - Miraflores Palace, which he built.

Next door is Parapara's *Casa de la Cultura*, a small community cultural center housed in the town's last remaining Colonial-era house that's in good repair. Inés, the lady taking care of it, takes a few minutes to tell us about the place. She says they hold crafts lessons, music and dance workshops, and they have a library. In the corner, a group of men are discussing upcoming activities in their sporting cooperative. In the room next door is where they practice their *llanero* music and their *Joropo*, Inés tells us. *El Llano es música*, Juan responds.

The library is blessedly ideology-free – the usual beat-up tomes of Eduardo Blanco and Romulo Gallegos coexist next to dusty tomes of Enciclopedia Salvat, but nothing by Luis Britto García or Eva Golinger. The books seem to have been read.

As we walk out, Inés goes back to her radio program. Everyone listens to the radio in these parts.

Back out in the plaza we meet a set of guys - ages between 30 and 50 - from one of the 23 (23!) Community Councils in town. Their big thing is Misión Vivienda: they've gotten the green light to build two dozen new houses in town, in a place called La Lechera. Basically, that means the government has promised them materials so they can build some new homes themselves. They hold weekly meetings out on the street in front of his house and vote on every aspect of the project.

But the guys are frustrated. The red tape around the Misión is driving them crazy. "I had to go up to San Juan to get the one permit rubber stamped so I could send the second request for building materials up to Caracas, and then we have to wait. Eventually I guess we'll rent a truck to go down to Calabozo to get the stuff but then we also need to work out the paperwork with the controllers who have to verify we didn't steal it."

He goes into detail on each part of the administrative obstacle course he needs to navigate just to get some building blocks and zinc roofing sheets for the self-built homes. It's taken him months. No new homes are up yet.

They are all chavista, but they're not sucking their thumbs. We ask about the opposition primary and while they're not planning to vote, they are pretty well aware of who the candidates are and they sure don't see it as a taboo to vote. "I guess some people in town are going to vote, and that's good: vote in February and then vote again in October. I don't know why the opposition says there's no democracy here," he says, pointing out the opposition propaganda hanging all over town.

It's hard to deny he has a point.

This particular crowd is probably out of the opposition's reach. They're very skeptical. "I just heard Henrique Capriles say that he hasn't taken away any resources from any of the Misiones in Miranda State. He must think we're stupid, because everybody knows the money for the Misiones comes from the National Government. Of course he hasn't taken away any money; he wasn't giving it to them in the first place! So if you start out lying to us..."

Capriles doesn't pass the credibility test with them, but when I ask them if they think they might be able to work with a Capriles administration they don't recoil in horror. They're skeptical rather than dismissive.

Then one of them launches into a rant, "And what about that Corina?! She's crazy! That shit about Popular Capitalism ... where did that come from? Man, if she was on 5% when she started, as soon as she said that she must have dropped to 3!"

The guy is snarling; his buddies are guffawing. Capriles inspires weariness, Maria Corina contempt.

Pablo Pérez they don't know what to think of. None of Perez's messages seem to have gotten across, so they don't really have an idea about him. They ask Juan why Zulianos just won't back the revolution.

At least they know who the candidates are, we think to ourselves. They've even watched some of the debates. The opposition doesn't have easy access to these guys, and a lot of the messages they're getting seemed filtered through VTV, but it's not a total shut-out either.

We ask them about crime. Contrary to the high-school kids, they say that recent infrastructure projects have brought people in from other towns, and bad stuff is happening. One of them even tells Quico that cocaine is available in town. We ask if they believe this is Chávez's fault, and they disagree.

"Mexico," one of them says, "is much worse," seemingly unaware that they are repeating PSUV talking points. "It's all the fault of the Americans who consume so many drugs. I know how that society is. I watch The Simpsons."

Down the street we meet a street-cleaning crew from the Alcaldía, the local government, sweeping the street. Parapara is a rural parish within the more urban Roscio municipality, which includes San Juan de los Morros, the State Capital. The mayor here is actually opposition, a former PSUV, now PPT guy called Franco Guerratana who got 37% of the votes in Parapara but 46% in San Juan (in a three-way race).

We stopped in our tracks when we realized they were all wearing different kinds of shirts – "Hay un Camino", "PSUV", "UNT." We ask about the apparel. They shrug and say they got the shirts and caps from different campaigns. Anything is good if it shields you from the unforgiving midday sun.

"Yeah, we're going to vote in the primary," one of the street cleaners tells us, "they're going to force us to. We work for the Alcaldía, see?"

These guys are a lot poorer and less educated than the Community Council guys in the plaza. They don't seem to have any real political ideas – what they believe in is clientelism.

"Of course, you have to vote for the guy who gives you a hand," one of them says, "así es la vaina."

But they're bitter. Sweeping the streets in Parapara for minimum wage makes for a hard life, and one in the group doesn't even have that.

"There used to be day labor here," he says, "guys in trucks would come and pick you up to work in the lemon fields, picking peppers or tending corn or the cattle. It's been years since that happened, though."

Skinny, rugged, wearing a *pelo'e'guama* hat, the guy is a dead ringer for *Juan Bimba*.[43]

We ask them about the Community Councils. They're scathing. "There are 23 community councils in Parapara: 22 of them do nothing. Nothing! They just grab the money. There's just one, up there in La Lechera, that's really trying to do something. The rest? Well, maybe they get a couple of jobs to hand out, and then they give them out to their cousins."

Everyone nods.

"That's what it is, it doesn't matter who has power here: if they have a job, some help, any kind of benefit, they're going to give it to their cousin."

Life is hard for these guys, ideology an unattainable luxury. Politics for them is a raw matter of power and survival: politicians have jobs to give out, they need jobs to survive. With private sector jobs extremely thin on the ground, finding a way into clientelist networks is a matter of life-or-death for them.

But lacking the education to set up their own corrupt networks, and lacking the family contacts and social capital to hook into existing ones, they're entirely forlorn. For now they sweep streets for minimum wage in the harsh mid-day sun.

Life in Parapara is no bed of roses. This is neither a revolutionary nirvana nor a seething opposition stronghold. It's a place where big words such as "socialism," "Cuba," "dignity," and

---

[43] A fictitious character, Juan Bimba is widely regarded as a caricature for the common peasant Venezuelan.

"fatherland" seem distant, far removed from people's actual concerns.

Back in 2007, Juan wrote that until the opposition had a presence in places like this it would be hard to compete with Chávez nationally. Today, the opposition has a tenuous reach into the town – largely shipped in from neighboring San Juan de los Morros – whether in terms of propaganda posters or of municipal jobs.

It's easy to exaggerate chavismo's dominance in the town, though. Hundreds of Paraparans do vote for the opposition, and always have.

But the coat-tail effects associated with having an opposition mayor are a little disappointing: in 2008, Franco Guerratana's machine certainly did pull votes over and above than the opposition trend, but that didn't really seem to carry over into 2009 and 2010.

Some opposition messages do get through, but they land in a town where chavista social organization – for good and for ill – is solidly entrenched.

The opposition has little chance of winning in Parapara. But at least they have something of a presence there.

That is a big improvement.

Primero Justicia: an inside peek
Posted on November 1, 2007 by Juan Cristobal

Eighteen months ago, some friends who work for Primero Justicia called me up and asked me if I would like to help edit the document containing the party's platform. Seeing as though Julio Borges had been working on a comprehensive proposal of his own for his presidential campaign, they didn't want the document to die along with his candidacy, and they decided they wanted to turn it into the party's platform.

I jumped at the opportunity, and I've been working on it since. Three weeks ago, I took part in the party's ideological congress, where the document would be discussed and approved. Here's my eyewitness account.

First off, I should make it clear that I don't consider myself a party insider. Although I do belong to Primero Justicia, I'm not really active in it. For starters, I don't live in Venezuela. My main motivation was out of loyalty, yes, but I was also driven by the challenge of writing a document that was comprehensive yet accessible, something that any middle-class Venezuelan with some education would be able to understand but, at the same time, something that public policy experts would think was more than rhetorical wish-wash.

The congress itself had its share of the good, the bad and the ugly.

The good: The event, held in the Eurobuilding's tent, was well-organized and filled to the rims with four thousand people from all over the country. Every state was represented, and there were even representatives of Venezuela's indigenous communities. I was expecting to find a lot of middle-class kids from Caracas' eastern neighborhoods, but I found a portrait of the country: young and old, men and women, union members and housewives, yuppies and workers. The crowd was a sight to see - all enthusiastic, ready to rock.

International visitors included former Bolivian president Jorge Quiroga and PAN (Mexico) congressman Rodrigo Cortés. Both spoke eloquently. Quiroga in particular impressed me with his ability to connect with the audience, telling us his country's experience as a warning that what happens in Venezuela affects the entire continent. (On a side note, Pres. Quiroga warned me about José Miguel Insulza, saying he and Chávez had a pact to get him elected to the OAS and that he would be Chávez's man in Chile in the next election.)

The Congress itself had many hurdles to overcome. The climate of intimidation in Caracas has reached the point where none of the capital's hotels were willing to hire out space to an opposition political party. Originally, it was supposed to take place on the campus of the Universidad Nueva Esparta, but they bailed two weeks before due to the government's pressure. It was a miracle that the Eurobuilding Hotel finally relented and allowed the event to be held there. Even then, just a day before the Congress, the guy in charge of supplying the podium flaked on account of government pressure, so the podium they ended up using was pretty makeshift.

One of the most positive aspects of the meeting was that everybody there understood the importance of the vote. Some of the loudest cheers came whenever a speaker warned against abstention, saying this was tantamount to handing the country over to Chávez.

The other important aspect was the sense that this is not a "caudillo" party but a cohesive group where everybody understands the importance of team-play. While all the party's leaders spoke, none stood out above the other and they all had more or less the same message. It didn't strike me as a party that revolved around a single person's personality.

Perhaps this is a consequence of the split that happened earlier this year, when Leopoldo López, Gerardo Blyde, Liliana Hernández and others left to join Manuel Rosales's UNT. Everyone I asked lamented their departure, but told me that the problem was that they were simply not team players, they did not believe in the organization or in its goals. While the party may have suffered through this split, it still looks healthy and, in a way, more coherent.

Truth is Blyde, Lopez, and Hernandez have seen their credibility suffer - after all, they said they left PJ because it had no internal democracy and no ideology. The irony is that now Primero Justicia is the only one of the country's two main opposition parties to have held internal elections and an ideological congress. Also worth noting is the fact that many of the people who left Primero Justicia have now joined UNT's top ranks without having been elected to any of their posts, which suggests to me their vehement pleas for internal party democracy were grandstanding.

The bad: If there is one thing lacking in this group is P.R. savvy. Media coverage of the event was a disaster, and even now, the party's ideological platform, its proposals to the country are not on the Internet.

I was shocked to find Venezuela's major newspapers gave us minimal coverage, and most of them focused on Quiroga's speech blasting the Chávez administration. There simply was no mention of the party's main proposals, including strengthening of Misiones, the pledge to raise oil output, the promise to provide Venezuelans with shares of PDVSA so they can use it as collateral for credit or as a pension fund and the firm stance regarding civilian control over the military.

While there is a bias against Primero Justicia in the Venezuelan press, the blame here goes both ways. If the media is against you, you hire an expert to get them to talk about you. If you want them to talk about you, you have to find a way to make it interesting for them to do so. I didn't see any of that.

Even internal communications are error-prone. For example, I'm stunned that the party's website was not functioning that day and, in fact, still isn't. An Ideological Congress is not something to be taken lightly, and independents and sympathizers may have wanted to take a peek at what exactly was being proposed. But if you go to the party's websites, you will find next to nothing about it.

This kind of thing left me feeling that the party is not quite ready for prime time, and this is something that has to be seriously addressed, as I told some of the party leaders I spoke to.

It was depressing for me to return to Chile and find that the Christian Democrats - a party that usually gets around 20% of the vote in Chile, in the same ball park as Primero Justicia's 11% - held its Ideological Congress that same weekend and this made the headlines in all the major newspapers here. There was even a thorough discussion of the outcome, since many felt the party was veering to the left. Instead, in Venezuela, Sunday's paper had a small corner story that talked about the Congress, and a two-page spread discussing Che Guevara and his legacy.

The ugly: I guess it would be snobbish of me to criticize the fact that the event was scheduled for 10 but began at 11:45. This is Venezuela, after all, and the party in a way reflects the country as a whole.

However, I can't get past the idea that Venezuelans, young and old alike, are hard-wired to think that giving a good political speech is the same as shouting. While none of the speakers were terrible, nobody stood out. The rhetorical style may be suited for Venezuela, but personally, it doesn't do much for me.

Julio Borges's speech was very good, but the guy is distant. He needs to tell a story, to connect with the crowd emotionally. While his comparisons of Primero Justicia's proposals vis-a-vis Socialism were on the mark on an intellectual level, it doesn't really resonate.

Carlos Ocariz did a little better in terms of connecting, but a little worse in terms of content. Henrique Capriles was simply awful, although he seemed to have the crowd going nuts which was surprising to me. The other guys were OK, but it was the people from the grassroots, from the "interior" of the country (Vargas or Portuguesa) who showed more promise and more preparation.

This is a young party, with lots accomplished so far but still a lot to learn. I was happy to put in my two-cents, and I sincerely wish them well. I hope they work out the kinks in the operation- if and when they do, they may just be a force to be reckoned with.

PS. - I feel terrible. As I write this, Primero Justicia is busy getting their asses kicked on the streets of Caracas and, in the process, trying to drive up Chávez's negatives. And here I am pontificating from my office...

Teodoro's strange isolation
Posted on March 12, 2006 by Quico

All signs are that Teodoro Petkoff will announce he's running for president before the end of this month. Conventional wisdom sees him as the strongest of the potential challengers. Personally, I admire the guy tremendously - I'm sure he'd make a fantastic president. Still, I can't help but worry about his electoral prospects - and for reasons that go well beyond the never ending, ultimately sterile controversy about CNE.

The structure of the Venezuelan electorate really hasn't changed in the last few years. Something like 25% of the electorate is strongly pro-Chávez, something like 20% is strongly anti-Chávez, and the largest chunk, over half, floats between the two camps. To win, an opposition candidate needs to hold on to the anti-Chávez base while attracting more than half of the floating voters.

Thing is, you can't attract those waverers if you don't know who they are, what they want and why the vote for who they vote for. You need a specific, thought-out strategy to identify them and target them, and I worry that Teodoro hasn't quite grasped this.

Floating voters are basically poor people, living in barrios and down-and-out urbanizaciones, without a university education, focused more on bread-and-butter issues than on ideological niceties. In the last few years most of them have voted for Chávez as part of a clientelist quid-pro-quo: my vote for your petrodollars. You don't win over waverers by waxing lyrical about freedom and democracy or denouncing *castrocomunismo*, you get their votes by persuading them they'll be better off with you in Miraflores than with Chávez.

Teodoro faces challenges all around. To begin with, he can't necessarily count on the anti-Chávez ultras. It's not just that the CNE polemic has left many of them unwilling to vote at all, it's that most of them are ideological conservative and instinctively distrust any leftish candidate. No matter how moderate Teodoro's stance gets, a good number of militant anti-Chavistas just can't stomach voting for a former *guerrillero*.

This would be okay if Teodoro could count on solid support from floating voters. And, in principle, waverers should love him: he's been a consistent critic of the more ideologically-strident elements of the Opposition, which are major culprits in floating voters' strong distaste for the Traditional Opposition.

But Teodoro is too much of an intellectual to be a darling of the non-ideological waverers. He's not willing to pander aggressively to them. He makes his pitch in terms so abstract ("a modern, democratic left") that you get the feeling many waverers just won't know what on earth he's talking about. Even if they do understand what he's getting at, the fact is you can't eat a "modern, democratic left" - too often, his language is too high fallutin' to resonate viscerally with people's day-to-day concerns. Needless to say, Teodoro can't make up the difference by spreading oil money around like his opponent can, which leaves you to wonder if he can really mobilize enough waverers to be competitive.

To my mind, Teodoro is oddly politically homeless for a putative opposition front-runner. His main strength - his ability to mete out memorable tongue lashings to both the government and the radical opposition - makes him as many enemies as friends, while leaving non-ideological voters basically cold. Fatally, his only natural constituency seems to be people like me: over-educated, instinctively moderate, incurably wonk-ish and respectably leftish types- an electoral dead-end if ever there was one.

If he's going to position himself to actually win an election, Teodoro is going to have to develop a far less abstract pitch, one that resonates with wavering voters at a gut level. Colorful denunciations of Chávez that peter out into abstractions about the state's role in development will not do the trick. Using dictionary words that get chuckles from university-educated readers might be a good way to prop up Tal Cual's circulation figures, but if his shtick is going to play in Caucagüita, Teodoro has to stop saying "inefable" once a paragraph.

To my mind, his best bet would be to just shamelessly plunder Roberto Smith's formidable rhetorical arsenal. Unlike Teodoro, Smith has thought through these issues systematically and worked diligently to figure out which rhetorical strategies can win over wavering voters. Focus grouping the hell out of your message to strategically brand the candidate is an admittedly gringo way of going about an election, but taking a scientific approach to pandering is far preferable to sticking to rhetorical lines that may "feel right" to a candidate but in fact turn off the very people he should be attracting.

Is Teodoro willing to go down this route, or is it below his dignity? Hmm ...

20 points for Borges
Posted on April 20, 2006 by Juan Cristobal

A few weeks ago, Quico asked me to post my thoughts on why I think Julio Borges is the best of the current group of non-Chavista pretenders. At the time, I hadn't really thought of Borges as superior to the other contenders (Petkoff, Rosales and Smith) because I believe any one of these four would do a better job than our friend Hugo. I did think, though, that Borges was being underestimated by non-Chavista talking heads. As I thought about this post, I concluded that Borges, like recent polls are showing, is indeed the leader of the non-chavista pack. What follows are 20 reasons why I believe this to be true.

Borges is, at heart, a philosopher. Chávez is a military man. Two disciplines cannot be more different.

Borges's father was a prominent Valencian neurologist, and his mother a Catalan immigrant and a well-respected bio analyst. Julio, the youngest of five siblings, was educated at Don Bosco and San Ignacio schools in Caracas – quite a distance from Chávez's rural upbringing in Sabaneta de Barinas. Although some might construe his upper middle-class upbringing as a handicap in reaching out to poorer voters, Borges is working hard to prove them wrong.

Unlike Chávez and many of the people governing with him, Borges attended university. Borges went on to study law at UCAB, philosophy at UCV and Boston University, and public policy at Oxford.

Whereas Chávez's character was shaped in the halls of the Military Academy and in the remnants of defunct guerrilla movements during Venezuela's most prosperous and corrupt period, Borges's character was formed in the student movements that propped up during the disastrous years of the end of the 1980s. His distaste for what the military did in 1989 and 1992 helped make him a firm believer in civilian control of the Armed Forces.

Among the field of candidates, Borges is the sole representative of the post-Black Friday generation, one that, in his words, "was born in a crisis, grew up hearing about the crisis and now lives and raises its children in the midst of a crisis." Borges has been trying to frame Venezuela's current woes as the failure of an entire generation, Chávez included. He has a point.

While some highbrow analysts derided the TV Show that made him famous, *Justicia Para Todos*, the show actually won international awards, and people in the barrios still remember him for it. In fact, lower-class voters participating in focus groups have identified Borges as having a strong character, in part because they recall Borges's alter ego in *Radio Rochela*, where the fake judge would throw his hammer in anger at the people in the court. And yet the show was not meant to be a vehicle for Borges's personality; it was meant to bring the idea of justices of the peace to people that have never had access to justice through the use of mass media. It seems to have served its purpose well.

In recent focus groups, lower-middle class voters have been asked to describe Borges, and the word that keeps coming up is "*arrecho*", a Venezuelan slang-word meaning "daring" or "with a strong character". They have also described him as fair and decisive.

One of the factors that distinguishes Borges's candidacy from the others is that it is rooted in a process to form a political party out of the ashes of the IVth Republic. Primero Justicia understand the links between the decline of Venezuelan democracy and the decline of political parties: traditional parties fell prey to rent seeking and corruption and ceased being agents for change and progress. However, it sees the demise of all political parties as a step backward for our democracy. Instead of the chavista phenomenon that sees in a populist caudill-esque and military "movement" the solution, Primero Justicia is a civilian political party, with multiple leaders, tendencies and yes, even in-fights. Right now, it is perhaps the only relevant political party in Venezuela. (Side note: inside sources from within the party tell me the rift between Borges's group and the Leopoldo López/Liliana Hernández faction is serious, although getting better).

Because of his background and personality, Borges can be portrayed as aloof, elitist and a bit snobbish. While none of this is true, Borges understands that as long as his enemies from either side of the spectrum are the ones portraying him on the media, he doesn't stand a chance. This realization, along with the need to differentiate Primero Justicia from the rest of the opposition pack, has led him to take to the streets and start meeting people face-to-face, bringing his message of "Popular Progress" and his persona to let voters form their own opinion about him.

Borges' proposals are rooted in sensible economic and social policy. Although the campaign is young and government programs have not been made public, we already have some information on Borges's proposals for the country.

The cornerstone of Primero Justicia's program is a deep reform of the justice system, with an increase in the number of judges, an expansion in the number of justices of the peace, and transparent mechanisms for naming and overseeing judges. The cornerstone of the chavista justice project is politicized judges few in number and in temporary positions. Organizations such as Human Rights Watch have warned of the dangers of the chavista stranglehold of the judiciary. Primero Justicia understands that the first step towards creating a civilized society that can provide progress for all is having an accessible and impartial justice system.

Borges's program will focus on improving current "Misiones" so that they do not exclude people on the basis of their political beliefs. Surprisingly, polls by Greenberg Research, among others, have found this to be the issue most likely to appeal to swing voters.

Borges is the only major candidate proposing a radical reform of oil production and the way it benefits people. Borges favors increasing Venezuela's oil production under the sensible notion that the only way the country will develop is by producing more of what we do best. In theory, Chávez also favors increasing production, as witnessed by several PDVSA expansion plans he has announced over the years but so far failed to implement.

Borges is the only candidate currently proposing direct cash layouts to all Venezuelans from excess oil profits. Borges believes that these funds could be used to set up a working national pensions system. They could also be used to fund youth training and universal health care. As the Constitution says, oil belongs to the people, not the State, and Borges believes it's time to start taking this seriously.

For several years now, Primero Justicia has been proposing legislation to tackle the high unemployment levels of the past seven years, including incentives to hire young people and women. This also includes an emphasis on favoring labor-intensive sectors such as construction and tourism. Chavista congressmen have duly shelved PJ's legal initiatives, and the result has been double-digit unemployment for more than five years now.

Borges favors massive title holding for barrio dwellers, as well as giving away or selling highly valued government land to those who need it most. One of Primero Justicia's main criticisms of the government (and in this they have been almost unique) is that the "deeds" or "titles" it occasionally gives out to slum-dwellers are not really transfers of property rights, but rather a primitive form of leasing. In part based on the influential work of people like Hernando de Soto, Primero Justicia believes that unless we are able to bring the enormous capital of our informal sector into formal society, under-privileged classes will never find their way up.

Borges has been the only candidate so far to embrace the idea of primaries for opposition candidates. He believes in unity, but he also believes this unity should come from the people, not from backroom dealings between political parties with self-appointed bargaining power and no voters.

Borges's role in the opposition has been marked by complicated decisions. In a move that probably halted the rise of his party, Borges and company decided to join forces with Fourth Republic dinosaurs like Pompeyo Márquez, Henry Ramos Allup and Enrique Mendoza in the now extinct Coordinadora Democrática. In spite of Primero Justicia representing a break both from chavismo and from parties such as AD and Copei, PJ was instrumental in forging unified candidates for the National Assembly. In spite of their uneasiness with old-style politicians, they have always been willing to play the unity card. This gives them ample room to be able to forge alliances in the future, an essential condition for post-Chávez governability.

Borges does not believe that arguing with the CNE should be the main focus of non-Chavista candidates. He knows that any negotiation with the current or future CNE is useless unless one has real popular support. In that sense, his current strategy of forging ahead with his campaign while at the same time embracing Sumate's conditions for electoral transparency is the correct one.

Borges is understated and unassuming. When I met him during our mutual years at UCAB, he seemed to be driven, intellectual and somewhat shy. He was not given to petty small talk, nor is he one who likes to hear the drone of his own voice for hours. It is hard to imagine him conducting a six-hour edition of Aló, Presidente.

Anti-politics taken to its logical conclusion
Posted on July 25, 2006 by Quico

Well, it had to come to this: Benjamin Rausseo, much better known as El Conde del Guacharo, has launched his presidential bid.

It's a bit of a challenge to explain who Mr. Rausseo is to foreign readers. Basically, he's a stand-up comedian who long ago launched a wildly successful, unabashedly ribald act as "El Conde del Guacharo" - a fast talking, obscenity-spewing, tell-it-like-it-is everyman from Oriente. Love his comedy or hate it, Er Conde is just about as far from a traditional politician as it's possible to imagine.

Not surprisingly, the question that dogs Rausseo at this stage is whether he is, you know, actually serious about this. It sure seems like he is: wearing a suit, making a gargantuan effort to contain the stream of utter obscenity that is the cornerstone of his comedy act, and fielding questions (mostly) seriously, he's making every effort to convey that this is not a joke.

Alarmingly, Rausseo seems to be the most talented campaigner the opposition has come up with so far. Making the most of his humble beginnings, but also wasting no opportunity to talk about his successful career in business (the guy built and owns a Theme Park in Margarita,) his soon-to-be-earned law degree and his polyglot abilities, Er Conde is packaging himself as the no-nonsense alternative to Chávez. He's the one opposition guy able to talk to regular Venezuelans in a language they can understand, able to level with them without condescending or patronizing, and able to stake out a dissident position that's solidly grounded in good old, popular common sense. When it comes to connecting with regular people on a gut level, he's just light-years ahead of Borges, Petkoff and Rosales...which is not surprising, since connecting with regular people on a gut level has been his job for 20 years.

Can his candidacy attain the Electoral Tsunami status he aspires to? Only time will tell. For now, I'll just note that his strategic positioning is excellent. Rausseo is selling himself with Roberto Smith-esque marketing savvy, but without Smith's hoity-toity Eastside-Caracas-via-Harvard baggage. His pitch is solidly centered on

Chávez's polling weak points (*"se acabó la regaladera de plata! primero los de acá, los demás que se pongan en fila!"*) and what he lacks in experience he more than makes up in charm, street cred, and *chispa*.

Other positives? Absolutely everyone knows who El Conde del Guacharo is - and almost everyone seems to like him: he is one candidate with no name-recognition problems, and low negatives. Moreover, he is one guy Chávez just can't run his usual playbook on: Rausseo's outsider aura and popular touch makes him the only candidate with a real chance to out-Chávez-Chávez, to out-feel people's pain, and to out-flank any personal attack. Actually, with his legendary, acerbic wit, trying to attack him would be a distinctly risky proposition for Chávez...who else could bitch-slap the guy the way El Conde could?

Remember how people said Teodoro was a good candidate because Chávez could not credibly dick him around? Well, it turned out that Chávez didn't have to dick him around, because Teodoro is such a hopeless campaigner Chávez can just ignore him. Rausseo, though, is the real thing: a guy who can't be ignored and can't (safely) be attacked.

It's amazing, alarming, depressing, just plain sad that it's come to this, but...I'm sort of excited about it.

Man(uel) of the hour
August 9, 2006 by Juan Cristobal

Manuel Rosales, two-term governor of the state of Zulia, in Western Venezuela, has just been confirmed as the single presidential candidate of a substantial portion of the opposition to Hugo Chávez's pseudo-socialist revolution. The announcement was made today in Caracas, after Venezuela's CNE decided yesterday that Rosales did not need to resign from his governorship but rather take a temporary leave of absence.

Zulia (where I am from, by the way) is Venezuela's most populous state. It is the home of a big chunk of Venezuela's oil wealth, as well as some of the best agricultural land in the country.

It is also the home of some of Venezuela's most distinctive cultural manifestations, such as *gaitas* and the cult of the Virgin of La Chinita. Maracaibo, the state capital, is Venezuela's second-largest city. Once a sprawling big town riddled with problems, it has sort of come of age, and the city looks cleaner and more prosperous than many other places in the country.

Both Quico and I have expressed our misgivings about Rosales on several occasions. Both of us have come forward in favor of other candidates, such as Rausseo or Borges. However, today is not the time to dwell on these issues. I think it is a good moment to pause and reflect on all that is positive about this announcement.

Rosales' announcement is the product of intense political negotiations that began several months ago. This process involved lengthy discussions between three main candidates, several less popular ones, and Venezuela's NGOs. The fact that these people could sit down, see the urgency of what is coming to us, understand that unity is of the utmost importance, and come up with a reasonable solution at the right time is an enormous step forward for the opposition. Long gone are the extensive deliberations of the extinct Coordinadora Democrática, where nothing was ever solved, nobody had the lead voice, there was no vision and the message was never clear.

Some people have expressed misgivings about Rosales being the product of negotiations and not the product of primaries. There are several reasons why this criticism rings a bit hollow:

a) It was well known that the organization of the primaries was facing numerous logistical problems;

b) enthusiasm for the primaries was dwindling;

c) voters were afraid of participating in the primaries and ending up in some government list where they would be punished;

d) Súmate was being distracted from its role by the government's continuous harassment; and

e) the primaries would have probably yielded a Rosales victory anyway.

The way that Rosales was selected is a positive development. It is possibly the first time that different factions in the opposition have sat down, discussed what the country needs and come up with a solution. It is a big step toward proving that the opposition is capable of governing Venezuela in spite of its heterogeneity.

It was also refreshing to see the way Teodoro Petkoff, Julio Borges and the rest of the candidates came out and supported Rosales. Special mention goes to Borges, who was Rosales' main challenger and who has immediately put his party's logistical and intellectual resources at his disposal. There are rumors Rosales will announce in the next few days that Borges will be his vice-president should he win, but the fact that Borges' support did not come with a quid pro quo is certainly positive for the future.

What does Rosales bring to the table? His two main assets are an efficient record as a public servant and two electoral victories over Chávez and his barrage of tricks. His record is evident in Zulia's improvements in roads and public services. Rosales has also shown political deftness, working with both the federal government and, especially, with Maracaibo's chavista mayor. All over Maracaibo, you see a healthy competition between the public works sponsored by city hall and the works sponsored by the governor (the competition reaches somewhat tacky levels, given the enormity of the colorful signs announcing this or that sidewalk is being brought to you by either the mayor or the governor).

Rosales has skillfully hung on to his job in spite of the CNE's tricks and opposition voter apathy. He is very popular in Zulia, and it is likely he will carry this state in the election, tricks or no tricks. Zulianos are Venezuela's most region-proud bunch, and we tend to be more pragmatic in our ideology. It's my impression that, as a whole, Zulianos seem to be less prone to left-wing populism. We believe in entrepreneurship and in private property more than the rest of the country, and we can be sure that Rosales will bring these issues to the table.

As for Rosales' proposals, we'll have more time to discuss these later. From what he has already said, they combine most of the proposals brought forward by Petkoff and Borges, including a direct mechanism to hand out oil rents and the improvement of the misiones. He has also come forward against the war-like mentality that seems to pervade in the government lately, even borrowing some of Rausseo's lines by saying that airplanes will be changed to schools and missiles will be changed to hospitals.

Finally, Rosales is the product of decentralization, a complex political process started in the late 80s that has not quite achieved as much as promised in spite of its popularity. Decentralization has come under attack from the current administration. Chávez, as all good military men, hates independent subordinates, and he has implemented numerous initiatives destined to take away what little power regional and local governments had. Rosales is sure to propose further decentralization as a way of bringing power back to the communities and the states.

As I said before, today is not a day to criticize. The opposition is showing great maturity in coming up with a concerted solution at this stage of the game. Let's wait and see what happens with other candidates such as Rausseo or Smith, as well as what AD decides to do. In the meantime, let's celebrate the hope of putting a zuliano in Miraflores for the first time in our history.

Things you learn from watching Globovision at high altitude
Posted on November 8, 2006 by Juan Cristobal

Last weekend, my family and I rented a cabin high in the Andes to get away from it all. What the picture from the brochure didn't show was that the cabin had a satellite dish, so one of the channels on offer was Globovisión.

So much for getting away from it all. I hadn't watched Globovisión in ages, so I decided to take in their coverage of Saturday's 26x26 walk-a-thon.

The enthusiastic, racially diverse crowd was impressive. Globo's broadcast was not.

For starters, the march got non-stop, wall-to-wall coverage all afternoon. All they did was show the crowds all the time, which is great if you're a Rosales supporter like me. But what's a NiNi to think? That Globovisión is spoon-feeding them their chosen candidate. What a turn-off.

From the studio, Alba Cecilia Mujica kept referring to Rosales, mantra-like, as "the national unity candidate, Manuel Rosales..." with a smile as wide as the Cheshire Cat's. Poor Alba Cecilia, you got the sense that covering this march is the most fun she's had in years. She really should get out more.

And while she's at it, she should try and be just a tiny bit more professional. I mean, when you use political catch-phrases like "the candidate of national unity," you play right into the hands of chavistas who allege outrageous media bias on the part of private TV stations. What is Globovisión up to? I thought. Is it that desperate for a whipping? Do they think they do us a favor by being so blatantly pro-Rosales?

I tried to picture a Fox News anchor talking about George Bush as "reformer with results George W. Bush", or "compassionate conservative President George W. Bush..." Not likely...even Fox News shows some restraint when whooping it up for their guy.

Hour after hour, it just kept getting worse.

"Ma'am, what's your name, what do you think of this march?" one reporter kept asking.

"My name is Beatríz, Beatríz Martínez, I walked from La Castellana, and I'm here because I'm happy, because we are finally going to get rid of this totalitarian, authoritarian regime!"

Whoa. So much for fear. The only thing missing from her statement was her cédula number and the name of the woman who does her toe nails, but you can probably find that in the Maisanta list under Martínez, Beatríz, La Castellana.

"Sir, what's your name, what do you think of this march?"

A 65-year old man who had obviously walked a lot - God bless him, I can barely make it to the bathroom some days and I'm half his age - answered "My name is Luis Méndez, and I'm happy because this march is the biggest since April 11th!"

Oh great, just what we need, more references to April 11th. Keep that up and NiNis will be lining up en masse on Dec. 3rd...to vote for Chávez!

"Ma'am, what's your name, what do you think of this march?"

"My name is Sofía Pérez, I'm marching from Chacaíto and I'm really happy because the march is very well organized." Uh huh. Wait, how much "organization" does a march actually require? It's hundreds of thousands of people walking from one end of the city to the other. Cops just have to stop traffic, street vendors do the rest. Oh well, I guess just making it home alive is a sign that it was a good march. Lots of marchers agreed, "excellent, very well organized." Opposition unity indeed!

A dozen or so of these interviews left me pining for a commercial break. Eventually, it came.

An ad for Rosales, "Atrevete te te", with a woman taking money out of an ATM using Mi Negra. In fact, all the ads I happened to catch were about Mi Negra. Funny how Rosales decided to focus his campaign on the issue Chávez is least vulnerable on, social policy. Wait, what were Rosales's proposals on crime and jobs, the two issues that all voters care about the most and rate the government's performance worst? Easy to forget...

Then it was back to the march. A shot of a very, very sweaty Rosales with an even sweatier Carlos Ocariz, making their way through a crowd somewhere in Petare. He tried to give a speech but Globovisión didn't have the sound and their camera was blocked by a string of plastic flags. Amateur hour at the OK Corral...

Oh well. Maybe they'll show some *políticos*. Here comes one... it's... it's... it's Antonio Ledezma! Ugh. The man is like a vapid drivel factory. I really can't recall the last time I heard him say anything smart, a fresh thought, a non-cliché. Does he even have a job? How does he support himself? Politicians...

Next up, the ineffable Liliana Hernández, or Ledezma with a wig. A VTV reporter had been asking her tough questions at the beginning of the march, and she was quite rude to him, telling him that "my taxes paid for your salary." Wait, Liliana, isn't that what we want, journalists who ask politicians tough questions? Why so prickly?

I mean, I hate VTV as much as the next guy, but do you have to be so rude, so intolerant, so... chavista? The guy was simply doing his job, the fact that VTV reporters don't do it when questioning chavistas is another issue. Why not take advantage of the opportunity to show that we are different, that we can handle the tough questions? I thought Rosales did that brilliantly the other day. But that's just beyond her. On second thought, Liliana is Iris Varela with a better hairdo.

More people from the march: the Chairman of the Teacher's Federation (who apparently didn't get the "fear" memo); an old man who kept harping on our poor reporter on the street, telling her that "Rosales was going to save Venezuela for beautiful women like yourself;" a poor guajira woman originally from Municipio Mara who was now living in Caracas. And all through, Globo kept up the same tone of breathless, misplaced boosterism. It was kind of sad.

I had to turn it off. The march was impressive, the enthusiasm of the people contagious. But Globovisión is shameful. This march did not merit uninterrupted coverage, and it sure as hell did not merit uninterrupted counter-productive inanity. Instead of asking marchers smart questions, it was like watching somebody else's vacation video. "This is me in El Escorial... this is Juanita at the Eiffel Tower, remember Juanita? That was so funny when you..."

Hours and hours of coverage geared to one type of voter only: the convinced Rosalista who is afraid of losing hope.

Why this tone? I think the answer comes down to fear. The fear of fear makes us fall into artificial highs, and it makes us lash out at unsuspecting passers-by.

I've been thinking a lot about the reactions to Quico's recent posts, and about the ones I am sure to get to this one, and I've concluded that part of our problem is that we fear Chávez.

When we turn away from people who are saying something we don't want to hear, when we say that we need a Kleenex handy to read a discouraging poll, when we build up our hope on the basis of something as hard to gauge as a march, when we accuse people of being chavistas if they express the possibility that the country may, perhaps, actually be about to vote for Chávez, we are simply acting out on fear.

Chávez knows we fear him. That's why his speech is so hateful, so full of incitement. He works to ignite our fear and makes us appear... well, fearful, or to use another word, squalid. It's a show put on for the benefit of poor voters who get a kick out of watching us tremble. It's like their own little French Revolution is playing inside their head; Chávez's tongue playing the part of guillotine.

For all his authoritarianism, his corruption and his incapacity, for all the hate that spews out of his *jeta*, I don't fear Chávez. If the country does indeed have a chavista majority, so be it. I don't need my values confirmed by a majority of Venezuelans. I know I'm right to oppose this thug, I know what he's doing is deeply wrong and dangerous, and 6, 8 or 10 million people will not change my mind.

Democracies are like that, sometimes a majority of people make mistakes for the best of reasons. For the best of reasons, a majority of gringos gave the presidency to a bumbling oligophrenic like George W. Bush, and for the best of reasons they just handed the House of Representatives to a dim-witted snob like Nancy Pelosi yesterday. Does that make them right? Probably not.

Me? I'm in this for the long-haul. I'll be working for Rosales from now until the election. But if Chávez wins another term, we'll have other chances, there will be other battles. We have to be careful and watch his every move, but we must remember that he has absolute power now, and if re-elected, he will continue having absolute power. Democracy will continue circling the drain, as Quico says.

I know I will live to see the end of this, and the end will probably not be pretty given how emotionally invested Chávez's supporters are in him. I'm not scared of his stupid referendum proposing the end of term limits. Bring it on! It will be that much sweeter when, finally, be it in 2010, 2012 or 2021, we defeat chavismo by defeating the man himself.

Some rhetorical questions nobody seems to ask
Posted on March 9, 2006 by Quico

Some rhetorical questions nobody seems to ask...

Can you summarize the political doctrines, policy positions and strategic visions of AD, Un Nuevo Tiempo, Proyecto Venezuela, Un Solo Pueblo Copei, Primero Justicia, Alianza Bravo Pueblo, Causa R and MAS, and how they differ?[44]

Can you explain, in substantive terms, how a future government headed by AD would be different from a future government headed by Un Nuevo Tiempo, Proyecto Venezuela, Un Solo Pueblo, Copei, Primero Justicia, Alianza Bravo Pueblo, Causa R or MAS?

Is the opposition to the Chávez experiment in any way strengthened by the existence, as separate parties, of AD, Un Nuevo Tiempo, Proyecto Venezuela, Un Solo Pueblo, Copei, Primero Justicia, Alianza Bravo Pueblo, Causa R and MAS?

Besides the need to multiply "leadership posts," can you provide any rationale for the existence, as separate parties, of AD, Un Nuevo Tiempo, Proyecto Venezuela, Un Solo Pueblo, Copei, Primero Justicia, Alianza Bravo Pueblo, Causa R and MAS?

Can you name a single instance, in Venezuelan history, of two distinct parties merging?

What do you think it says about the public spiritedness of Henry Ramos, Manuel Rosales, Henrique Salas Romer, William

---

[44] These are all opposition political parties. Some, like AD, are the parties that held sway for most of the period before Chávez.

Ojeda, Cesar Perez Vivas, Julio Borges, Antonio Ledezma, Andres Velasquez and Leopoldo Puchi (plus assorted hangers on) that AD, Un Nuevo Tiempo, Proyecto Venezuela, Un Solo Pueblo, Copei, Primero Justicia, Alianza Bravo Pueblo, Causa R and MAS continue to exist as separate parties?

What do you think it says about the conception of the nature of politics of Henry Ramos, Manuel Rosales, Henrique Salas Romer, William Ojeda, Cesar Perez Vivas, Julio Borges, Antonio Ledezma, Andres Velasquez and Leopoldo Puchi (plus assorted hangers on) that AD, Un Nuevo Tiempo, Proyecto Venezuela, Un Solo Pueblo, Copei, Primero Justicia, Alianza Bravo Pueblo, Causa R and MAS continue to exist as separate parties?

What do you think it says about the Opposition's political culture that AD, Un Nuevo Tiempo, Proyecto Venezuela, Un Solo Pueblo, Copei, Primero Justicia, Alianza Bravo Pueblo, Causa R and MAS continue to exist as separate parties?

Why, in your opinion, is it that these questions are not part of the political debate in Venezuela?

What I'm getting at is that Opposition politicos seem to have a warped understanding of what a political party is.

A political party is supposed to be an institutional mechanism that aligns and coordinates the political activities of broad sectors of society sharing a basic vision even if, unsurprisingly, its members disagree on various points.

In order to aggregate their strengths, party members come to understand that they have to accept a measure of discipline, a broad commitment to cooperate, to sing from a single hymn sheet even if they might each quibble with some of the notes. This doesn't mean that they contract out their judgment to party leaders, or that they stop discussing their disagreements. It means that they agree to process their disagreements through an institutional mechanism that prevents their petty disputes from impairing their collective ability to act effectively in the broader political sphere.

For these reasons, in most Western countries politicians understand that for a political party to be at all effective, it needs to be broad. Ken Livingstone can share a political party with Tony Blair, Dennis Kucinich with Joe Lieberman, and Felipe Gonzalez with Rodriguez Zapatero.

Does that mean they stop disagreeing? No. It means that they understand that, on balance, their agreements outweigh their disagreements and that the benefits, in terms of political effectiveness, they get from processing their disagreements inside a single organization outweigh the costs of fragmentation.

This line of reasoning just doesn't seem to occur to the Venezuelan Opposition, where parties proliferate not because their leaders disagree on anything substantial, but simply because each would rather be a bigger fish in a smaller pond than a smaller fish in a bigger pond.

The costs of this attitude, in terms of disorganization, disaggregation, mixed messages, wasteful bickering, intra-coalition competition and overall incoherence barely figure in their calculation. So parties proliferate ad infinitum, with a cacique-to-indio ratio that increases exponentially until none of the parties is able to be at all effective...or even to exist, in any meaningful sense, beyond the confines of a TV studio.

It's hardly surprising that a political opposition "organized" in this way can't lead the anti-Chávez movement, and ends up, instead, reacting to waves of opinion it can't control.

My point in raising these questions - especially the last one - is that Chávez is a big, big problem - so big, in fact, that the obsessive concern with attacking his government stifles debate on a series of lesser, but still very important problems - like the little matter of the self-defeating fragmentation of opposition parties. It's always more comfortable for an Antonio Ledezma or a Cesar Perez Vivas to rant against Chávez than to question the crazy structure of the opposition.[45]

So they don't. And we don't. And so we're ineffective...in great part, because we can't be bothered to sort out a political organization within the anti-Chávez camp that might make us effective.

One political prisoner's ordeal
Posted on March 19, 2010 by Quico

What the government is doing to Judge Maria Lourdes Afiuni staggers the mind. No other single story captures Venezuela's slide to dictatorship quite like hers.

Jailed summarily simply for doing her job, Judge Afiuni was sent to Los Teques Women's Penitentiary, where she's in the extraordinarily dangerous situation of having to wait for trial surrounded by violent offenders, including several whom she herself sentenced.

For her first two weeks in Los Teques, her jail cell there didn't have a lock on the door, leaving her terrifyingly exposed to some of the most dangerous, violent women in Venezuela. At one point, her fellow inmates tried to set her on fire – literally. Her relatives get threatened with a similar fate each time they try to visit her. These days, she is in virtual solitary confinement: too scared to leave her 25 square foot cell.

The ironies pile up fast with this case. Judge Afiuni was jailed after she had the temerity to order the release of another political prisoner. Afiuni released Eligio Cedeño because the state was way past its legal deadline for launching a trial against him, so he'd been sitting in jail for over two years merely waiting for his day in court.

---

[45] Ledezma is the current Metropolitan Mayor of Caracas. Pérez Vivas is the current governor of the state of Táchira. Both come from the discredited parties that ruled Venezuela prior to Chávez.

That was three months ago. Judge Afiuni's been sitting in jail ever since, waiting for her preliminary hearing. By law (COPP Article 330) the preliminary hearing must be held no later than 20 days after the Public Prosecutor files formal charges. Judge Afiuni was charged on January 26th. It's been almost two months since then...but her prelim keeps getting delayed because...well, just because.

Remember, sitting in jail surrounded by violent offenders she put there, Judge Afiuni's life is at serious risk every single day the state stalls. Considering the circumstances that brought her to jail in the first place, what judge would risk joining her by ordering her release?

Carlos Andrés Pérez – 1922-2010 – fashion victim
Posted on December 26, 2010 by Quico

Carlos Andrés Pérez, who dominated Venezuela's social democratic landscape for over a quarter of a century, has died at the age of 88, on Christmas day.

CAP, as he was universally known, is harder to eulogize than most. Variously described as a corruption-enabling populist, a far-sighted visionary, a proto-Chávez, a champion of third world autonomy in the Cold War, a neoliberal despot, and the godfather of Spanish Democracy, CAP was all of those things and none.

To my mind, we should remember him, first and foremost, as a man of his time...in fact, a man too much of his time.

His two presidencies – 1974-1979 and 1989-1993 – were famously at odds with one another. The determined statist of the 70s gave way completely to the liberal reformer of the 90s. There seemed to be no thread linking the two, beyond the man himself and his steely determination to bring to Venezuela the most up-to-date international thinking on development.

The result wasn't a catastrophe: it was two catastrophes.

It's easy to forget now, but the kinds of Big Push, import-substitution industrialization strategies that CAP implemented with such relish in the 1970s were cutting edge stuff at the time. Academics at big name think tanks, hoity toity universities and, of course, throughout the UN System were convinced that without a major state-sponsored drive to coordinate investment, third world countries would remain mired in a peripheral position in the World System, staying poor forever.

Grandiose projects, like the expansion of Sidor behind high tariff walls, were part of the standard World Bank prescription for development back then. CAP positioned himself as an international leader for this movement. Chávez, for one, can barely sleep at night knowing the history books will always credit CAP with having nationalized the oil industry.

The ISI recipe, unfortunately, was badly flawed from the start. In the 1970s, like much of the International Development community, CAP failed to foresee the intractable coordination problems involved in mobilizing the huge new resources unlocked by the 70s oil boom, and the sprawling incentives for corruption they would generate.

The outcome, in terms of Dutch Disease, wasteful investment and plain old graft is perhaps best illustrated by the heaping piles of rusting junk you can still see if you look closely by the side of the runway as you fly into some Venezuelan airports. Snow-plows and aircraft de-icing equipment have been gathering dust there ever since the late 70s, when they were bought as part of airport modernization kits. That the inclusion of Cold Weather components hiked up the price was, of course, a feature rather than a bug from the point of view of the bureaucrats taking a cut of the contract...

CAP's big push of the 70s set in motion a chain of events that would turn Venezuela – at that point the fastest growing economy in the world over the previous 40 years – into the basket case it would become over the next four decades.

Mutatis mutandi – and almost everything was mutandi - it was the same story in the late 80s and early 90s, when CAP drank deeply from the cup of the Washington Consensus and tried to implement it, "shock therapy" style, before there was any kind of political, well, consensus for it inside Venezuela. The outcome, in terms of political instability, wholesale contempt for the institutions of democracy and, ultimately, the rise of authoritarian politics is too well known to rehash in an obituary.

Once again, CAP set out to apply the recipes handed down from the big development institutions. Once again he badly mangled the political economy of reform, with catastrophic results over the medium term.

An Intellectual Fashion Victim until the end, Carlos Andrés Pérez stands as an icon of Venezuela's failed integration into the World Economy, of its inability to process the currents of international ideas into a viable recipe for broad-based prosperity. In attempt after attempt to bring the country up-to-date with the latest in development thinking, CAP sunk it deeper and deeper into a morass of economic dysfunction and moral degeneracy that was bound, sooner or later, to morph into the tragedy now all around us.

It was the Venezuela traumatized and weakened by CAP's serial mishandling of reform that found its institutions too frail to withstand Chávez's authoritarian onslaught. And in that sense it was CAP – far more than his pardon-wielding Christian Democratic nemesis – who is to blame for Venezuela's relapse into dictatorship.

The candidate for people who hate politics
Posted on October 2, 2011 by Quico

Yesterday's campaign launch speech to the Primero Justicia party conference by Miranda governor Henrique Capriles Radonski was none too subtle about how he intends to position himself: as the candidate for people who hate politics.

Capriles's spiel is calculatedly, militantly non-confrontational. His total rhetorical focus on the future implies a militant refusal to even talk about the last 13 years except in the most oblique way.

I think this is canny. People are exhausted with all these years of hyperpolarization. That big, swing-voter rich segment right in the middle of the electorate is full of people who have no interest at all in re-litigating the ideological squabbles of the Chávez era for the umpteenth time.

In fact, they were already sick to death of the ideological fight in 2004. They turned off a long time ago, learned to tune out the *cadenas* and the headlines and the news bulletins and the boring uncle who only talks about politics years ago. They're too busy making a living (and trying to stay alive) to really pay attention to a squabble that's as predictable as it is irrelevant to them.

Reaching these people is obviously a major challenge. And that's a problem, because they will almost certainly decide the election next year.

Capriles is making a carefully targeted play for their votes precisely by positioning himself outside the hyper-polarized back and forth. This is what all that "future focus" stuff is about: an implicit promise to Ni-Ni Nation that a vote for me is a vote to bury, once and for all, the fallow disputes of the Chávez era.

Another way to say this is that Capriles is running a General Election campaign in the primary season. In an American context, that's what overwhelming front-runners typically do: if you're fairly sure the nomination is yours, there's no need to pander so much to the extremes and risk alienating the voters you'll have to appeal to win the General. But, of course, it's a risky strategy, because the fire-breathing Chávez-hating right wing is going to be hugely over-represented in the Primaries, and there's no question as to who is dishing out the red meat they crave these days.

The dynamic of a primary fight is going to create strong pressure for Capriles to come out swinging against Chávez in much stronger terms. But now that he's told us that his campaign's entire rationale is avoiding that stance, can he do so without shooting himself in the foot?

Veremos...

Stepping back
Posted on February 15, 2012 by Quico

Chavismo's generalized freak-out over the selection of a Nazi Zionist gay fraudster TFP-member bent on world domination as Opposition Unity Candidate has been troubling to watch, but stepping back, what are we likely to remember about Sunday?[46]

1. The marginalization of the old guard: AD's inability to mobilize a majority for its candidate in any state other than Delta Amacuro – the only state outside of Zulia where Pablo Pérez won, barely – was remarkable. So too was Copei's inability to even come close to delivering Táchira, where Capriles trounced Pérez. This dramatically re-arranges the incentives within the MUD. It empowers Capriles and his allies, while it marginalizes the remaining toxic assets around the unity table (cough-cough-ramosallup-cough.) Capriles probably has no choice but to cozy up to the UNT-machine in Zulia, which it will need in October. But the rest of the Old Guard will find its room to maneuver severely constrained.

2. Early and disciplined beats late and scattered: Capriles's candidacy was announced in September of 2010. Pérez announced in August of 2011. Capriles had a clear message from the start, whereas Pérez and Machado tried out different things ("Por tu futuro Seguro," "Tarjeta única," "Abajo cadenas," "Vota duro," "Capitalismo popular"). Even Leopoldo seemed confused, talking about "La Mejor Venezuela" while jumping over office furniture. Ultimately, the voter knew exactly what the Capriles campaign was about. Did they know what the other ones were about? Relentless discipline and an early start carried the day.

---

[46] The opposition's presidential candidate Henrique Capriles easily won the opposition's primary on February 12, 2012. He was immediately called a Nazi, a Zionist, an extreme right-winger, and a homosexual by mainstream chavista news outlets.

3. The collapse of opposition radicalism: With less than 5% of the vote between them, the opposition's three radicals discovered the actual limits to their brand of politics. The fact that one of the three was the smartest, most articulate, hardest-working candidate in the race, and was well-funded to boot, only underscores that the problem was the message. The *cabezas calientes* will remain hot-headed, but their claim to represent anything beyond a marginal fringe has lost any credibility. This is a good and blessed thing.

4. The possibility of competing without a lot of resources: Let's face it, if turnout estimates were low before Sunday's vote, it's largely because we thought mobilizing people on a shoestring was going to be hard. Without proper access to the air-waves, running campaigns that were precariously funded at best, it was far from clear we would be able to turn out more than a million and a half people or so. We doubled that, even though the nation's millions of public employees were essentially forbidden to participate.

5. Opinion polls worked: You've heard it, I've heard it, the mantra-like repetition: *"Esas encuestas son chimbas"* – the polls don't work. There is this perception that proper polling is impossible to do in Venezuela. This is nonsense. Putting aside Jesse Chacón's absurd rants, serious pollsters such as Datanálisis, Consultores 21, and Varianzas not only predicted a Capriles win, but also a few of the local races. For example, Datanálisis correctly predicted Muchacho would beat the incumbent Graterón in tiny Chacao. Varianzas correctly predicted Uzcátegui would beat Blyde, albeit they got the margin wrong, probably due to some late developments in that race. Datanálisis predicted Ocariz would beat Mendoza. All in all, a good day for serious pollsters.

6. The Government's political radar is faltering: It seems clear chavismo expected much, much lower turnout, and was caught off-guard by the results, having to improvise a rash power play for the voter rolls that ended up being easily

defused by the MUD. As the premiere consumers of their own insane propaganda, chavistas have crippled their own ability to understand what is going on around them.

7. Caracas Chronicles for the win: If you read Caracas Chronicles, you knew there were no national exit polls, so immediately you would have known some people were echoing completely made-up numbers. If you read Caracas Chronicles, you knew about the brilliant quick count, designed by loyal reader and friend Omar, which nailed the results almost to a T. If you read Caracas Chronicles, you were also among the first to know Capriles had won the election. We work hard for you guys and we put our credibility on the line. When we call an election, we try to do it quickly and accurately. We make mistakes sometimes, but we try to get things right. And we can recognize BS from a mile away. Keep that in mind next October 7th.

V

Chavista additions to our daily lexicon

Chavismo is nothing if not a spectacle. The Chávez era has been, sometimes quite literally, a reality show in which things get named without even existing, in which Presidents sing and talk about their bowel movements, and in which troop movements are ordered – all on live TV.

Whether it's a catchy slogan, changing the name of the country, making headlines on international issues, or introducing new philosophies, Hugo Chávez has brilliantly used rhetoric as one of his main weapons. As innocent bystanders, we have fallen prey to these new idioms, and we spent quite some time on the blog using them, analyzing what they meant, and pondering how they made us feel.

Our navel-gazing and our willingness to play along to the strings of the chavista agenda was proof positive that, indeed, "Chávez nos tiene locos." Chávez's uncanny ability to turn everything he did into a "show" kept us glued to our seats.

The "democratic revolution" is a contradiction in terms
Posted on April 11, 2006 by Quico

At the center of the Chávez Revolution we have a contradiction in terms. In democracies dissent is healthy, and alternation is the norm. In revolutions dissent is treason, and alternations are impossible.

You can be democratic or you can be revolutionary. You can't be both.

The strategic ambiguity inherent to this oxymoron is unsustainable. Chávez has been particularly successful at maintaining the fiction that the two concepts can co-exist within a single political project. They can't.

The essence of a revolutionary regime is permanence. The essence of a democratic regime is alternation. "*¡No volverán!*" is the essential revolutionary slogan – the ideological rejection of the possibility of alternation. A regime founded on the promise of a slogan such as that incubates skepticism about its commitment to democracy.

The prominence of "*no volverán*" as a chavista slogan explains much of the opposition's basic unwillingness to believe in this or any other chavista appointed-electoral authority. "After all," their thinking goes "they have already announced it clearly – *no volveremos.*" Seen in this light, any and every CNE concession is a sop to international opinion. The radical opposition sees the revolution as purely revolutionary, the "democratic" part as little more than window-dressing.

I think that's a mistake. The tension encapsulated in the oxymoron is the defining characteristic of chavismo. The government long ago decided that its ultimate goals can only be met if Chávez can retain some minimally plausible claim to democratic legitimacy. Without the strategic ambiguity embodied in the phrase, chavismo would not be chavismo.

The opposition, by withdrawing from the vote, has tried to force the government's hand, to push it into resolving the tension between democracy and revolution by becoming frankly and exclusively revolutionary (and thereby, anti-democratic.) That is a trap the government has not and will not fall into.

The balancing act the government is pushed to attempt is necessarily precarious – although that's momentarily obscured by the oil bonanza. Absent the oil windfall, the tensions inherent in chavismo's foundational oxymoron will become harder and harder to manage. The only question is whether the opposition will be in any way able to capitalize on those difficulties when the time comes.

Democracy implies a clear delineation of the conceptual boundaries between "party," "government," "state," and "nation."

Democracy conceives of the state as the institutional incarnation of the nation, something larger and more permanent than the government. The state is led but not owned by the government. The government is led but not owned by the party in power.

Democracy conceives of politics as the realm of legitimate competition between parties for temporary control of the government. In a democracy, governments come and go but the state is permanent, because it transcends partisan differences - understood as normal and healthy - and accommodates the periodic changes in control of the government that naturally result from elections.

Revolution, as Chávez understands it, is a refutation of this understanding. It starts from a rejection of the conceptual differentiation between party, government, state and nation. It expresses itself in the drive to establish permanent control over the government, the state and the nation while flattening the conceptual boundaries between them. This process takes place both on a symbolic and a substantive level.

Symbolically, Chávez has mixed partisan with national symbols from the start. By adopting the *Libertador's* name, his original political vehicle - the Bolivarian Revolutionary Movement - broke the long established norm that lifted Bolivar, the primary symbol of a unitary national identity, above the partisan fray.

Once in power, the co-optation of Bolivar's name for partisan purposes reached undreamed-of new heights, from the subtle process that has made the word "bolivariano" basically synonymous with "chavista" to the decision to stick the now hyper-politicized label in the country's official title.

"Bolivarianism" - for 150 years the glue that held together our national identity - has morphed into a locus of official partisan identification, while remaining a locus of national identity. This process tends to meld partisan loyalty with patriotism, undermining the possibility of a non-partisan national identification. Dissenters are left without even a country they can call their own - literally, since the politicization of bolivarianism turned "República Bolivariana de Venezuela" more into a provocation than a description.

Later, the revolution moved to strip away the neutrality of even the most basic symbols of national allegiance, politicizing the nation's flag and its coat of arms. (Can the National Anthem be far behind?)

Time and time again, loci of identification that had served to bind the nation together have been turned into symbolic wedges, into instruments for the de-legitimation of dissent and the marginalization of dissenters. Hand in hand with this process, the revolution works to transform the unquestioning acceptance of Chávez's every utterance from a free expression of opinion into a litmus test of patriotic allegiance.

So the cries of "traitor" and "vendepatria" increasingly launched against those who dissent are in no way coincidental: they're the logical outcome of the conceptual flattening at the center of the revolution. In the chavista imagination, party, government, state, and nation have been melded into a single undifferentiated soup. Having erased those distinctions, chavistas have lost sight of the notion, fundamental to democracy, that citizens can oppose the government without opposing the state, or object to the party without betraying the nation. Swimming in the undifferentiated conceptual stew that is the revolutionary party/government/state/

nation nexus, chavistas cannot recognize the distinction between disagreement and treason.

On a substantive level, the revolution also seeks to stamp its mark permanently on the instruments of state power in ways that further flatten the conceptual distinctions that sustain democracy. State resources are used openly and systematically for partisan purposes. Courts come to serve the revolution rather than the state - a political rather than a national project. PDVSA is turned into an appendage of Chávez's political program. The Armed Forces morph slowly but surely into a praetorian guard, where loyalty to the party becomes indistinguishable, to participants, from loyalty to the nation.

On both the symbolic and the substantive level, these revolutionary moves are in direct contradiction with the conceptual apparatus that sustains democracy. They are intended to negate the possibility of alternation. They do so by erasing the conceptual distinctions that give meaning to the democratic process, to the process of partisan competition for control over the government within the context of a permanent, transcendent state conceived as the institutional expression of the unity of the nation.

As such, revolutionary values strike at the heart of democratic system. Flattening the distinction between party, government, state and nation, they leave any future government in the position of having to lead an explicitly chavista state, of commanding an Armed Force that conceives of itself as the protector of the revolution, of governing through a personalized bureaucracy, under a flag and coat-of-arms willfully manipulated into symbols of chavista hegemony.

Why is it so hard to reach Chávez's 30%?
Posted on April 19, 2004 by Quico

or...

Why those soporific speeches at the end of opposition rallies are such a bad sign...

This has been an ongoing debate in the Comments section, and it's a tough nut to crack. I don't have the answers – but I do have some idea about the questions we need to ask ourselves to come up with those answers.

The opposition tends to have a somewhat naive, 19th century-esque notion that it's the content of a political message that matters. And of course content matters, but it's not the only thing, or even the most important thing.

Chávez's credibility with "his" 30% has more to do with style, identity, and use of language than it does with content. You can see this when you see Diosdado Cabello gives a speech. He says the same things Chávez says, but he says them with all of the soul ripped out. Result? Diosdado can't really fire up the crowds, or the opposition's anger.

Style is crucial. Chávez adopts a rhetorical pose of always speaking to his audience as their notional equal. He never pulls rank, never talks down to people, never condescends. Within the construct of his speech, he builds a sense of respecting his listener, of speaking to him on his level.

This was revolutionary when Chávez started doing it in 1998, and today, astonishingly, he remains the only public figure in the country who talks this way. The reason so many people associate the opposition with the old regime, if you ask me, is that opposition politicos still use the rhetorical conventions of the old regime – and it was those conventions, as much as the corruption, mismanagement, and substantive failure of the old system that people voted against in 1998 and 2000.

Chávez talks to the poor. The opposition talks at the poor. Chávez talks like the poor. The opposition talks about the poor. Chávez takes the poor as real, living, breathing human beings. The opposition treats the poor as an abstraction, an academic problem, a set of mathematical relationships on a social indicators statistical report.

Is there any doubt why Chávez connects and – so often – the opposition doesn't?

Identity: Chávez grew up poor. He knows how to tap into that fount of credibility and use it to connect emotionally with the audience. Too many opposition leaders did not grow up poor, and cannot hope to match Chávez's credibility here. (This also explains why they have such a hard time treating the poor as actual people rather than abstractions.)

Worse still, the opposition leaders who did grow up poor seem to feel ill-at-ease bringing it up or using those stories politically. Quite unlike a John Edwards or even a Bill Clinton, they seem to have no idea how to "give legs" to their life stories. Ever listen to Horacio Medina describe his upbringing as a kid of *conserje* in Caracas? From a more rhetorically skillful politician, the line could be devastating. From a bashful, shifty-eyed Medina, it's thoroughly forgettable.

The opposition further alienates itself from Chávez's 30% through its choice of words. Unlike in English, where simplicity and economy are considered the cardinal virtues of usage, in Spanish linguistic virtuosity demands that you use lots of big fancy words. Strunk and White's famous stricture to "omit needless words" makes no sense at all in the context of Spanish – something that took me years to learn when I edited VenEconomy.

Chávez is a lexical rebel in this regard. He talks as though he had read Strunk and White. His speeches may be unbearably long, but they are not verbose. He shuns long words, shuns any word not likely to be understood in a barrio, and if he's forced to use a fancy word, he takes the time to explain its meaning patiently to the audience. Chávez goes far out of his way to make sure his message is not just understood, but understandable.

The opposition has failed miserably to learn from Chávez in this realm. Opposition speeches are still full of *bodrios inefables* and people *manteniendo la sindéresis* and denunciations of *contumacia* and the *abdicación de las obligaciones deontológicas* of the regime - all, of course, in the name of helping the needy. It's funny, but even the formulation opposition politicos use to define the poor - "*los mas necesitados*" - is itself oddly convoluted and probably not that understandable to ... *los mas necesitados* themselves.

The problem is not to come up with a new political program. The problem is to come up with a new discourse, a new way of facilitating political communication between people.

To my mind, the opposition should get over its shyness and just copy Chávez's method. You can't argue with success! The opposition has no reason to be ashamed of imitating a superior strategy - just ask Bill Clinton and Tony Blair how effectively a political discourse can be borrowed once it's been developed.

Many will read this and be horrified by the notion. "Eternalizing chavista-style rhetoric in the political sphere? *Ni locos!*"

It's an understandable reaction, part of an overall, virulent rejection of the craziness of the chavista project. But it's counterproductive. The opposition needs to learn the lesson of 1998, a lesson it still hasn't learned: you cannot hope to mobilize the masses with a discourse understandable only to the elite, you cannot hope to win if you continue to exclude millions of people from political participation by raising the lexical bar of participation so high that millions of people cannot meet it. You can't convince someone who can't understand the words you use!

Undoubtedly there are many in the opposition who were more than happy with the cozy control over political life they could maintain so long as only they and their college-educated peers could understand the stories in El Universal and only that social class was even able to discuss the affairs of the nation. That era is over, finished, buried for good. That's not a bad thing, that's a good thing. Politics means, and will mean, something much broader in Venezuela from here on out, simply because through his rhetoric, Chávez has opened the doors of the political realm to any number of people who were informally (but decisively) excluded from it in the past.

These are the new realities of political communications in Venezuela. The opposition had better adapt to them, accept them, and embrace them, because it can't roll them back.

The half-assed totalitarian
Posted on November 12, 2002 by Quico

I'm reading Christopher Hitchens' new book on George Orwell at the moment, and enjoying it immensely. As I read about Orwell's horror at Stalin's tactics, it's hard not to relate it to events here, which are at once so similar and so vastly different to 1930s Russia. What Orwell makes clear, what he made his reputation writing about, is the way that the systematic denial of the truth is the cognitive cornerstone to totalitarianism. Mangling reality wasn't just something Stalin did accidentally: it was at the center of his control of society. And while there are many, obvious differences between the two, Hitchens' book shows up some terrifying parallelisms between Chávez and Stalin, at least in terms of their attitudes to reality.

Take, for instance, Orwell's satirical take of the rhetoric coming out of Moscow during the dark years of the pre-war purges:

"To get the full sense of our ignorance as to what is really happening in the USSR," he writes, sometime in the mid 1930s, "it's worth trying to translate the most sensational Russian event of the past two years, the Trotskyist trials, into English terms. Make the necessary adjustments, let Left be Right and Right be Left, and Trotsky be Churchill, and you get something like this:

Mr. Winston Churchill, now in exile in Portugal, is plotting to overthrow the British Empire and establish Communism in England. By the use of unlimited Russian money he has succeeded in building up a huge Churchillite organization which includes members of Parliament, factory managers, Roman Catholic bishops, and practically the whole of the Primrose League. Almost every day some dastardly act of sabotage is laid bare – sometimes a plot to blow up the House of Lords, sometimes an outbreak of foot and mouth disease in the Royal racing-stables. 80% of the Beefeaters at the Tower of London are discovered to be agents of the plot. A high official at the Post Office admits brazenly to having embezzled 5 million pounds and also to having committed lese majesté by drawing moustaches on postage stamps. Lord Nuffield, after a 7-hour interrogation, confesses that ever since 1920 he has been fomenting strikes in his own factories. And meanwhile the Churchillites never cease from proclaiming that it is they who are the real defenders of Capitalism...

"Anyone who has followed the Russian trials," Orwell comments, "knows that this is scarcely a parody. From our point of view the whole thing is not merely incredible as a genuine conspiracy; it is next door to incredible as a frame-up. It is simply a dark mystery, of which the only sizable fact – sinister enough in its way – is that communists over here regard it as a good advertisement for Communism."

Now, think about this, and think about Chávez' Venezuela in terms of this.

When we hear MVR congressman Raul Esté telling us that on November 4th the gunshots at a chavista march were fired by undercover Chacao policemen who had infiltrated the chavista protest but forgotten to change their boots, when we're told on State TV (channel 8) that the Plaza Altamira protest is a satanist/neonazi plot spearheaded by right-wing opposition activist Alejandro Peña Esclusa, when we're told that the Metropolitan Police routinely drops tear gas canisters on perfectly peaceful chavista demonstrators for no good reason, when MVR deputy Pedro Carreño tells us that Carabobo governor Henrique Salas Feo's *Operación Alegría* street-sweepers are a highly trained corps of provocateurs who sneak into chavista marches, when Chávez tells us that an offhand comment by a CNN correspondent proves that the opposition planned and organized the April 11th massacre...

when we hear things like that, isn't there a more than evident streak of totalitarian truth-twisting to the rhetoric?

Isn't there an obvious and alarming parallelism between the ways these statements mangle the truth beyond all recognition for partisan gain? Aren't these items "next door to incredible as frame-ups"?

Yet, the differences are just as telling. What made Stalin *Stalin* is that state-lies held a monopoly of the information available to common people in Russia. His aggressive convolution of reality was paired with a willingness to use as much violence as it took to crush anyone who questioned the state line. Stalinism wasn't just about routinely making up impossibly far-fetched lies; it was about making it compulsory to believe them. It was about routinely using impossible lies as the justification for putting bullets in people's heads, or sending them for long sojourns in Siberia.

Chávez won't go all the way, which explains why the Chávez era has been one-part-tragedy, two-parts-farce.

Without total control over people's access to information, twisted state lies are laid bare before the end of the day, becoming a farcical joke rather than a source of deep terror. Not only is it not compulsory to believe the crap the government peddles, but making fun of various chavista lies has become a kind of pass-time for the middle classes.

To make a proper totalitarian leader, you have to balance off your willingness to mangle the truth with an equal dose of cruelty and violence – Chávez just can't strike that balance, because he's just not comfortable enough using violence to achieve political ends.

Thank God. People are realizing that Chávez isn't really willing to use massive, indiscriminate violence to stay in power. Think about it: this is a country where military intelligence raids are foiled by pissed-off, pot-banging housewives who block the access roads with their cars and laugh at the heavily-armed, ski-masked intelligence officers when they demand to be let through.

Think that's a problem that Stalin had?

Fear and loathing in La Campiña
Posted on November 10, 2006 by Quico

Four years ago, I was working for VenEconomy out of their Sabana Grande offices. Lucky me, I was living in La Campiña, so I had the rare privilege of being able to walk to work every day. Granted, I did get mugged three times in a year and a half, but at least I didn't have to deal with the traffic.

My "commute" took me right by PDVSA headquarters on *Avenida Libertador* twice a day. This was late 2002 – and, as you'll remember, during the oil strike a group of chavistas decided to camp out more or less permanently in front of PDVSA – a sort of *"rojo, rojito"* counterpoint to the generals of Plaza Altamira. So twice a day, every day of the week, I had to walk straight through this little throng of militant chavistas just so I could get to the office where I'd spend the rest of my day criticizing them.

Looking very much like the anti-chavista sifrino I am, this experience was more than a little disconcerting. Pretty soon, I realized I would need some camouflage. Rummaging through the wares the street-vendors at the camp were peddling, I found a bandanna that read *"Chávez los tiene locos-* "Chávez makes them crazy."

Looking at it sideways, I realized I kind of liked it.

It dawned on me that this was the only chavista slogan I actually agree with. After all, by December, 2002 – with Globovisión playing *"Y deciiiiiimos siiiiiii a la esperanzaaaaaa!"* on a continuous loop all day long – I was sure the opposition had gone off the deep end. This was a chavista slogan I could make my own!

So for months on end I wore this silly thing on my head on my way to work. There was something appealingly ironic about having to wear it for my own protection. I felt like I was playing a secret joke on the government, like their attempt to impose a new identity on me was as crazy as the ribbon claimed Chávez was making me. I could laugh about it because I was certain that, though they might be able to dictate what I put over my head, they will never control what's in it.

"Chávez makes them crazy." When you think about it, it's a really odd slogan. Where else do you find a leader who boasts about undermining the mental health of his opponents? Why is this something to brag about? What does it say about Chavista values that managing to get under our skin is actually a cherished revolutionary achievement? And what is it about Chávez, in the final analysis, that's driving us crazy?

I think Juan came close to answering this the other day when he noted that:

"Chávez knows we fear him. That's why his speech is so hateful, so full of incitement. He works to ignite our fear and makes us appear... well, fearful, or to use another word, squalid. It's a show put on for the benefit of poor voters who get a kick out of watching us tremble. It's like their own little French Revolution is playing inside their head; Chávez's tongue playing the part of guillotine."

Part of what's driving us crazy is the realization that Chávez actually gains politically when he baits us – that the more he puts us down, the more his supporters get off on it. Strident divisiveness is not part of Chávez's political strategy – it is his strategy.

There's an element of symbolic warfare at play here. Driving us crazy is important for chavismo because it's part of a strategy to "re-signify" the country.

This is a word I'm borrowing from pollster Oscar Schemel, who said:

The current political struggle is chiefly over interpretations and meanings. While the elites and the middle class fight to impose their own notions about democracy and citizenship, the poor majority, chavista and non-chavista, is refuting and re-signifying those same ideas. A new culture is emerging, and it's re-signifying and deactivating our received ideas about politics, amidst a social and symbolic struggle to redefine democracy, development and social relations.

Regardless of what we may or may not think will happen in December, beyond the polls and predictions and allegations, there are two things I have learned this week. The first is something we can all agree on, that Rosales still has a shot, because the only poll that counts is the one in December 3rd. The second is more controversial, and it's that most of us would find it incredibly difficult to deal with the possibility that there may be more of "them" than there are of "us."

The reasons for this go back to Chávez himself. Because Chávez's attempt at re-signification is, in the end, an attempt to redefine our identity, to change who we are.

The attempt isn't subtle. From changing the national coat of arms to adding extra stars to the flag to splashing a partisan tag across our damn passports and *cédulas*, the revolution has not been bashful in its attempt is to enshrine its ideology, its phraseology and its iconography permanently into the symbolic fabric of our national identity. The goal is to establish chavismo as the ideology of the State and not merely of the government – partly, of course, by erasing the distinction between the two.

Chavismo's symbolic agenda is fundamentally exclusionary – it is about excluding us, subduing us, about banishing our values, our thoughts and our understanding of what democracy is and how it should work. Its goal is to impose a new symbolic order where the way we think is "un-Venezuelan." What's serious, what drives us crazy, is that Chavismo has launched a bold and ruthless drive to redefine "our" national identity in terms that expressly exclude "us" from it.

Is it any wonder the guy is driving us crazy? Is it any mystery why his supporters are proud of that?

My fellow bloggers and I have been getting some very strong, deeply emotional reactions in the last few weeks from committed readers, people we respect and value and spend lots of our time writing for. What is curious is that what sparked this controversy is something that wouldn't be that controversial in a working democracy: our honest opinion, based on research that may or may not be right, that more people may be planning to vote for one candidate than for another.

What's clear is that, for many in the opposition, the proposition that we might be in the minority is impossible to fathom; a banned thought, something unsayable, unthinkable – certainly unbloggable.

Why are we so touchy about this? I think Juan's right: deep down, we are dead scared of losing the battle over the meaning of Venezuelan-ness.

Our understanding of democracy, which we had always taken as the unchanging center of our national identity may be about to die...and we've convinced ourselves that it will die, if it turns out that we are in the minority at the end.

Suddenly under siege, feeling itself dependent on majority support for its viability, our identity has turned defensive. Paraphrasing, J.M. Briceño Guerrero, our certainty of being a majority has turned oddly defensive...

it's as though we were speaking rather in the imperative: "be the majority" – layered over an unspoken "it would be unbearable not to be so", all of which rides on the strongly repressed sense that "horror, we aren't!", which only bolsters the imperative: "become the majority right now!" which again turns into the indicative, now superstitious and magical: "we are the majority."

We have fallen into a trap, believing that if there are more of them than there are of us, Chávez's attempt to re-signify Venezuelan-ness has succeeded. It's as though contemplating the possibility that more people want to vote for Chávez than for Rosales is contemplating, symbolically speaking, our own ethnic cleansing – the annihilation of our identity.

But we're wrong about this. Who we are, what we are, our right to be dissenters and fully Venezuelan at the same time can be sustained even if we are in the minority. A new, exclusionary definition of Venezuelan-ness cannot be sustained over the active resistance of just under half the country; it's just that we act as if it could. Only the belief that this election is a matter of survival leads us to say things like "everything is in play this December."

Well, everything is not in play. Don't get me wrong, this is an important election, one that we really, really need to win. But if we don't, we will continue our struggle. Unless, that is, we lose the battle inside ourselves; we start wearing our bandannas on the insides of our heads.

In the end, I got so attached to this little trinket, to this souvenir of my struggle to survive amid the symbolic onslaught, that I brought it with me when I came to Europe. I like to glance at it when JVR starts baiting us for the cameras, when Chávez starts to rant. It reminds me that the more we lose our cool, the more we advance their agenda.

Because when the other side's goal is to make you crazy, the only way to fight back is to stay sane.

The revolution's endlessly malleable bogeymen
Posted on February 4, 2006 by Quico

This line, from Hutton's take on last year's Youth Festival, got me thinking:

"When I was here in 2000-2002 I don't remember anyone using the word imperialism. The subject just didn't come up."

It's interesting to consider the way Chávez's rhetorical bogeymen have transmogrified over the years. If I remember correctly, it went something like this:

1994-1998: Corruption

1999-2000: Puntofijismo

2001-2002: The Oligarchy

2002-2004: Coup-mongering

2005- : American Imperialism

Am I missing a bogeyman here? Do the dates look about right? It would take some fairly stomach-turning research in the Aló, Presidente archives to confirm - I'm just not up to it.

What's weird is the way the switchover is never explicitly justified or even acknowledged and yet, once it happens, it's absolute, Orwellian. This revolution has always been about opposing imperialism, we have never been at war with Eurasia.

A fundamental unseriousness
Posted on March 20, 2011 by Quico

If it had the slightest interest in such things, chavismo could build an honest, cogent, powerful case against international intervention in Libya.

It could point out the thicket of contradictions that has led the United States to, at once, attack one Arab government (Libya) that is murdering its pro-democracy demonstrators while continuing to send weapons and "development aid" to another Arab government (Yemen) that is murdering its pro-democracy demonstrators.

It could note that Europe is now fighting an army equipped with European weapons bought with the proceeds of oil sales to Europe – a creature very much of its own making.

It could skewer the myth of "Arab support" for the intervention, pointing out the way governments busy violently squashing their own pro-democracy movements – Syria, Algeria, Saudi Arabia, Bahrain – had the tremendous balls to vote to request a no-fly zone over a country doing the same thing – though, admittedly on a much bigger scale.

It could ask whether those governments aren't simply working to deflect attention from their own authoritarian outrages by keeping Al Jazeera and the BBC focused squarely on Libya ... and out of their hair.

It could point to the extraordinary position of the Saudi theocracy, which is now supporting two interventionist adventures at once: one to quash the democratic aspirations of Bahrainis, the other to stop Gadhafi from quashing the democratic aspirations of Libyans.

It could note what a funny coincidence it is that the U.S. only seems to mount its enormously high horse to attack its enemies, but continues to support its allies as they do more or less the same thing.

Chavismo could, in other words, make a serious, honest, bracing critique of the U.N.-mandated intervention in Libya.

But it won't.

In order to make that critique, it would have to face facts it remains ideologically committed to ignoring. It won't because it lacks the intellectual integrity to squarely acknowledge Gadhafi's indiscriminate use of military weapons against civilians.

It won't because it has chosen to portray a sophomoric, deeply ahistorical narrative of the conflict where the allies are only out to get Libya's oil ... as though Repsol, Wintershall, Total, Eni, OMV, Shell, the Oasis Group, Chevron, Marathon, ExxonMobil, and BP hadn't been getting Libya's oil just fine for the last eight years, thank you very much.

It won't because Chávez remains determined to question the one aspect of the attack that's actually beyond doubt: its international legality.

It won't because it lacks even the modicum of seriousness it takes to act minimally responsibly on the international stage.

It won't because it insists on treating the truth as a kind of play-doh to be molded around its ideological pre-commitments.

It won't, in the end, because Hugo Chávez's principled refusal to let reality dictate terms to him is different from Muammar Gadhafi's only in degree, not in kind.

Big oil has landed: Hugo Chávez in Copenhagen
Posted on December 16, 2009 by Quico and Juan Cristobal

What do you think would happen if the head of one of the world's five largest oil companies started lecturing the UN Climate Change Conference in Copenhagen about the evils of global warming?

How do you think the most esteemed delegates to the world's premier forum on the pressing issue of our time would react if a man who's leveraged his control over hundreds of billions of dollars' worth of oil rents into a spot in Forbes' list of the world's 100 most powerful people ... started to tell them what they need to do to save the planet?

Why, they'd fall all over themselves cheering him, obviously.

Hugo Chávez's Copenhagen speech today was such an event, though on its face, the speech itself was boilerplate. The Venezuelan strongman delivered his usual twenty-minute anti-capitalist tirade, full of quasi-religious rhetoric about saving the world and such. Developing world delegates ate it up with mustard, spiraling into rapturous applause each time he blamed the rich countries for "destroying the planet."

It's insane. Cheering Chávez as he lectures you on climate change is like cheering Joseph Fritzl as he lectures you on fatherhood.

As far as Chávez can tell, it's not CO_2 that's changing the climate, it's "capitalism." The specific mechanism through which this happens, the whole pesky issue of the actual fuel that generates all that carbon, the bucketful of petrodollars he makes out of the whole dirty business...the less talked about such things, the better.

Chávez's green-standing, echoed by his hapless delegation and the minions in his vast media empire, stands in sharp contrast with the actual policies Venezuela has put in place.

Instead of taxing oil consumption, Chávez has spent a decade subsidizing it, making Venezuelan gasoline the cheapest in the planet. In fact, in real terms, gasoline is 85% cheaper in Venezuela today than it was when Chávez came to power ten years ago. The price of a liter of gas has not moved in ten years, while accumulated inflation is 655%.

This is a leader who subsidizes not just gas but car sales, a man whose idea of foreign aid is giving cut-price fuel oil to people … in Boston. A gallon of fuel in Caracas costs less than a lollypop, a policy Chávez has no intention of relenting on. The man responsible for feeding oil junkies the world over - that's the guy who brought down the house in Copenhagen?

Talk about a real climate scandal.

In the days leading to the Summit, some in Venezuela wondered what the country's position would be. Chávez has rarely discussed the complexities of how climate change and the policies to stop it can affect Venezuela. You wouldn't expect him to: any decision that seriously cuts demand for oil at Copenhagen would directly undermine the whole material basis of his power.

Although Chávez has famously adopted every third-world, anti-imperialist, "us vs. them" pose in the book, it's not like the developing world was coming to Copenhagen with a unified voice. The Chinese and Indians do not want to sacrifice their development, the Africans are desperate for action sprinkled with a little bit of cash, and the Saudis would prefer the status quo. Countries like Bolivia have a real interest in curbing greenhouse emissions, which is causing melting glaciers. Bolivia's vast reserves of lithium, which can be used to power the batteries in hybrid vehicles, mean it is poised to reap the benefits of a green economy.

Yet, Venezuela's position was a big question mark.

Chávez's speech cleared up it up. He embraced the environmental movement and gleefully served as a spokesman for countries such as Cuba and Bolivia, highly vulnerable to changing weather patterns.

But the world would be foolish to confuse rhetoric with values.

Chávez knows the end of the oil era would kill the goose that lays the golden eggs. He will peddle his oil while denouncing everyone else for burning it. He will demand a binding agreement but will not tolerate any imposition on his insane environmental policies.

This gasp-inducing pileup of ironies and contradictions can only be interpreted as a joke. Hugo Chávez came into the global warming summit and made a big hot mess of it. Thankfully, at least some of the world's newspapers took note and shunned him.

The rest of the delegates - at least the ones looking for progress on this issue - should do the same.

The Eudomarian Republic of Venezuela
Posted on March 5, 2008 by Juan Cristobal

"Como vaya viniendo, vamos viendo..."[47] Eudomar Santos, character in the legendary 1990s soap opera Por Estas Calles.

Venezuelan President Chávez recently announced that he was deploying thousands of soldiers to the border after Colombia bombed a FARC base in Ecuadorian territory. His government also announced the land border would be closed to all traffic, and expelled all Colombian Embassy officials while it announced it was bringing home all personnel from the Venezuelan Embassy in Colombia.

It remains to be seen whether all these announcements are part of an actual policy and consistent with some established goal. It's not clear what objectives Venezuela is pursuing with this unilateral action, or how long all this is going to last. The reason given so far, "to ward off a possible Colombian attack," has little to do with what has actually transpired, which differs from what has been announced.

---

[47] The phrase roughly translates into "We'll play it by ear..." or "we'll make something up as w ego along." It refers to Venezuelans' seeming inability to plan ahead.

Take the military mobilizations. Reports abound in Caracas that this is all a bluff. General Raúl Baduel said yesterday that it was all part of a "reality show" and a "media event."[48] Stories from Caracas and the Pentagon hint that troop movement has been minimal, and that the little there has been was put on just for show since the Venezuelan army does not have the plan, the logistics, or the operational capacity to mobilize thousands of soldiers to its border in three days.

In the meantime, Interior Minister Rodríguez Chacín blasted local media for reporting the troop movements, threatening to charge them with treason. Apparently the Minister thinks that the media should shut up about the movement of tanks in heavily populated areas during broad daylight.

Perhaps the Minister should ask himself why Chávez announced the troop mobilizations on national TV if they were, in fact, supposed to be secret. Perhaps they should have declared some sort of media blackout to prevent this sort of thing from getting out. Perhaps they should ask themselves if it's reasonable to allege the Colombian army, an institution with the technology to identify guerrilla camps inside Ecuador and pinpoint an attack, an institution aided by the technology of the US government, is relying on Globovisión to know where Venezuelan troops are headed.

But it's all just a show.

There is an undeniable whiff of improvisation in everything the government is doing. The Foreign Ministry, for example, is acting like a teenage child, making up responses on the hoof to the Colombian government's serious allegations like, well, like a country that doesn't need diplomacy and brains because it has oil.

One of Foreign Minister Nicolás Maduro's most embarrassing responses was his claim that $300 million was simply too much money, suggesting it would take four rooms the size of the National Assembly to store that amount of cash. Maduro thinks this shows that the Colombian allegation of Chávez's financing of the FARC

---

[48] By this point, Baduel had split with Chávez and was now giving opinions contrary to the government. He is currently a political prisoner.

was a lie. Apparently the Minister thinks the whole world operates in cash.

Sounds like the kind of reasoning you overhear on a bus. "En la parada por favor!"

The Agriculture Minister announces the borders have shut down, which is akin to the Environment Minister announcing troop deployments (come to think of it, we may live to see the day). Meanwhile, people in the border say that, while traffic has slowed, it has not closed completely. Today, Chávez's burly Defense Minister said that he has received no orders to close the border.

No policy details are offered, no clear goals are set out, no end date is provided, no two spokespeople can agree. It's all dependent on Chávez's next whim. It's all improvised, it's all a show, unless... well, unless things change.

Como vaya viniendo, vamos viendo.

Venezuela's Narcissist-in-Chief
Posted on January 28, 2003 by Quico

[The OpEd I would have liked to write for the Wall Street Journal – and would've written, if I'd had a more pliable editor and 1800 words to play with.]

If you're looking for insight into Venezuela's political crisis, section 301.81 of the American Psychiatric Association's Diagnostic and Statistical Manual is an excellent place to start.

The entry reads eerily like a brief character sketch of Venezuela's embattled president, Hugo Chávez: "Has a grandiose sense of self-importance; is preoccupied with fantasies of unlimited success, power, brilliance; requires excessive admiration; has unreasonable expectations of automatic compliance with his expectations; shows arrogant behaviors or attitudes, etc." Actually, it's the DSM-IV's diagnostic criteria for Narcissistic Personality Disorder (NPD.)

Venezuelan psychiatrists long ago pegged Chávez as a textbook example of NPD. According to the DSM-IV, a patient has NPD if he meets five of the nine diagnostic criteria. But Dr. Álvaro Requena, a respected Venezuelan psychiatrist, says Chávez "meets all nine of the diagnostic criteria." Dr. Arturo Rodríguez Milliet, a colleague, finds "a striking consensus on that diagnosis" among Caracas psychiatrists. Not that it really takes an expert: you only need to watch Chávez's weekly five-hour talk-show on state television once to understand the extent of his narcissism.

Of course, lots of politicians have some narcissistic traits – Washington, D.C. is notorious for the size of its egos. NPD, however, is what happens when those traits run amok. People with NPD are so intimately convinced of the crushing weight of their historical significance that they lose the ability to interact with the world in anything like a reasonable way.

Narcissism and political power make an explosive combination. As Dr. Sam Vaknin, author of Malignant Self Love: Narcissism Revisited, puts it, "the narcissist's grandiose self-delusions and fantasies of omnipotence and omniscience are exacerbated by real life authority." And President Chávez has amassed more real life authority than anyone in Venezuela's contemporary history.

But those grandiose self-delusions co-exist with a fragile sense of self-worth, often masking deep insecurities. As Dr. Vaknin writes, "the narcissist's personality is so precariously balanced that he cannot tolerate even a hint of criticism and disagreement."

In Venezuela, over the last four years, this has led to a systematic winnowing of the president's pool of confidants, as people with views that differ even slightly from the Comandante's have fallen out of favor. Only sycophants and yes-men survive in Chávez's inner circle. What's perverse about that mechanism is that some people close to him have clearly learned to manipulate his narcissism for their personal purposes. Once you've caught on that feeding the president's narcissism is the way to get ahead in palace politics, what's the reasonable response? Feeding the president's narcissism, of course.

Over time, this has left Chávez worryingly isolated. It's probably been months since the president has been brought face to face with ideas different than his own, with versions of reality that don't conform to his own sense of grandeur. Under those circumstances, anyone's sense of reality would suffer. But if you've started out with narcissistic tendencies, that level of isolation is liable to push you over the edge altogether. With no critical thinkers around anymore, no one willing to sit him down and tell him the awful truth, there are no checks left on his pathological relationship with reality.

It's important to bear this in mind as you read the news coming out of Venezuela these days. Last week, for instance, the president repeated again and again that there is no strike in Venezuela's key oil industry, just a conspiracy by a few privileged executives who have sabotaged its installations. Exuding confidence, he assured Venezuelans that production had risen to about 1.5 million barrels per day and said the industry would return to normal soon. The remarks were picked up by the world's journalists more or less at face value. An unsuspecting reader would probably have believed him.

Meanwhile, back in reality, Venezuelans faced lines over 24 hours long to pump gas, and more and more households reverted to cooking with firewood for absence of kitchen butane. Independent experts estimated production at 450,000 b/d at best, and the nation was refining 90% less oil than usual. Nine out of every ten oil workers were off the job, and the nation faced its gravest fiscal crisis in a century.

To a narcissist, though, none of that matters. As Dr. Milliet points out, "his discourse might be dissonant with reality, but it's internally coherent." Chávez's only concern is to preserve his romantic vision of himself as a fearless leader of the downtrodden in their fight against an evil oligarchy. If the facts don't happen to fit that narrative structure, then that's too bad for the facts. So it's not that Chávez lies, per se, it's that he's locked up within a small, tight circle of confidants that feed an aberrant relationship with reality. To lie is to knowingly deceive. Chávez doesn't lie. He just makes up the truth.

Obviously, there are more than a few inconveniences to having a pathological narcissist as president. For instance, it's almost impossible for narcissists to admit to past mistakes and make amends. The narcissist's chief, overriding psychological goal is to preserve his grandiose self-image, his sense of being a larger-than-life world historical force for good and justice. Honestly admitting any mistake, no matter how banal, requires a level of self-awareness and a sense for one's own limitations that runs directly counter to the forces that drive a narcissist's personality. So for all the crocodile tears on April 14th, Chávez cannot, never has, and never will sincerely make amends. It's just beyond him.

Once you have a basic understanding of how their pathological personality structures drive the behavior of people with NPD, Hugo Chávez is an open book. Lots of little puzzles about the way the President behaves are suddenly cleared up. For instance, you start to understand why Chávez sees no adversaries around him, only enemies. It makes sense: the more he becomes convinced of his "fantasies of unlimited success, power and brilliance" the harder it is for him to accept that anyone might have an honest disagreement with him.

Chávez is a man in rebellion against his own fallibility. "As far as he can see," explains Dr. Requena, "if anyone disagrees with him, that can only be because they are wrong, and maliciously wrong."

People with NPD are strongly sensitive to what psychiatrists call "narcissist injury" – the psychic discombobulation that comes from any input that undermines or negates the fantasies that dominate their mindscape. Chávez clearly experiences disagreement and dissent as narcissist injury and as any psychiatrist can tell you, an injured narcissist is liable to lash out with virulent rage. Often, his slurs are almost comically overstated. He insists on describing Venezuela's huge, diverse, and mostly democratic opposition movement as a "conspiracy" led by a tiny cabal of "coup-plotters, saboteurs and terrorists." These attacks not only demonstrate the tragic extent of his disconnect with reality, they have also thoroughly poisoned the political atmosphere in Caracas, creating what's been described as a "cold civil war."

But it's not just a matter of some overly sensitive folk taking offense at some rude remarks. Chávez's brand of intolerance has turned the Venezuelan state into the most autocratic in the Americas short of the one led by his hero, Fidel Castro. It's no coincidence. In Dr. Milliet's view, "narcissism leads directly to an autocratic approach to power."

President Chávez has systematically placed diehard loyalists in key posts throughout the state apparatus. When you come to understand his behavior in terms of NPD, that's not at all surprising: someone who understands the world as a struggle between people who agree with everything he says and does vs. evil will obviously do everything in his power to place unconditional allies in every position of power. And indeed, today, every nominally independent watchdog institution in Venezuela, from the Supreme Court to the Auditor General's office, is run by a presidential crony. With the National Assembly operating like a branch office of the presidential palace, the formal checks-and-balances written into the constitution have become a farce.

The case of the Attorney General is especially worrying. With nothing like a special counsel statute and no state criminal jurisdiction, the A.G. must approve every single criminal investigation and prosecution in Venezuela. Control this post, and you have total veto power over the entire penal system. For this reason, the A.G. is not a cabinet position in Venezuela like it is in the US. Because of its key role in fighting corruption and keeping watch over the legality of the government's actions, the A.G. is set up as a fully independent, apolitical office in the Venezuelan constitution. But that clearly wouldn't do for Chávez. For this most sensitive of offices, Chávez tapped perhaps his most unconditional ally, a doggedly loyal chavista fresh from a stint as Vice President.

Not surprisingly, not a single pro-Chávez official has been convicted of anything, ever, despite numerous and well-documented allegations of serious corruption, and a mountain of evidence to suggest the government has organized its civilian supporters into armed militias. Chávez loyalists realize they're beyond the reach of the law, and behave accordingly. A growing list of armed attacks on opposition attests to the fact that the president's shock troops act under a kind of tacit blanket amnesty: several times the attackers have been fully identified by amateur video footage, but the government has never made the slightest attempt to arrest any of them.

Once Chávez had every branch of government safely under his thumb, he set out to control society as a whole. On that score, he's been far less successful. An early attempt to grab the labor movement backfired disastrously when union members elected his most ardent critic to head the country's main labor federation. The independent news media has responded to four years of presidential threats, and insults by becoming strident, single-minded opponents of his government. Even the discredited old political parties that Chávez once thrived on vilifying have made something of a comeback.

In short, Venezuelans have wised up to the dangers of having a narcissist president, and they're now fully mobilized against him. Credible independent polls suggest some 60-65% of the voters want the president to resign. Most importantly, a remarkable proportion of those who oppose Chávez do so vehemently, actively, on the streets.

Venezuelans will not surrender their freedom to a narcissist-autocrat. The massive opposition movement has made the country impossible to govern, leaving only two options: a presidential transition or ongoing chaos. Many here worry that as his hold on power slips, Chávez could lash out, deploying the kind of widespread, indiscriminate violence he has so far shunned. The United States must make it clear that it will not tolerate such actions – not to the narcissist-in-chief, who is beyond reasoning with, but to his associates.

Only the CNE retains a measure of independent credibility from both sides. Nothing will be possible unless both sides solemnly pledge to accept CNEs eventual decision. They should do this right now.

The reality is that CNE has become a beacon of hope in Venezuelan society. On the verge of the presidential recall, CNE stands as the sole exception, the sole entity of the state that Hugo Chávez cannot control at his pleasure, and my feeling is that, despite its 3-2 nominal chavista majority, a genuinely independent CNE is the biggest problem in Hugo Chávez's immediate future. All five members of CNE must be uniformly lauded for putting legality ahead of party loyalty so far - a precedent that could serve as the seed for a true democratic awakening in the post-Chávez period.

Some may say I'm a dreamer, but I'm not the only one

The goal of a new, more dynamic, more participative and much, much more inclusive Venezuela is now within striking distance. The country need not be dominated by a pathological narcissist much longer.

How the Soto twins learned to stop worrying and love the Opposition
Posted on February 8, 2012 by Quico

It was a Sunday evening back in 2007 when Adán Soto sat down at the Zulia Governor's mansion to eat some *arepas peladas* with his nemesis, Manuel Rosales.

It wasn't an easy meeting for either of them: for an ardent Chávez supporter and long-time co-op member like Soto, even being there felt like a betrayal. This being Maracaibo, though, there was precious little beating around the bush.

"I hope you don't get mad, but I'm going to tell you a *verga*," said the governor right off the bat, "I don't believe in co-operatives."

Adán Soto looked him up and down and replied, "well, I hope you don't get angry either, because I don't believe in you."

At the time, Adán Soto and his identical twin brother, Adaulfo, were hardcore chavistas, as were their whole families. When

Chávez got big into Co-ops back in 2002 they started one up, to make cement blocks. Later on, when Chávez started to promote Community Councils, the twins made sure to be front and center in their neighborhood council.

Fast forward to 2012, and the *morochos* are now among the most visible opposition activists in their community, building low-income housing for needy families in partnership with Zulia's opposition-run state government and supplying building materials to people throughout the state.

The story of the Soto Twins' transformation is a case study in careful retail politicking, the kind of minute, result-oriented work at the community level the opposition will need to get very good at quickly if it wins on October 7th. Here's how it happened.

For years, the Soto twins had been touchstones in their little corner of *Brisas del Lago*, a barrio within the sprawling slum municipality of San Francisco, just south of Maracaibo, in the shadow of the *Puente Sobre el Lago*. Just under a quarter of Maracuchos live in the area, making it something like Maracaibo's Petare.

San Francisco was the kind of place where joining every chavista organization around seemed like common sense to people like the *morochos*. They're the kind of family that neighbors instinctively turned to for help solving everyday concerns: de facto community leaders, *de toda la vida*.

At first, landing a string of government contracts was no trouble for the co-op, thanks to a contact at Corpozulia (the Zuliano version of CVG). Trouble started in 2007, when Adán decided to go to the government for a loan.

They asked for Bs.1,000 million, but after several trips to Caracas and all kinds of hurdles, the money never materialized.

In part, starting a co-op together with a close blood relative ran afoul of chavista rules on nepotism (cuz we know how Chávez loathes nepotism.) But there was no way Adán was going to cut off Adaulfo – the two have always worked as a team. "We were born together and I guess we'll die together, because we're together all the time," he says.

This ruled out a loan, which wreaked havoc with the co-op's finances. To add insult to injury, Corpozulia was chronically late with payments as well.

Into this breach stepped Angel Sánchez, at the time the UNT chairman of the Zulia State Legislative Assembly, representing Municipio San Francisco.

"The first time, when we went up to the community council the twins helped run, they wouldn't even let us in the door," Angel recalls. "They started to tell me about the 40 years of deceiving the people, and I tried to tell them we'd come to tell them about this social program, but they didn't even let me talk."

"Thankfully the people who were there stepped in saying, 'c'mon man, let him talk, ¿qué vaina es? Just as we listened to you we should listen to him,' and seeing people's reaction, they let me talk."

Sánchez jumped at the chance to tell them about the governor's plans to set up a soup kitchen in the community, and some sports projects, as well as his plan to set up a hair salon in the barrio. Faced with strong support at the meeting, the twins had to give way. A first, tentative approach had been made.

"We didn't trust him, of course," says Adán, "but, man, we needed a loan."

It was only after the first soup kitchen had been set up that Adán worked up the nerve to ask Angel about financing. Seeing an opening, Angel grabbed him and took him to the governor's mansion in Maracaibo to meet Rosales in person.

Angel smiles thinking back on that scene "He was telling me 'no man, the thing is I'm a chavista' and I had to keep going back and telling him 'brother, I don't give a shit if you're chavista or not chavista or red or yellow or from Mars, we're going over there!'"

He took him into Maracaibo where Rosales served him some *arepas* and within half an hour, the deal was done. Within a few weeks, a Bs.400 million line of credit was theirs.

The Governor's loan allowed the co-op to grow, buying new machinery and expanding their production capacity. But the Soto twins would pay a high price for the deal.

"The first thing they did is throw us out of the Communal Council", Adán says. "There are people in my family who haven't spoken to me since."

Over the next five years, the twins realized they'd been blacklisted. "The old payments never came through," Adán tells me, "but the new contracts dried up too...Corpozulia, PDVSA, the municipal government, Fundacomunal...we never got another contract out of them."

Oddly, though, they're still getting price-controlled Cement from the nationalized cement plant down the road. "I'm guessing not everyone in management there is really chavista," he says.

Cut off from Central Government financing altogether, the twins had no choice but to lean more and more heavily on the opposition-run State government. The State government pays on time and business is good, but they still run into trouble with the chavista municipal government on an almost daily basis. "If it's not a cop hassling me, it's somebody hitting me up for cash," Adán says.

As if on cue, while I'm there, a guy shows up in a massive Alcaldía de San Francisco SUV and tells him he represents a Communal Radio Station down the street. He wants Bs.150 a month worth of advertising from the Co-op.

It's phrased as a request, but it feels like a shake-down. At any rate, it's a small enough sum that Adán agrees to pay. The radio station only broadcasts to a 15-block radius and the co-op doesn't really need advertising. But the twins are in no position to chase yet another fight with the chavista mayor.

"We've struck a pretty good working relationship with the new governor, Pablo Pérez," he says, describing how Pérez pushed them to move from mere block makers into actual home builders. "He gave us a contract to build 20 houses here in *Brisas del Lago* and told us if that went well he'd approve another 20. Well, we made the first 20 in just five weeks, so the second contract he gave us was for 44 houses."

The twins are building those now, and hope another deal for 44 more houses comes through in their Barrio. Adán tells me they've identified around 1,000 shanties around in need of "rancho-replacement" – basically tearing down a sub-standard shanty to build a proper house on the same land for the same family.

The co-op has plenty of room to grow.

When I ask Adán about the future, he's wary. Constant harassment from the municipal government makes him fearful about what might happen if they lose the state government as well. Miraflores is way out of his radar screen.

"If we managed to get rid of this crooked mayor here and kept the State government too, I really think our co-op has a big future," Adán says.

More future than past, I'm tempted to add.

Would you like to get Haier than you've ever been in your life?
Posted on January 30, 2012 by Quico

Amazingly, some bits of Bolivarian bureaucracy actually do work properly. Among them is the system for giving out passports, which has morphed from insane, Kafkaesque ordeal to freakishly quick and stress-free *trámite* in the last few years: a 10 minute web form, some copies, a bank deposit, and then you wait a few days for an email giving you an automatically-generated appointment at a Saime office. Easy pleasy.

Alas, my appointment turned out to be in Ocumare del Tuy, about an hour and a half southwest of Caracas. No problem, I trekked on out there, parked, and set out across the Plaza Bolívar to the Saime office.

Except something seemed to be going on in the Plaza.

A bunch of olive-green tents were set up, with people queuing to get to rows of lap-top enabled *operativo* workers. Soldiers with AKs guarded the whole thing. From the center of the square, we were soon treated to a rousing recording of Chávez – yes, Chávez – singing the National Anthem, followed by a recording of the PSUV party anthem at full blast.

Some kind of incestuous PSUV-Army-Pueblo clusterfuck, no doubt – but I had no time for it, I needed my passport.

At the Saime office I really had to pinch myself to believe I wasn't dreaming it all or back in Quebec somehow – official paperwork was never meant to be this straightforward and hassle-free. It's un-Venezuelan, if you ask me.

Ten minutes later, *trámite* done, I'm walking back across Ocumare's Plaza Bolívar and notice the preliminaries are over. An MC has taken up the mike and is in the middle of the square. With his best fake VTV Telonero voice, he starts announcing, "and now, we proceed to assign this brand new washing machine to Mrs. Fulanita De Tal". Only then do I notice the big lines of huge Haier cardboard boxes in the middle of the square.

"Ah claro," I think to myself, "they're giving out appliances!"

Welcome to Misión Mi Casa Bien Equipada: the government's Chinese appliance clientelist spree. Chávez claims some 3 million appliances, TVs and AC units will be distributed at knock-down prices through the misión before the year is out. (Consider: there are 6 million households in Venezuela.)

Everything on offer is Haier branded and, I suspect, the operational face of the infamous, hyper-opaque $30+ billion Export-Loans-for-Future-Oil deal with the Chinese, where Chávez gets paid for tomorrow's oil barrels with today's clientelist goodies.

At first I thought the Misión was a straight-out giveaway, but poking around online I see it's more like a subsidy within a subsidy. You do have to pay for your Haier products, but the government sells you the stuff at deeply discounted prices, then lets you pay back at very low interest rate loans from state-owned banks, but only if you're in the "qualified" category.

As you can already intuit from that, there's a nightmarish amount of bureaucracy involved in getting the appliances, complete with the inevitable baffling bureaucratic holdups and corrupt scams that can't fail to spring up when you start selling 10 bolivar bills for Bs.6.

After all, if the government is going to sell you a 42" flat screen TV for Bs.3,327 and that same TV goes for Bs.6,500-10,000 down the street, why wouldn't you just turn around and re-sell it? And if you were a Misión worker living on a Bs.2,500 monthly wage and your job consisted entirely in handling out those TVs, wouldn't you be tempted to cut out the middleman and cash in on the deal yourself?

In fact, it's when you start getting into the numbers that you realize just how insane the Misión really is – because those same 42" Haier flat screens that the government sells for a low, low Bs.3,327 retail for $450 on Amazon.com.

But wait, at the official exchange rate, $450 is less than Bs.2,000!

There's more. A 12 cu.ft. Haier fridge sells for Bs.2,628 at the Misión. At the official rate, that's $611. But go to the States and you can get that same fridge for $499.

In other words, the Misión's products aren't actually cheap at all. They seem cheap, though, but only because the rest of Venezuela's economy is so pathologically distorted.

Those $499 gringos have to pay Amazon.com for that fridge buy close to Bs.4,150 on the parallel market, which is what the same fridge ends up costing in private shops here. The misión price is only cheap compared to the insanely inflated cost you face if you're shut out of access to price-controlled dollars.

Really, that's all a convoluted way of saying that the government isn't really subsidizing the appliances, or even the credit for the appliances: what they're subsidizing is the dollars that buy the appliances.

(Or, rather, they're subsidizing the government's access to the dollars that buy the yuan that denominate the swap for future oil shipments that buy the appliances – nothing is simple with these people!)

The galloping opacity of the set-up is both the point, and totally beside the point.

From the beneficiaries' point of view, all that's visible is that the *turco coño'e'madre especulador* in the shop down the street wanted to charge me Bs.4,150 for a fridge whose "fair cost" is just Bs.2,628, and the one reason I can take it home is that Chávez really cares about me.

The politics of manipulated resentment and manufactured loyalty are that straightforward.

How the opposition begins to disarm the heady-cocktail of petro-largess and emotional attachment chavismo has built through misiones like this one isn't at all clear. The one thing I note is that from the beneficiaries' point of view, the key shortcoming to the system is obvious: to hop onto the Misión bandwagon, you first have to jump through a never ending set of administrative hoops, hoops that make no sense to people and shut out many who feel legitimately entitled to the stuff on offer.

Promise to make access to *Misión Mi Casa Bien Equipada* as straightforward and hassle-free as getting a passport, and you might just get somewhere with them.

Cubazuela chronicles
Posted on July 14, 2011B by Juan Cristobal

"This is where I bring the Cubans," he says.

I'm with my buddy Joaquín. We're in one of those upscale Caracas cafés that makes you wonder what people in Venezuela complain about.

The place would not look out of place in a Scandinavian architecture magazine. We are surrounded by sumptuous food from all over the world, and by what has to be Caracas' most beautiful people, the crème of Chacao fauna. A couple of ladies-who-lunch sit next to me, busily chatting about makeup. Three intellectual wannabes sit across the hall discussing Chávez's yet-to-be-disclosed illness. The post-modern *criollo* sound of Huáscar Barradas, at just the right volume, fills the air. In short, it's one of the few remaining post-modern Venezuelan oases.

"Wow," I respond. "You must really like them. This place is pretty nice."

"No, no, no. I bring them so they can feel sorry about their miserable little lives. I hate those *coñuemadres*."

Joaquín has been a friend since college. He had always been interested in government work, but after graduating, he couldn't get hired by the Caldera administration, so he went into private business instead. Resentful about the IVth Republic's antics, he voted for Chávez, but quickly realized his government was going nowhere.

After a brief stint abroad, *saudade* for his country was strong, so he decided to head back. This was 2003, right when things were in upheaval and the entire government was being renovated.

Thanks to lifelong leftie connections and a brief dabbling with subversion, Joaquín was deemed a perfect fit for the growing chavista bureaucracy. He is now a middle manager at a government office, making BsF 4.500 a month, in charge of, among other things, international relations.

In other words, he is in charge of dealing with the Cubans.

"It always has to be the Cubans," he says. "You can't really bring experts from other parts of the world. The Cubans take precedence."

I ask him why the bad attitude toward the Cubans. After all, it's not their fault.

"It's the way they behave when they come," he says, "their sense of entitlement. I don't care how good their education is, they think that just because Chávez has a man-crush, they can come here and treat us like savages, like they're coming to do our job for us. And you cannot believe how uneducated they really are – they're twenty years behind on everything. Even when they write, their grammar is bad."

He tells me how it usually goes. The Cubans send them a list of the people that will be coming, typically for a one-month stay. The Venezuelan entity in charge of their trip has to pay for their airfare.

"And then, usually a day before their trip, they call you up to tell you they can't come because their passport is expired."

According to Joaquín, the passports of all the Cuban bureaucrats are held in some vault in Havana. Their handlers only check the passports a few days before they have to travel, and it's frequently the case that the passports are expired. This means their plane tickets have to be changed at the last minute.

And who picks up the tab for the enormous fees the airlines charge? *Doña Petra de la esquina*, that's who.

Negotiations with the Cubans begin and end with discussions of their daily stipends. They don't really care what they are coming for. According to Joaquín, all they care about is how much money they are going to receive. Inevitably, tensions arise with the local underpaid bureaucracy.

"After a few of these trips, I began to realize how connected they really are. One time they asked for a daily stipend that I thought was excessive, so I told them that we were considering whether they would get any stipend at all. A half hour later, the Minister calls me up. He tells me that the Cubans have informed him that we are not open to giving them what they need, and that if I'm not going to help them, I have to resign."

"The Cuban minister called you?!" I ask, slightly confused.

"No, no. The Venezuelan minister, my boss's boss's boss. The Cubans have a direct line to those guys."

He tells me of the Cubans' resentment at Venezuelans' way of life. The Cuban he brought to the café was a particularly annoying one, who got angry because Joaquín was sending him emails via his Blackberry.

"Oh right," he apparently wrote, "you send me messages from your little thingy. Lucky you."

"The worst part," he says, "is having to take them shopping."

It turns out the Cubans are terrified of walking the streets in Caracas. Aside from the crime problem, which is much worse than in their country, they have felt intimidated by Venezuelan shopkeepers. More than once, they have been kicked out of trendy stores because of their accents.

And stores are what they want to see, everything from TVs to underwear, from jeans to medicine. El Palacio del Blumer is a particular favorite. The Venezuelans who accompany them help carry their bags, pay for their bills, ask questions, and arrange the shipping.

"We even have to pay the excess luggage fees," he says. "Boxes of flat-screen TVs, suitcases, you name it. We max out the allowed limit on each trip."

You can imagine the resentment this breeds on the local bureaucracy. Luckily, Joaquín is single and he makes ends meet, but BsF 4.500, though considered a great salary in Venezuela, is peanuts for a professional with graduate studies abroad. A secretary, or a doorman, make but a portion of that. They're not stupid – they see what the institutions' budget is used on.

The dislike of the Cubans seems to run deep in the Venezuelan state apparatus' rank-and-file.

I know Joaquín is not chavista, but I ask him about his bosses. Are they all convinced chavistas? Don't they see this simply isn't working?

"Oh, they're very critical. They started out believing in the revolution, the ones higher up. But they know this isn't working anymore. They go to the marches and wear red, but what choice do they have? It's not like before."

Still, I tell him, I bet they go and vote chavista anyway.

"Yeah," he tells me. "I think so too. Because, you see, this doesn't work, but at least now they are getting their slice of the pie. At least now, they're inside the bubble, working on something they like, and they are being taken into account. They know that if Chávez goes, so does their job."

"It's all a matter of survival," he says.

I munch on my profiteroles, while I still can, wondering what this place will become once the Havanization of Caracas is complete.

The eager eunuch
Posted on December 15, 2010 by Quico

The deepening state of collective insanity also known as the Bolivarian Republic has plumbed bizarre new depths over the last few days. But the news item that really struck me was this clip with Congressman-elect (and frighteningly talented demagogue-in-training) Robert Serra eagerly rushing to register his view that the body he's just been elected to should be stripped of most of its powers before he's even taken office.

The entire Enabling Law episode is simply bizarre. Because, let's just remind ourselves that the legislature whose power Chávez is moving to strip isn't some opposition-controlled behemoth: it's a place where unquestioning chavista partisans control 59% of the seats! There's no real chance of the new Assembly substantially slowing, let alone reversing, any part of the Chávez agenda. Even so, eager new chavista pols who you might think would relish the chance to legislate for the first time in their young lives are all signed up to the plan to Ledezimate it.

You may remember Serra as the frighteningly silver tongued die-hard chavista student drafted in to insult the Manos Blancas movement when its representatives managed to get a speaking slot at the National Assembly some years ago.

These days, he's one of the 59% of A.N. members who represent 48% of Venezuela's voters. Yet Serra isn't trying to reassure his boss that the body he is about to join is going to be just as pliant as the outgoing one. He isn't trying to tell Chávez that he can leave it to them, that they've got his back. No!

Instead, implicitly, he says "you're right, mi comandante. The 98 PSUV deputies elected? We're pretty useless...best to bypass us altogether."

Which, in the end, shows he's no fool.

Robert Serra understands what Chávez has worked hard to ensure everyone in Venezuela understands. Power rests with him, and only with him. If you want a share of it, your overriding priority is to ingratiate yourself with the president. I mean, duh!

The tenth anniversary of a slap in the face
Posted on July 27, 2009 by Quico

It was hard, this weekend, seeing those images of Hugo Chávez celebrating the tenth anniversary of the 1999 Constituent Assembly. Presidential satchels and speeches; pomp and (what passes for) circumstance (in the Bolivarian Republic.) All this public splendor to celebrate the drafting of a constitution that, as Teodoro Petkoff's *bon mot* has it, reads more and more like a subversive pamphlet, so far removed are its norms from the day-to-day reality of the way power is exercised in Venezuela.

Those of us who like to write about the way the constitution is nullified, day-by-day, in Venezuela have something of a long-tail problem: a relatively small number of flashy, highly visible violations (you know the list: the right to private property, the separation of powers, the apolitical nature of the military) grab all the attention, while a much larger constellation of less spectacular outrages barely merit a mention. Call them the B-List Violations: a long list of also-rans in the unconstitutionality stakes.

My own impotent outrage typically centers on the almost-entirely-forgotten Article 23. It's an article of staggering ambition that, for some reason, you almost never hear anything about. Article 23 actually makes international human rights treaties constitutionally binding within Venezuela, as well as directly applicable by all Venezuelan courts.

That means that, in theory, you should be able to go up to a Venezuelan judge and cite your rights in, for instance, article 13 of the American Convention on Human Rights (to wit: the right to free expression may not be restricted via indirect means, such as the abuse of official controls on newsprint, on radio frequencies, or of inputs and goods used to broadcast information, in order to impede the free communication of ideas) and that norm is supposed to have constitutional status, superseding any and all Venezuelan legislation on the matter. Taken seriously, Article 23 would revolutionize Venezuelan justice.

Somehow, though, the TSJ never got the memo, and neither did anyone else. It's just weird: nobody seems to know about Article 23. You never hear Marta Colomina all huffed up and horrified at its total desuetude. And Prof. Colomina very rarely passes up the chance to get all huffed up and horrified.

But it's there, Article 23. Not because aliens from the planet Zorgon put it there. Not because the CIA conspired to sneak it in. It's there because the 94%-chavista constituent assembly put it there in 1999. You know the one I'm talking about, right? The one Chávez went to commemorate this weekend? That one!

Today in TalCual, Miranda State Education Director Juan Maragall focuses on another of these also-rans. Everybody knows that the Constitution says that tenured judges have to earn their seats through "public competitions" - *concursos públicos de oposición* - where political criteria cannot be taken into consideration. But did you know that, according to article 104, the same thing applies to school teachers? Few outside the profession know that...nor should they, as article 104 has become another serial dust-gatherer.

In practice the main qualification you need to get a nice, steady job warping the minds of small children ... is a PSUV membership card.

Of course, if you're accepted into the profession without a *concurso* you don't get tenure. You can only be taken on as a substitute or interim teacher, meaning you can be fired by the Education Ministry at any time and for any reason, or no reason at all. Totally exposed, you end up becoming a kind of lower-court-judge-of-the-classroom: at all times, you are one-insufficiently-chavista-remark away from seeing your livelihood vanish.

In Maragall's phrase, the practice of appointing most teachers as interim or substitutes has started to spawn its own juridical framework. Recent Education Ministry resolutions make it a prerequisite to have entered the profession as a sub, or as an interim teacher - that is, discretionally - before you can even go to *concurso*. So, the status quo is that you can now only opt for tenure if you've been picked discretionally, *a dedo*, without your credentials ever having been evaluated in open competition.

That's how easy it is to upend the Venezuelan Constitution. No need to bother with referendums or amendments or reforms or any of that jazz. An education ministry resolution does the job.

It'd be an interesting, if somewhat morbid, exercise to go through all 350 articles of the 1999 constitution and try to figure out precisely how many have been subverted like this, sotto voce, without anyone much talking about it or acknowledging it out loud or even quite realizing that it's happened.

And amid all this, VTV forces us to watch Chávez celebrating the tenth anniversary of... what, exactly? It's never been clear to me. Over time, I've come to see the 1999 Assembly as one of the most bizarrely nonsensical public spectacles in these ten years of intensely bizarre public spectacle.

The best way I can make sense of it is that for Chávez, the Constitution is a fetish. Not in the contemporary, sexual sense of the term, but in the older anthropological one: a kind of amulet, a magical thing whose powers are embodied in its physicality, in its life as object, and are quite independent of anything actually written inside. It's the little book itself that interests Chávez, the physical embodiment of his claim to legitimacy. But his claim, ultimately, is mystical rather than legal - based on a metaphysical consubstantiation of leader and pueblo that cannot be mediated through anything as humdrum as a set of formal legal rules.

And so the little blue book came to be used as a kind of magic charm, waved around in inverse proportion to how often it was actually read, much less interpreted or - heaven forbid - applied.

In the end, reading the constitution - taking it seriously as text - is a profoundly counterrevolutionary thing to do. It can only lead to the kind of apostasy you keep finding in this blog - hell, earlier in this post, even - where an interpretative discourse is developed to compare the legal standard set out in the text to the reality instantiated day-to-day by those who wield power in Venezuela.

Discourses like those are inherently destabilizing to a regime like Chávez's. They insert human intelligence where it is least wanted, least tolerable, and most dangerous. When you take the Constitution seriously as text, when you set out to interpret it rationally, you interpose yourself between the caudillo and the masses, limiting and qualifying his claim to authority over them.

To do so is to meddle in the mystical link between them. And chavismo cannot put up with such an affront: it needs to silence it. Because, in the end, to read the Constitution with fresh eyes is as close to apostasy as you can come in the secular religion that is chavismo.

Crafting a chavista court
Posted on May 20, 2009 by Quico

Five years ago today, the court-packing Organic Statute of the Supreme Tribunal of Justice came into effect. As I've recently discussed, I think that event should be recognized as the moment when Venezuela ceased to be a constitutional democracy in any recognizable sense.

To continue our commemoration of the event that made our justice Simply Red and our democracy Simply Dead, I've asked Venezuelan Legal Scholar Raul Sanchez Urribarri to contribute his thoughts on the state of Venezuela's legal system.

Raul says: On January 26, 2006, in the opening act of the Judicial Branch's activities for that year, Venezuelan Chief Justice Omar Mora Diaz, speaking in front of Chávez and other prominent political figures, proudly stated that the Venezuelan judiciary was, at last, free from external political interference. The AD & COPEI era of judicial submissiveness was gone, and a new time of true judicial power had arrived. Shortly afterwards, several judges started spontaneously singing "Uh, ah! Chávez no se va!" showing everybody what judicial independence meant in Chavista jargon.

We know our judiciary –especially the Supreme Court – has always been weak compared with other political actors, especially the *cogollos* of the AD & COPEI era and their acolytes in the Judicial Council (Consejo de la Judicatura). But we have reached new lows in the current regime: the old tribes at least had the minimum sense not to chant political slogans in their robes. How did it come to this?

It would be too easy to just blame Chávez. In public, he has never showed too much deference to *Dos Pilitas*. From the (in)famous letter sent to the Supreme Court justices back in 1999, to his public use of expletives to refer to decisions that didn't go his way, Chávez frequently showed contempt for the idea of leaving justices alone to do their job and interpret the law as they see fit (or to freely express their policy preferences, as judges arguably do in established democracies). These open interventions can only psych-out judges, usually threatening and constraining them from reaching any decision that would not match the regime's (a.k.a. Chávez's) preferred outcome.

However, Chávez's public Court bashing probably is not all – or even most – of what this is about. Chavismo uses other tools to manipulate the courts. Like everywhere else, the most important mechanism is the appointment of sympathetic judges. In a democracy, this takes place following institutional rules that allow for the meaningful participation of a variety of actors, and respecting the rules of judicial tenure, probably the most important guarantee of judicial independence. Conversely, in non-democracies or dysfunctional democratic regimes, these rules are changed or completely bypassed: Judges are dismissed, forced to resign, or the court's size and composition is changed to reflect the rulers' wishes (a.k.a. court-packing).

Under Chávez, the Supreme Court has been reshuffled three times - late-1999, late-2000 and 2004 - and all three episodes have aimed to create Chavista majorities. But some majorities have been more Chavista than others. After the first two tries, the Chavista majority crumbled as soon as the ruling coalition responsible for its appointment broke apart.

Take, for example, the late-2000 appointees. Many of those justices people used to call "Chavista!" were really Miquilenista judges who understood that they owed their appointment not to Chávez but to their political boss, former Interior Minister and Chávez-mentor turned opposition Luis Miquilena. As a result, as soon as Miquilena flipped on Chávez, the justices did the same and, coupled with the very few judges who had connections with other parties, formed a solid 10-judge group strongly committed to the opposition cause. This group went far as stating, in a majority decision of the Court's entire roster, that the events of April 11-14, 2002 were not a coup. The feeble Chavista majority in the Constitutional Chamber was barely able to overcome this deadlock through their controversial use of that chamber's alleged pre-eminence over other Chambers in the Court and over the Court in its entirety, reliably voting 3 against 2 in favor of the government in every major decision, including those that paved the way to the 2004 recall referendum.

To (re)create a majority, the 2004 Chavista majority in the National Assembly decided to expand and pack the Court, using the excuse of needing to pass the pending Organic Statute of the Venezuelan Supreme Court (LOTSJ). At the time, this proposal gained even more steam, since there was some fear among Chavistas about the prospects of losing the recall referendum against Chávez or achieving a narrow victory. Basically, they needed the Court as insurance in case of trouble.

The main culprit in this second packing-plan is clear: Luis Velásquez Alvaray. Velásquez had an agenda of his own - to reach the Supreme Court and, specifically, the Comisión Judicial, a body in charge of appointing Venezuela's judges, to create a new judicial network or tribe that responded to his will.

We remember well how far Velásquez Alvaray and his buddies were willing to go to get the new Statute passed - they ended up modifying the National Assembly's Rules of Order to get the Statute approved, steamrolling all opposition, even if that involved turning the statute into the messiest, most inarticulate piece of legislation in Venezuela's contemporary history. Possibly even more than the crude political hatchet job it represents, it's the amazing amateurishness of the LOTSJ's drafting that makes serious lawyers cringe.

The Law passed and the new justices were appointed, Velásquez Alvaray among them. Ironically, Velásquez would last just a short time in the Court. Picking a fight with the wrong people and being blatantly corrupt at the same time was probably too much a stretch for someone with such little juridical credentials!

Now, what did they achieve with the last wave of court-packing? This time, the court apparently turned more Chavista than ever before, right?

That's one plausible interpretation - especially since every magistrate is now absolutely clear that the only boss around is Chávez. Only a handful of justices with ties to the opposition dare to vote against the government line - among them, former Miquilenistas like Rondon Haaz at the Constitutional Chamber. Moreover, since the new justices arrived in the Court, the judiciary as a whole has been more willing than ever to stretch or trespass the boundaries of acceptable legal interpretation to favor the regime, tearing down a minimal image of legitimacy that is necessary to perform its role. Just think about the Supreme Court's endorsement of the closing of RCTV last year, the use of criminal prosecution against political opponents, and a very long "etc."

On the other hand, some things have not changed. Beyond the evident commitment that most Supreme Court justices have to Chávez's cause lies an ever-divided court. Justices still compete, sometimes bitterly, for business, favors and to secure judicial appointments for allies in the lower courts. More importantly, since the 2004 law, many of them became tokens of prominent legislators in the National Assembly. Additionally, despite a decline in the court's willingness to protect plaintiffs' rights against the government – a phenomenon that several Venezuelan legal scholars have already highlighted – the opposition still goes to the courts.

This might sound puzzling, but it is also reasonable: the courts, especially the Supreme Court, are a highly visible venue for opposition politicians to keep showing that they are fighting for their constituency – in our case, that they are challenging the tyrant and his servants by all possible means, even if this is otherwise absolutely useless, even when their claims are constitutionally plausible.

So, on the one hand, the Court fails to control both the President and the Legislature, ceasing to do what is most important in a liberal democracy. That is probably fine with Chavismo, since they are already clear that their regime is not liberal-democratic. But many things have not changed. As in the past, networks of justices, judges, politicians and lawyers work to exploit the court for rent-seeking and personal benefit. In the legal world in Venezuela, everybody knows that several judges (not all of them) are willing to sell decisions to the highest bidder, and even guarantee that the decision will not be overturned on appeal by sharing the profits with their superiors. Everyone knows that many attorneys work as ruling-brokers, and not as legal practitioners; this used to be the case before Chávez and it essentially remains the same. And everyone knows that justices of the Court and politicians struggle to get judges appointed who then pledge loyalty to them – just like they once did with their old-regime designators.

In fact, the judiciary changed for the worse without addressing any of the underlying problems. Judges without tenure or a sense of it are less secure than ever that they will be in the bench tomorrow. Every time you see a discussion about 'improving the courts' and whatnot in the National Assembly, bear in mind that what we are really witnessing is a fight between different factions to control the judicial goldmine. So, in addition to being politically dependent, and sing songs to praise Chávez their noble leader, many of them know that even this is not enough, because the day somebody else is powerful in the legislature or the court, their post is at greater risk than ever. Making money while you are in the court all of the sudden starts making a lot of sense..

That is Chavista justice in a nutshell - a judiciary that remains politically dependent, not only on Chávez, but on rapacious politicians inside and outside the Venezuelan court system. But not everything is bleak. As in the past, there are a few real heroes that work as justices, judges, lawyers and public defenders with the goal of building the rule of law in Venezuela. Quietly, they believe that wearing red T-shirts, going to demonstrations or singing Chavista songs in the court is inappropriate for honorable public servants. And they are worthy of our utmost respect, and at least a bit of hope.

Chávez, totalitarianism, and the fecklesness of the opposition
Posted on May 5, 2003 by Quico

These days, it seems to happen alarmingly often. And it makes me shudder each time. Antichavista talking heads keep describing the Chávez government as a "totalitarian regime." Like nazism or Stalinism, or Pol Pot's Cambodia.

But do they stop to think about what that actually means?

It takes a bit of a re-read of Hannah Arendt to realize afresh the scale of the historical travesty perpetrated when Venezuelans liken our half-baked autocracy to actual totalitarianism. As a Jew who lived through the holocaust, Arendt knew a thing or two about what real totalitarianism is like, of the scale of human suffering it inflicts. Reserving the term mostly for the regimes of Stalin and Hitler, she dissected it with clinical precision.

The first thing to understand about "totalitarianism" is that the term has a precise meaning. It's not just some loose synonym for dictatorship, autocracy, and authoritarianism. For Arendt, it's a unique form of state power, a conceptual category all its own.

Totalitarianism isn't about losing any inhibition in the use mass-scale violence to stay in power: mere dictatorships reach that level all the time. Totalitarianism of the brand pioneered in Germany and Russia in the 1930s goes much further than that. Its aim is not just to silence all sources of political dissent. Its goal is to dominate the totality of each and every thought and activity of each and every citizen each and every day.

As Arendt explains in The Origins of Totalitarianism, this form of political organization is not to be confused with dictatorship, which is much more common historically. Dictatorial violence is politically motivated, politically-rational violence. It's violence that "makes sense" if your main goal is to hang on to power.

Totalitarianism isn't like that. The Stalinist purges could not be explained in those terms. Stalin was willing to put Soviet society through immense dislocation, not just in human but in economic and military terms, even though as Arendt puts it,

"None of these immense sacrifices in human life was motivated by a raison d'état in the old sense of the term. None of the liquidated social strata was hostile to the regime or likely to become hostile to the regime. Active organized opposition had ceased to exist by 1930."

In the Soviet Union, dictatorial terror (which is distinguished from totalitarian terror insofar as it threatens only authentic opponents, not harmless citizens without political views,) had been grim enough to suffocate all political life, open or clandestine, even before Lenin's death.

But totalitarianism is not content with that. Going beyond the bounds of the political sphere as traditionally understood, Stalin's totalitarian violence was about gaining total power over everything anyone in Russia did or thought.

In a chilling passage, Arendt explains what this means:

If totalitarianism takes its own claim seriously, it must finish once and for all with 'the neutrality of chess,' that is, with the autonomous existence of any activity whatsoever. The lovers of 'chess for the sake of chess,' are not absolutely atomized elements in a mass society whose completely heterogenous uniformity is one of the primary conditions for totalitarianism. From the point of view of totalitarian rulers, a society devoted to chess for the sake of chess is only in degree different and less dangerous than a class of farmers for the sake of farming.

This is what the "total" in "totalitarian" means – a system of government that will use any amount of violence it takes to control literally everything that happens in that society – even something as seemingly harmless as a citizen's relationship towards chess. Authoritarianism might be contented merely with absolute control over the political sphere. Totalitarianism is about total control over everything – about eradicating any basis for social organization not dominated by a central authority.

To achieve this level of control, the state must destroy any alternative links that could imaginably call into question any citizen's loyalty – it must "atomize" its citizens, destroying any alternative objects of identification or repositories of loyalty they might have. This it does through fear:

"Mass atomization in Soviet society was achieved by the skillful use of repeated purges which invariably precede actual group liquidation. In order to destroy all social and family ties, the purges are conducted in such a way as to threaten with the same fate the defendant and all his ordinary relations, from mere acquaintances up to his closest friends and relatives."

"The consequence of the simple and ingenious device of guilt by association is that as soon as a man is accused, his former friends are transformed immediately into his bitterest enemies; in order to save their own skins, they volunteer information and rush in with denunciations to corroborate the nonexistent evidence against him; this obviously is the only way to prove their own trustworthiness. Retrospectively, they will try to prove that their acquaintance or friendship with the accused was only a pretext for spying on him and revealing him as a saboteur, a Trotskyite, a foreign spy, or a Fascist. Merit being gauged by the number of your denunciations of your closest comrades, it is obvious that the most elementary caution demands that one avoid all intimate contacts, if possible – not in order to prevent discovery of one's own secret thoughts , but rather to eliminate, in the almost certain case of future trouble, all persons who might have not only an ordinary interest in your denunciation but an irresistible need to bring about your ruin simply because they are in danger of their own lives."

"In the last analysis, it has been through the development of this device to its farthest and most fantastic extremes that Bolshevik rulers have succeeded in creating an atomized and individualized society the like of which we have never seen before."

Take a minute to think about that passage, about the extent of domination, terror and violence it reveals, the next time you hear Antonio Ledezma describe the Chávez government as totalitarian.

"Totalitarian governments," Arendt concludes,

"are mass organizations of atomized, isolated individuals. Compared with all other parties and movements, their most conspicuous external characteristic is their demand for total, unrestricted, unconditional and unalterable loyalty of the individual member. Such loyalty can be expected only from the completely isolated human being who, without any other social ties to family, friends, comrades, or even mere acquaintances, derives

his sense of having a place in the world only from his belonging to a movement, his membership in the party. Totalitarian domination is something that no state and no mere apparatus of violence can achieve, namely, the permanent domination of each single individual in each and every sphere of life."

In other words, make no mistake about it: if the Chávez regime was "totalitarian", I would be dead, and so would you.

The tendency to call the Chávez government "totalitarian" lays bare, to my mind, a worrying contempt for history, a kind of idiotic indifference towards the past. The comparison is so shrill, so obviously detached from any kind of serious consideration, that it suggests to me a deeply worrying contempt for the meaning of the words used in the public sphere.

Yet the charge is so commonplace it's become almost a cliché, constantly hurled through the media by opposition leaders who've clearly never stopped to consider that if they lived in anything even approaching the kind of regime they claim to be oppose, making such a statement in public would certainly cost them their lives.

VI

The war of 2002-2004

This was a painful chapter to edit.

From 2002 until the Recall Referendum of 2004, Venezuela´s two factions engaged in an intense political confrontation that led to large street demonstrations, a crippling two-month general strike, a coup, and an unprecedented recall referendum that saw Hugo Chávez win at the ballot box. The Referendum itself marked Chávez's definitive consolidation in power. It also sealed the opposition's fate for many years to come.

On the topic of the April 11th coup, we've struggled to clarify what it meant and who was (or wasn't) involved. As the years have passed, we've learned more information about those events, so our narrative has also evolved. Sadly, the elusive Truth Commission that would solve any lingering doubts remains one of many unfulfilled chavista promises.

On the Recall Referendum, we went from believing in fraud to believing in our defeat. Our initial shock at losing gave way to an incredulous questioning of the truth – what we thought was the truth, what we were led to believe was the truth, and what people continue to mistakenly insist is the truth. We hope the chronological order in which the posts on the Referendum are presented paints a picture of our evolution on the subject. To this day, the idea that different factions within the opposition will reach consensus on what happened on August 16, 2004 remains out of reach.

What is the main lesson from those years? Don't leave the politics of the opposition to hacks.

We have a pile of mistakes left behind from those years to prove it.

The untold story of Venezuela's 2002 April crisis
Posted on April 14, 2004 by Quico

The conventional wisdom about Venezuela's brief coup attempt in April 2002 is almost entirely wrong. The real story is much weirder, and much more interesting.

The events that gripped Venezuela from April 11th to April 14th, 2002 will keep historians busy for decades to come. In the space of four days the country cycled through three presidents. Venezuelans watched appalled as an elected official emptied his gun in the direction of an opposition march in broad daylight. They saw tanks rolling on the streets of Caracas, they heard the armed forces' top-ranking general announce the resignation of President Chávez, and they saw a right-wing clique take total control of the state. The private TV and radio stations that could have covered the chaos were first shut down by the government and then conspired to suppress the news of his return. It's a lot to cover in a single essay, so bear with me.

First, a note of caution: the task of de-mystifying the coup is made especially difficult by the lush propagandistic undergrowth that now covers nearly every aspect of the story, a version that obscures or distorts nearly everything of importance that happened that weekend.

Since 2002, polite opinion outside Venezuela has hardened around an impossibly simplistic version of events, one that fits in snugly with first world perceptions of Latin America as a passive CIA stomping ground, where an all-powerful Uncle Sam makes all the important decisions and the "natives" grin and bear it.

It's not surprising this account has gained such a wide following. It spares people the trouble of having to learn about the details of the crisis that led to the coup. It exempts indignation-rich readers from having to wade through a mass of incomplete, often contradictory information on their way to an evidence-based understanding of what happened. And, of course, it has a powerful and extremely well-funded patron in the Venezuelan government itself.

Helped along by the tireless propagandizing of The Revolution Will Not be Televised and Eva Golinger's Chávez Code, as well as by Chávez's own politically motivated endorsement, this version now dominates first-world accounts of the coup.

The only trouble is that large parts of it are incompatible with the record.

The alternative account you'll find here is evidence-based and, unavoidably, pretty long and terribly unsatisfying. I can't spin a nice, simple, satisfying tale explaining what happened that weekend: too much evidence is missing, too many accounts are contradictory, and especially because the entire episode has never been credibly investigated by an impartial public body. What I can do is give you a sense for the complexities of the April Crisis, of what we can actually say we know and what we're left to speculate about.

I understand the temptation to massively simplify this story is strong. We all want good guys and bad guys, a "neat" story that ties all the loose ends. Anybody who tries to peddle you a "neat" story about April 2002 is just lying. The evidence on record supports only messiness.

So the first thing is to accept that there's no way to convey what happened in 800 words without massively distorting the story. Whether you favor the Chavez government or oppose it, you can't understand what actually happened without throwing some cherished but unsustainable certainties into the pyre.

The truth, I'm afraid, makes for some uncomfortable reading for both sides.

Much of the material the following is based on comes from Sandra La Fuente and Alfredo Meza's excellent book El Acertijo de Abril (The April Riddle) – an oasis of fair reporting in a sea of political propagandizing on the subject. The two have worked hard to produce a book of confirmed facts, not spin or supposition. Of course, any errors are mine.

An atypical coup

Though the psychedelic four-day whirlwind of events is commonly described as a "short-lived coup," or a "failed coup attempt," the word "coup" obscures as much as it reveals about the April Crisis. At the heart of this convoluted story is an attempt to implant an unconstitutional government, for sure. It's no less true that the April crisis witnessed a series of events that fall completely outside the territory of the traditional Latin American coup d'état.

Rather than a neatly organized conspiracy, sprung on an unsuspecting government in a way designed to maximize the element of surprise, what we have is a chaotic, fast escalating crisis, with parallel brinksmanship strategies leading to a quick succession of events that got well ahead of either side's planning.

I mean, who ever heard of a Latin American coup where the coupsters "forget" to gain military control over the seat of government? One where they have no overall plan, no settled leadership, and end up improvising a strategy minute-by-minute as they go along? And who's ever heard of a Latin American coup where the overthrown President had a specific, worked-out plan to provoke the crisis that eventually toppled him?

One thing is clear: whatever April 11th was, it was not your typical, 50s style CIA-hatched plot.

So what actually happened?

Factor #1: The march

By 9:00 am on April 11th, it was already clear this would not be a normal day. A very large number of Caraqueños had gathered to demand the president's resignation. The crowd, variously estimated between half a million and 800,000 strong, came out on just twelve hours' notice. It was, then, the single largest political demonstration in Venezuela since 1958.

Why did several hundred thousand people decide to march to demand the resignation of a president they had democratically elected twice, by huge majorities, in the preceding 3 years?

Without going into a long detour on just how it is that the political crisis caused by the appointment of seven leftist academics and bureaucrats to the board of the state oil company, PDVSA, caused a crisis capable of escalating so explosively, I'll say that April 11th was the culmination of five months of increasingly vicious political fighting between the government and the opposition: a fight marked by reckless brinksmanship on both sides, with parallel escalation strategies that anyone could see could only end in a crisis.

Whether one side or another might have been able to pre-empt this crisis with a conciliatory gesture will remain one of those imponderables that historians argue about. The reality is that neither side was in a mood to give in. The opposition bitterly accused the government of seeking to impose an elected dictatorship, while the government saw the opposition as little more than a cabal of reactionary wreckers. By early April, the sense of crisis was palpable, with Venezuelans riveted to the unfolding political drama on TV. By the time April 11th rolled around, a violent denouement could surprise no one.

It can't really be denied that, throughout this highly volatile period, President Chávez gave free rein to his trademark hyper-confrontational style. The perception at the time in the opposition camp was that the government was consciously seeking to provoke a crisis.

Two years later, Chávez confirmed this perception explicitly, in a speech to the National Assembly. He boasted that, having failed to capture complete control of the oil bureaucracy in his first three years in power, he had worked out a plan – Plan Colina – to escalate the PDVSA conflict, and appointed a task force to focus on this goal. By raising tensions to unprecedented heights inside the company, Chávez hoped to identify and flush out all those who did not back him unquestioningly.

"Sometimes it is necessary to provoke a crisis," he said.

It worked.

Chávez's belligerence grew throughout early 2002, culminating in his theatrical firing of seven top PDVSA officials who had resisted the new board appointments. The private media responded in kind, showering the country with highly inflammatory anti-government propaganda around the clock. The tenor of the political diatribe grew increasingly vicious throughout those early months, with the opposition increasingly questioning Chávez's right to hold power and Chávez increasingly questioning the opposition's right to participate in public life at all.

By April 9th, when the opposition-run National Labor Federation and Employers' Federations called a General Work-Stoppage, basic civility had completely broken down. Each side vowed to crush the other. The private airwaves were dominated by anti-government propaganda, and Chávez used his power to "chain" the national broadcast media (i.e. to force them to all broadcast a government message, live) to an unprecedented extent. By my count, there were over 20 such "cadena" broadcasts on April 9th alone, most of them devoted to straight-out government propaganda rather than official information.

That the opposition media gave up any notion of journalistic balance in attacking the government can't really be denied. It was war out there. At the same time, it's clear that an atmosphere of extreme tension was just what Chávez had been seeking. Plan Colina can be seen as an effort to systematically piss off government critics in the media, the unions, the Catholic Church, and any other institution he could not control: a red rag consciously designed to lure them out into indefensible positions.

To understand the confrontational extreme the government had reached, consider this: the proximate cause of the crisis was the appointment of that new PDVSA board. On April 10th – the day before the coup – those newly appointed PDVSA board members, sensing the mood of national emergency, tendered their resignations to Chávez, apparently hoping that their sacrifice could avert the crisis everyone could see looming.

Had this gesture been made public, it might – might – have been enough to defuse the entire crisis. But Chávez chose to keep their offer to resign secret – a decision entirely at odds with any kind of innocent explanation that would portray the president as a victim of a conspiracy.

Within 24 hours, he had hundreds of thousands of protesters on the streets of Caracas.

Factor #2: The bait-and-switch

The opposition protesters brought together on April 11th did not know they were about to set off on an insurrectional adventure to the presidential palace.

They believed the march would last just a few kilometers, from Parque del Este Metro station to the PDVSA building (now Bolivarian University) in Chuao. Both are on the East side of Caracas, 7 miles east of Miraflores Palace, which sits in the Central district to the west of the city.

In the months after the crisis, testimony given to a National Assembly investigating committee revealed that opposition leaders had planned a risky bait-and-switch on their own supporters.

The night before the march, they had agreed that, once the march reached PDVSA Chuao, they would call on their followers to march west, the entire way to the presidential palace, to demand Chávez's resignation. The decision to re-route the march would be presented as a spur-of-the-moment thing, and given the extremely emotionally charged atmosphere of those days, there was no doubt that the marchers would follow their leaders west. Faced with 800,000 angry marchers right on his doorstep, Chávez would have no choice but to resign.

One of the most interesting revelations in Sandra La Fuente and Alfredo Meza's book is that the government knew of this plan by the evening of April 10th. An agent from the Asamblea Popular Revolucionaria (the people who bring us Aporrea.org) "Directorate of Social Intelligence" had infiltrated the meeting. He communicated news of the plan back to headquarters.

Even government opponents must understand that, in a situation like that, the government had no choice but to protect itself from what was, without exaggeration, an insurrectional march. That's normal.

From a public-order point of view, the problem was not difficult: Chávez continued to command the Guardia Nacional – a military-run internal security force along the lines of the Gendarmes in France or the Guardia Civil in Spain – which is trained and equipped to deal with public-order problems.

With 12 hours advance notice, it would have been straightforward for the Guardia Nacional to block the march's route to Miraflores. Simply by blocking off the end of Avenida Bolívar, the Guardia could have kept the marchers a safe distance away from Miraflores Palace. Had they done so, the march might have turned into another of many political rallies. There would have been speeches and slogans, and eventually the marchers would have packed it in and gone home.

This is not how Chávez reacted. Instead, he came up with a two-pronged plan to defend the palace.

First, his political machine – again led by the Asamblea Popular Revolucionaria – gathered some 3,000 supporters to surround Miraflores for a counter-demonstration to face down the opposition marchers. La Fuente and Meza confirm that guns were handed out by pro-Chávez politicians to the crowd, though only after the shooting started.

At least a handful of those Chávez supporters were caught on video shooting south, apparently in the direction of the opposition march. Though it is not clear – because no serious investigation was ever carried out – whether those shooters are responsible for any of the deaths down below, it's plain that much of the chavista self-defense strategy relied on deploying armed civilian supporters around Miraflores, so much so that the Presidential Guard Regiment had set up a field hospital to prepare to treat casualties in the parking lot of its Palacio Blanco headquarters, just across the road from Miraflores.

Factor #3: Plan Avila

The decision to arm government supporters outside Miraflores was serious enough, but it's the second part of the government's reaction that really got Chávez into trouble with the army.

At 10:30 am, according to recordings of military radio frequencies made by opposition supporters, Chávez personally ordered the activation of Plan Ávila. Now, those two words will mean little to foreign readers, but they will send chills down the spine of any Venezuelan.

Plan Ávila is an army-run contingency plan designed to quell serious disturbances in Caracas.

The plan had only ever been activated once before, during the massive looting that broke out on February 27th and 28th, 1989. The police and the Guardia Nacional had been overrun by the riots, and the decision to deploy the army with orders to shoot looters on sight resulted in a bloodbath.

The army killed at least 277 people during Plan Ávila '89, perhaps as many as a thousand – an outrage that gave rise to the first wave of home-grown human rights NGOs in Venezuela.

Cofavic, (the Victims and Family Members Committee), an NGO set up to help the relatives of the victims, spent years pushing for an international human rights investigation headed by OAS's Inter-American Human Rights Commission. Eventually, the commission found against Venezuela, ordering the government to pay restitution to the families of the victims. The court also ordered Venezuela to disclose the operational details of the plan, previously protected by military secrecy laws, and to bring Plan Avila into line with international human rights law.

It's no surprise why Plan Avila had such lethal consequences when it was first implemented in 1989. The Venezuelan army has no riot gear, no non-lethal weapons at its disposal, no training in crowd control. Plan Ávila means setting loose a bunch of 18-year-olds carrying semi-automatic rifles packing live ammo against a civilian population: a recipe for massive bloodletting.

The order to activate Plan Avila set off alarm bells in the military establishment, and for good reason. If the plan had been controversial in 1989, when it was deployed to quell violent looting by armed groups of people, its application against the largest political march Venezuela had seen in its history threatened disaster. It was far too easy to picture just one young conscript losing his cool and firing on the (mostly) unarmed crowd, even if no such orders were given.

For the brass, it was plain that applying Plan Ávila in those conditions risked causing a Tiananmen-style political massacre.

By a quirk of fate, April 11th, 2002 was also the day when the International Criminal Court Treaty came into force worldwide. With the arrest of Pinochet in London fresh in their minds, top officers were only too aware that human rights abuses have no statute of limitation.

To their unending credit, the two key military officers at the top of the Plan Avila chain of command simply did the math and simply refused to follow the President's orders. As confirmed by the subsequent hearings in the National Assembly, this is the key decision that set off the chain of events that weekend.

Factor #4: Rosendo and Vásquez Velasco

Who were those two officers, and why did they act the way they did? Was their disobedience part of an insurrectional plot? Were they U.S. stooges? Or did they act on principle?

Major General Manuel Rosendo, a personal friend of Chávez and one-time baseball teammate, was head of CUFAN, the Armed Forces Unified Command. A Chávez confidant who had been intimately involved in contingency planning for precisely the kind of event they were facing, General Rosendo was seen as a Chavista hardliner until that afternoon. Rosendo was an unambiguous hate-figure in opposition circles due to the openly political, pro-Chávez speech he gave during the Independence Day celebrations in July 2001. By any measure, Rosendo was part of Chávez's inner circle.

After the crisis, General Rosendo testified to the National Assembly that he had participated in contingency planning with Chávez, members of his cabinet and of his party on April 7th. It was at that meeting, Rosendo said, that chavista politicians first aired the plan to mobilize armed civilians to protect the presidential palace in case of major trouble. General Rosendo pleaded with the President not to allow such paramilitary tactics into Venezuelan politics, sensing the potential for bloodletting.

Chávez dismissed his concerns.

On the 10th, just a day before the coup, Rosendo sent a long, emotionally-charged letter to Chávez beseeching him to establish a dialogue with the opposition leaders to defuse the brewing crisis. This suggests that Rosendo was not aware of Plan Colina, or of Chávez's decision to keep secret the PDVSA Board's offer to resign. Otherwise, he would have known that Chávez's policy of relentless escalation had been decided long before.

Rosendo's position matters because, legally speaking, it is the head of CUFAN who has the power to hand the order to activate contingency plans like Plan Avila down the chain of command.

When the order came, Rosendo balked. That decision, Rosendo's refusal to implement a direct order from his Commander-in-Chief, was the breaking point, the second when the until-then flimsy but still intact chain of command shattered.

Above Rosendo - in the chain of command, but outside the Plan Ávila loop - we find Major General Efrain Vásquez Velasco, the top ranking officer in the Venezuelan army. Seen as a moderate until that point, Vásquez Velasco was on good terms with the government. Upon hearing that Chávez had ordered Plan Ávila activated, Vásquez Velazco quickly supported Rosendo's insubordination.,

As we will see, Vásquez Velasco's decisions that weekend were not those of a man angling for power himself, or of one working closely with any sort of organized conspiratorial clique. If anything, Vásquez Velasco spent the weekend on the back foot, struggling to keep up with events, and basically unprepared to take charge of the situation at each critical juncture.

It's important to grasp that these were the two people whose decisions precipitated the chain of events that led to Chávez's fall later that night - two very high-ranking army officers trusted by Chávez, who balked at a patently unconstitutional order. Neither Rosendo nor Vásquez Velasco could seriously be considered coup-plotters: intensely spied on by chavista intelligence officers, they had been judged trustworthy enough to keep in key command posts.

A tiny aside: you can tell a lot about the intellectual honesty of any account of the coup you read by its handling of the Plan Ávila episode. The standard chavista version of the coup simply omits mention of it altogether. Despite the mountains of testimony and documentary evidence on the central role that the order to activate Plan Ávila played in cracking the military chain of command that afternoon, the official version simply sweeps the entire issue under the rug.

Instead, it places the bulk of responsibility on a supposed American intervention backed by evidence that is, at best, circumstantial. The cleansing of Plan Ávila from the Official History of the April Crisis must be one of the most blatant acts of self-serving historical manipulation in the Chávez era.

To recall the earthquake unleashed by the Plan Ávila order is not, however, to say that there was no military conspiracy afoot that day. As shown on the private TV stations on April 12th (and, with great glee, in The Revolution will not be Televised) there surely was a conspiracy - several conspiracies, in fact - led by lower-ranking army soldiers, Guardia Nacional and Navy officers who strongly opposed Chávez's evident confrontational and authoritarian streak.

It is important to grasp, however, that the watershed event of the day, the decision to disobey the Plan Ávila order, was not made by the conspirators, but by members of the chavista inner circle who do not appear to have been in contact with them. The conspirators swung into action only later that night, once Vásquez Velasco and

Rosendo had forced Chávez into a corner. April 11th was a coup, but it was not made by coupsters!

My April 11th

I spent most of April 11th running around Caracas with a camera crew – consisting of my friend Megan with her Cannon XL1, and our jolly oversized Scottish translator/bodyguard Hamish. We were working on a freelance project when the crisis broke. Alas, we were not inside the palace.

At 11:00 am, we were in Chuao when the march leaders 'spontaneously' announced the change of route. I had to be at my newsroom by 11:30 to write VenEconomy's daily 2-minute radio spot for RCR, to be broadcast an hour later. I took a taxi back to the office, and in a feverish hurry wrote a spot warning that the country would need to give itself a new government shortly and that this new government would to be as broad-based and conciliatory as possible, including even moderate chavistas, in order to have any credibility or staying power.

I include that tidbit not just for the Cassandra-ish gloating rights, but to show that even by the early in the afternoon, before the killings and the military about-faces and the rest, it was clear that the popular mobilization against Chávez was too widespread to simply go away somehow. It was also clear that the government had hours to go, and that whoever replaced Chávez needed to take the high road if it was to have any credibility and staying power at all. In fact, for the last several days, the entire country had been awash in speculation and rumors about impending coups. You hardly needed some crystal ball to intuit the road we were heading down.

This is an important point, because some strands of revisionist history have taken to citing memos sent from the US Embassy in Caracas back to Washington, warning that a coup was imminent, as somehow proving US involvement with the coup, or some sort "insider knowledge" about coup planning. This kind of accusation is entirely fatuous: the only thing you needed to know a coup was in the works in Venezuela in April, 2002 was a working TV set and an open pair of eyes.

But I digress. Radio-spot duly written, I caught another taxi and went right downtown to meet the crew at Avenida Bolivar, where I figured the marchers would arrive at around 2:00 pm or so. Three hours for a seven-mile march seemed about right to me. We sat down to have lunch, keeping one eye on the TV sets, but before we'd quite finished, we saw the first few marchers beginning to pour into Avenida Bolívar, directly outside our lunch spot. It must have been about 1:30 p.m.

At the same time, General Lucas Rincón, the Chavista hardliner who was then highest ranking officer in the Venezuelan Armed Forces, went on a *cadena nacional* to try to dispel rumors that Chávez had resigned, and to reaffirm the Armed Forces' commitment to the government. Rincón gave his speech with a mobile phone clutched to his ear the entire time, giving the none-too-subtle impression that his words were being dictated to him in real time.

We left the *tasca* and started to walk along with the marchers, trying to get some shots of what we could all sense would be a historic day. Marching down the street, I kept reassuring the crew: 'It's ok, they had three hours to prepare. We'll obviously run into a Guardia Nacional roadblock at the end of the *Avenida*.'

I didn't know it at the time, but they actually had twelve hours to prepare, not three. Even so, the end of the *avenida* came and, lo and behold: no roadblock.

With nothing to slow the march down, we kept on walking the remaining six or seven blocks to Miraflores Palace. To my consternation, I gradually realized that, insane as that seemed, there would be no Guardia barricade at all, just a bunch of gun-toting chavistas waiting for us on the other side.

Finally, just one block south of the palace, a very thin line of Metropolitan Police officers (i.e. people commanded by the opposition mayor of Caracas) stood trying to keep the opposition crowd at bay.

They had no riot gear, no gas masks, nothing. The most radical of the opposition marchers simply walked right past them, through a no-man's-land just one block deep, to the other side, where a similarly thin line of *Guardias Nacionales* – who did have riot gear and gas masks, and a whole lot of tear gas, to boot – tried to keep the pro-Chávez demonstrators away from the opposition.

The mood of the vast opposition crowd turned at this point, from the carefree party atmosphere of the street march to something angrier and more confrontational. The next hour is a blur of street skirmishes, tear gas, and any number of explosions that sounded like fireworks but could well have been gunshots - I, for one, can't tell the difference. The thin line of *Guardias* had enough tear gas on hand to keep the two sides more or less apart for a while, but opposition hot-heads kept charging at them. The atmosphere was impossibly tense, and soon, it became clear to me that this would not end without significant violence.

By 3:30 we retreated from the Calvario stairs towards Avenida Baralt. Jumpy as hell, I kept trying to persuade Megan to just get out of there – whatever footage we might get out of the melee didn't seem worth the ration of lead that would come with it. After we got some shots on Avenida Baralt - with the chavistas on Llaguno Bridge clearly visible - a man walked up to us. Megan swung the camera to film him. He put his hand over the lens and said, "No, you can't film me. I just came to tell you that you should get out of here. You'll be picked off in particular because of the camera. Get out, now."

So we did.

We didn't get a single recognizable shot of the guy, so I have no way of knowing who he was. An infiltrated DISIP suddenly gripped with a spasm of conscience? A guardian angel? I have no idea. I do know that five photographers and cameramen were wounded that day, and one of them, Jorge Tortoza, was killed. For all I know, that guy saved Megan's life.

We started walking, in the mass of confusion, first south and then back towards the east side. At that time – 4:00 or so – a huge opposition crowd was still walking west on Avenida Mexico, towards the palace. The streets were filled with people, rumors and confusion. For a while, the marchers chanted, simply, "Ejercito cagon! Ejercito cagon!" – the Army is chicken shit, as a way to urge the officers to join the protests in defiance of Chávez.

About five minutes after leaving Avenida Baralt, I turned on my pocket radio to scan for news. To my astonishment, what I heard was Chávez's voice. Incredibly, he had called yet another *cadena nacional* – a simultaneous live broadcast that all TV channels and radio stations.

The first news blackout of the weekend was on.

I didn't know it at the time, but the *cadena* started only minutes after the start of the shootout that left 20 dead and over 100 injured – most of them on Avenida Baralt, the street I'd been standing on five minutes earlier. Because there were so many loud bangs in the air, people did not initially realize that shooting had started. Many of the first to be wounded figured they had been hit with a rock or a bottle: only gradually did people realize that live shooting had started.

The sequence of those first few minutes after the *cadena* started is particularly confusing. It appears that a set of Policia Metropolitana (opposition-led) anti-riot vehicles charged up Avenida Baralt. The chavistas claim the cops shot first, the cops claim the opposite.[49] One way or another, a big firefight started between the two. According to many, there were also sharpshooters spreading bullets from various building tops, though none were ever photographed or identified.

Today, we know that there were deaths on both sides. Because no proper investigation has ever been held, it is not possible to know exactly who started shooting, why and when exactly. We do know that, via the cadena, the government had taken a decisive step to block reporting of the shooting taking place just feet from the palace.

---

[49] Writer Brian Nelson has published photos of chavistas shooting south from street level on Avenida Baralt before the cops even showed up.

Since I had a radio instead of a TV, I did not see what millions of Venezuelans saw. Enraged at Chávez's decision to give a rambling speech in the middle of a national emergency, the private TV stations split their screens down the middle. On one side you saw the president speaking, while on the other side you saw live video images of the shooting spree taking place just meters away.

For more than two long hours during perhaps the worst episode of political violence in Venezuela since the 60s, Chávez continued to speak while people died outside his door. He never stopped talking, never did anything to stop the shooting. Every few minutes, an army officer would enter the frame and slip the president a bit of paper containing a casualty tally, which Chávez would read, and then continue talking in his most natural voice.

Not all the shooting that day happened on Avenida Baralt. Both pro- and anti-government protesters died at several other locations in the vicinity. Minutes after the start of the shooting on Avenida Baralt, one man was killed standing directly behind Miraflores, in the Chavista march on Avenida Urdaneta – well away from line-of-sight from the Hotel Eden and the opposition march. The shots, according to police investigations, came from the Bolero building.

Also, the *Guardia Nacional* troops that had been keeping the opposition marchers away from Miraflores eventually ran out of tear gas and started shooting live rounds into the crowd.

One of the most puzzling subplots here concerns the arrests made by the police at the Hotel Ausonia on the 11th, where several foreigners were arrested with guns and a small quantity of drugs. They were jailed until April 16th, and then released unconditionally by a court under the restored Chávez government. They immediately vanished.

Who were they? The government has hinted they were opposition sharpshooters, but forensic tests did not show they had fired weapons recently. They were never questioned or arrested after the 16th, and may well have been ordinary criminals who chose the wrong hotel at the wrong time. But who can be sure?

Chávez's speech continued through 5:30 in the afternoon. Towards the end he announced he was shutting down the country's main TV stations in response to their conspiratorial actions against him. Little did he know that by the time that decision was made, it was too late for a cover-up: the private TV channels had already split their screens and broadcast live images of the massacre, so everyone in the country more or less knew what was happening.

The next few hours were a time of utter confusion. In Caracas, the terrestrial TV towers were taken over by the *Guardia Nacional*. However, the private broadcasters remained on the air in the rest of the country, and in Caracas via satellite. Like a lot of other people in town I made my way to the house of my nearest satellite-dish-owning relative (in my case, my sister Ana.) We sat there astonished watching the news coverage of the violence. It was the first time in our lives we had seen people killed in large numbers for political reasons. The sense of crisis grew minute by minute.

By 10:00 pm, Chávez's former number-2 man, Luis Miquilena, went on television to openly denounce the government's power play. Given his large following in congress and the supreme tribunal – since he had been given primary responsibility for selecting pro-Chávez officers to those posts – Miquilena's desertion opened the door, in the eyes of many, to the possibility of a constitutional solution to the crisis. Within hours of his "cadena", Chávez's congressional majority had vanished.

Then came the *coup de grace*. A Venevisión camera crew managed, through an outstanding bit of bravado, to get actual images of some government supporters shooting down into Avenida Baralt from Llaguno Bridge, which is really an overpass that crosses the avenue. The images were the only direct evidence of people shooting that was available that night. In the atmosphere of sheer confusion, it was not immediately clear that anyone was shooting in the other direction. The private TV stations repeated the footage again, and again and again, giving the impression that the opposition march had been ambushed by government supporters.

One of the gunmen was identified as Richard Peñalver, a pro-Chávez municipal council member in the district where I lived – an elected official. The footage showed him emptying his gun with glee towards the south of the bridge, the area where the opposition march had spent much of the afternoon. At the time, the footage seemed incredibly damning, and whatever support Chávez still enjoyed within the Armed Forces quickly crumbled.

Now, viewers of The Revolution Will Not Be Televised [50] know that as far as chavistas are concerned, the footage of Puente Llaguno was a blatant manipulation. Amateur video taken from a different angle and made public later showed no protesters on the southern part of Avenida Baralt while the chavistas fired.

The argument, presented as definitive on the film, is hardly enlightening. The film suggests, but does not quite say, that the opposition march had not yet reached Avenida Baralt at that point. It entirely glosses over the question of who shot the civilian marchers who were killed or wounded on the southern part of the avenue. Witness statements suggest the Llaguno Gunmen only got their guns after the shooting had started, and were filmed shooting well into the gun battle, while the opposition marchers who died appear to have fallen in the first few minutes of the shootout. One must regard the official excuse of the Llaguno gunmen – that it's okay because they were shooting at the opposition-led Metropolitan Police – as borderline nonsensical.

Then there was the confusing episode of the tank column filmed going from Fuerte Tiuna through the highway towards Miraflores Palace. If you saw The Revolution Will Not Be Televised, you'll recognize the scene, but you may be surprised to find out that contrary to the spin put on it by the film, the tank movements were not part of the coup.

---

[50] The Revolution Will Not Be Televised is a documentary about April 11th made by foreign filmmakers who happened to be inside Miraflores Palace during the time of the march and the subsequent coup. It has become an indispensable piece of propaganda for the Chávez government, encapsulating the chavista version of events that day. It has been carefully rebutted by opposition filmmakers and analysts, but the debate about the film rages on.

In fact, they were ordered by Chávez. The Ayala Tank Battalion was among the last to stay loyal to Chávez that evening, and they answered his call to surround the palace with military armor.

By the time the tanks reached Miraflores, the vast bulk of the army had risen up against Chávez, and there were reportedly threats to bomb the palace from the air, Pinochet-style. Of course, if you're facing an F-16 strike, a tank on the street is about as useful as an ashtray on a motorcycle, so the tanks really played no role. On advice from Havana, and owing no doubt also to his own psychological disposition, Chávez rejected the offer of martyrdom and gave himself up, showing up at *Fuerte Tiuna* wearing (illegally) his military field uniform.

Chaos in Fuerte Tiuna

At midday and through the afternoon, Rosendo and Vásquez Velasco had planned to go to Miraflores and tender their resignations to Chávez, explaining why they could not implement his orders in accordance to international human rights law – nothing more. But as the evening wore on, more and more active-duty military officers came forward to withdraw their support for the government and demand Chávez's resignation. The small conspiratorial cliques that had formed between military friends all burst into the open at once.

A reporter friend of mine actually went to *Fuerte Tiuna* that night to witness the toppling of the government as it happened. There was so much confusion at the fort that he was allowed to slip in and mingle with the assembling generals.

The story he tells is one of sheer confusion, with a bewildering array of generals milling around trying to decide what to do, while opposition civilians hung around different cubicles drafting God knows what on the PCs they could find. Chief among them: opposition "leading light" Allan Brewer Carias, together of course with Pedro Carmona and others, including even Orlando Urdaneta, a popular though extreme right-wing actor and comedian.

By the middle of the evening, private TV broadcasters were back on the air in Caracas, and the state-run TV channel had been abandoned by its chavista managers, fearing retribution. Amusingly, if you tuned in to Channel 8 that evening, you were faced with 30 year old nature documentaries about little ducklings...the last tape hastily thrown on the air as the managers ran.

As it became clearer and clearer that the government was in the process of falling, the Chávez regime started to "melt away." Any number of pro-Chávez officials and political activists went into hiding.

A confused set of negotiations ensued between Chávez and a now openly rebellious army. The conversations were complex, chaotic and confusing. By most accounts, Chávez agreed in principle to resign if he was guaranteed safe passage for himself and his entire family to Cuba. But splits between the rebellious officers were evident: one group, the pragmatists, wanted to just send him off into exile and start afresh. A second group, the maximalists, argued that Chávez should be tried in Venezuela for the afternoon's deaths and that, in any case, he could become a deeply destabilizing figure if allowed to flee to Cuba.

The military chain of command had gone all to hell, and the evening became a kind of civic-military free for all. Though nominally still in charge, Vásquez Velasco had lost control of the coup.

At around 2:40 a.m. on what was already April 12th, much of the nation was still glued to TV coverage of the crisis. Suddenly, one last cadena: General Lucas Rincón, the highest ranking general of the armed forces and a chavista loyal enough to have earned a third sun (equivalent to five stars in the US) despite never having fought a war, comes on the screen. He's flanked by what remains of the pro-Chávez high command of the Armed Forces.

Rincón read a prepared statement. Using an oddly convoluted formulation heavy in the passive voice that left unclear exactly who had done the asking, Rincón announced that President Chávez had been asked to resign, a request "which he accepted." ("La cual acectó ..." was the soon infamous formulation, mispronunciation and all) Rincón proceeded to tender his resignation together with that of the other pro-Chávez generals, leaving the change-of-president an apparently done deal. Celebrations rang out through the east of Caracas.

According to his later congressional testimony, Rincón then went to sleep.

(Bafflingly, Rincon remains a member of Chávez's inner. He was never disciplined for announcing – falsely – the president's resignation the entire country.)

By dawn, the best organized of the conspiratorial cliques managed to wrest control of the situation. Financed by a shadowy arms dealer by the name of Isaac Pérez Recao, the group included General Enrique Medina Gomez – at the time Venezuela's military attache in Washington DC - Allan Brewer Carias, right-wing lawyer Daniel Romero, Carmona, the top brass of the navy, and in particular Fedecámaras, the conservative National Chamber of Commerce.

Due largely to their long standing contacts with the late Cardinal Ignacio Velazco – then the influential head of the Catholic Church in Venezuela – they persuaded Vásquez Velasco to accept Pedro Carmona, head of Fedecámaras – as an interim president. Vásquez Velasco, eager to put the country back in civilian hands as soon as possible, accepted.

In the weeks following those events, this takeover by the right-wing conspirators came to be known as the 'coup-within-a-coup', and to my mind this remains the best way to describe what actually took place.

Who exactly controlled this group has been a subject of heated controversy ever since. Though Perez Recao took most of the blame, some well-informed sources are sure General Medina Gomez was the real boss. Certainly, Medina Gomez flew back from Washington to Caracas just days before the coup – a sign, to some, that the conspirators knew a day of reckoning was coming and they were working to put all their pieces in place before a showdown.

April 12th: The Carmonada

The day after the coup most people woke up to hear that Pedro Carmona would be the new president and he would make a statement on his course of action. Carmona had been one of the most prominent leaders in the anti-Chávez movement, so his appointment seemed almost natural to many. That morning, the private media refused to ask the evident question: who had chosen Carmona? And by what authority?

That same morning, the White House Press Secretary made a shocking pronouncement that has been used again and again to paint the Bush administration as co-conspirators of Perez Recao, Carmona and company.

As reported by CNN:

"Chávez supporters, on orders, fired on unarmed, peaceful demonstrators," White House press secretary Ari Fleischer said, referring to Thursday's violence that killed 12 people and wounded dozens more. "Venezuelan military and police refused to fire … and refused to support the government's role in human rights violations."

Fleischer's statement leaves out half the story. It wasn't only chavistas firing, but at that point in time, there was no way to find out who else had been firing in the mayhem. Nor could Fleischer be sure that the Chavistas were firing on those they appeared to be firing on. The second part of the statement is factually correct, though, and of course always conveniently left out of Bush-whacking accounts of the coup.

The second thing to notice is that Fleischer's main blunder was to speak prematurely. The White House statement was made several hours before Carmona's provisional government decree had been made public. The statement did not explicitly recognize the new government, largely because the new government had not yet been established.

Though it was retroactively read as a statement of support for Carmona's government, the White House statement preceded the Carmona decree. In fact, according to sources in Miraflores that day, the Carmona Decree hadn't even been finalized at the time Fleischer spoke. Ari jumped the gun. By speaking out of turn, he wrote a kind of blank check of US support for whatever Carmona might choose to do – a trust Carmona clearly didn't deserve.

Social hour in Miraflores

Back in Miraflores, the scene remained chaotic. On the one hand, dozens of job-hunting opposition politicians had turned up for a chance at the spoils. At the same time intense efforts were taking place behind the scenes to get Carmona to reconsider.

While chavista propagandists have associated the coupsters with far right-wing figures associated with Catholic groups like Opus Dei, the truth is more slippery. Though one prominent Opus Dei member, Pepe Rodriguez Iturbe, was named Foreign Minister, other Opus Dei-associated figures like Gustavo Linares Benzo were working to prevent Carmona's power play. In fact, Linares Benzo spent the day lobbying against Carmona's plans. He proposed a plan to ask the National Assembly to convene and, with Miquilenista votes, certify the "permanent absence" of the president from his post, paving the way to a constitutional transition. Linares Benzo's proposals garnered some support from the assembled, but Carmona doesn't seem to have seriously considered them.

Other political figures showed their mettle that day. Cecilia Sosa, the head of the *adeca encopetada* faction and former Chief Magistrate of the old pre-Chávez Supreme Court, is often seen as a bit of a right-wing extremist. That day, however, she had the law firmly in mind. Sosa faced Carmona down personally just minutes before he read out his decree, explaining to him bluntly that there was no imaginable legal basis for handing him the presidency.

"That has already been decided, Dr. Sosa, that has already been decided," is the only response she got from him.

The decree eventually drafted and read by Daniel Romero dripped with excesses. At one pen-stroke, on authority granted to them by no one, the decree shut down all federal institutions: the Supreme Tribunal, the National Assembly, all of them. It suspended 49 Chávez-imposed laws, and even changed the official name of the country back to the pre-Chávez "Republica de Venezuela."

In return, the decree pledged elections that Carmona would not participate in within one year. In the interim there would be a kind of legal void, with no elected institutions operating at the national level and nearly limitless power put in the hands of the interim president and an appointed "consultative board." Carmona then went on to swear himself in as "interim president," vowing to pave the way to the restoration of the validity of the Constitution – which is very different from pledging to obey it.

The antichavistas assembled in Miraflores that day cheered the decree wildly, intoxicated with the sense of victory. But the roster of people who sought to legitimize the decree by signing it was worrying. Most of them were hard right, business-class types. When the announcer called for "the representative of the Workers' Federation to come forward," no one turned up ... and for good reason. Alfredo Ramos, the only CTV member in the room, later explained that he refuses, on principle, to sign any document he hasn't read carefully beforehand.

First fissures appear

As Carmona signed his decree, Carlos Ortega, the head of the Venezuelan Workers' Federation, was 300 kilometers west in his home state of Falcón. Though Ortega and Carmona had acted as a team in leading the protest movement until April 11th, Carmona had distanced himself in the final 48 hours. By leaving, Ortega wanted to make it perfectly clear that he had no part in putting together the transitional government. This breakdown in the CTV-Fedecámaras alliance, at the most sensitive moment, may have been enough to doom the coup. So long as the anti-Chávez alliance could claim to speak for both employers and workers, it could plausibly represent the whole nation. With labor out of the equation, the movement was reduced to a business-led power play.

The situation in the barracks was not much better.

When Vásquez Velasco agreed to make Carmona president, he had naturally expected to earn the Defense Ministry in return. Instead, Carmona stunned the military by naming a Navy man as defense minister. Vice-admiral Hector Ramirez Perez was close to Carmona, Admiral Molina Tamayo and arms-dealer Perez Recao, but it was doubtful whether a Navy officer could really establish control of the army at such a delicate time. To his shock, Vásquez Velasco heard a rumor that Carmona was planning to send him out of the country, to serve as the military attaché in the Venezuelan Embassy in Madrid.

Perhaps because he was a Navy man, Ramirez Perez neglected some of the most basic elements of effective coup-plotting. Inexplicably, he made no effort to ensure loyal anti-Chávez troops took control of the Presidential palace. The pro-Chávez Presidential Guard of Honor regiment was left in place and in military control of Miraflores even as Carmona and his people moved in.

Moreover, the new regime had not shown itself overly concerned with calming the calls for revenge coming from some in the opposition side. The entire leadership of the Chavista government went underground, and a kind of witch-hunt broke down to find them, along with the shooters seen in the previous night's endlessly repeated video.

At some point, a rumor started making the rounds that Chávez's vice-President, Diosdado Cabello, had sought asylum at the Cuban embassy in Chuao. An angry mob was soon on the scene demanding his scalp.

The rumor was not true, but the crowd was belligerent, so the Cuban Ambassador, German Sánchez Otero, called the opposition mayor of the area, Henrique Capriles, to come and save his skin. This Capriles did, as best he could, in an emotionally-charged atmosphere. At the time, Sanchez Otero thanked him. Later, the government prosecuted and jailed Capriles for "leading the riots" outside the Cuban embassy that day.

Similarly, the mayor of Chacao, Leopoldo Lopez, had tried to protect Chávez's Interior Minister Ramón Rodríguez Chacín, who was arrested at an East-side apartment. An angry mob had gathered to witness the event: many tried to get punches in to Rodríguez Chacín as he was escorted into police vehicles. The footage was shown repeatedly on opposition news stations that day.

Other chavistas, like self-described Human Rights activist Tarek William Saab, were also arrested that day. In a show of democratic fortitude, a few anti-Chávez activists spent the day pleading with the Carmona authorities to release them. Teodoro Petkoff, Milagros Socorro, and Ruth Capriles need to be singled out for praise. It would have been far easier and more comfortable for them to look the other way that day. In fact, faced with the recent jailing of opposition activists, chavistas like Saab have shown how much easier it is to look the other way than to denounce injustices your own side perpetrates.

By the evening of April 12th, the coup was starting to unravel. Vásquez Velasco, stunned by the sweeping illegality of Carmona's regime, started to say out loud that in refusing Chávez's order the day before, he had intended to protect the Constitution, not to establish a de facto regime. The CTV continued to stay well away from Miraflores and rumors started to circulate more and more insistently that Chávez had not, in fact, resigned, and that no signed resignation letter existed.

By that evening, the US embassy was fully aware of what a blunder Fleischer's statement had been that morning. US Ambassador Charles Shapiro reportedly called Carmona to urge him to think again, particularly on the very sensitive matter of dissolving the elected National Assembly.

This is another key detail that's normally suppressed from standard the-US-did-it versions of the story. How you interpret this fact depends on your general attitude to US foreign policy, I suppose. But to me, if the Assembly had certified Chávez's absence, it would be hard to call this a coup – so Shapiro's call was, to my mind, an attempt to avert an illegal handover of power, to keep the process within constitutional bounds.

Pedro Carmona rejected Ambassador Shapiro, saying he could not be seen to backtrack on his first major decision. The following day, a desperately isolated Carmona would offer to reverse this position, agreeing to convene the National Assembly after all. By then, it was too late.

Carmona's biggest problem, though, was that he failed to obtain the one thing he needed to give his rule any semblance of legitimacy: a signed resignation letter. As the hours passed, and especially in pro-Chávez circles, rumors grew that Chávez had refused to sign a resignation letter and had therefore been kidnapped. It was the international media that carried this story first, in particular CNN, which even had a telephone interview from someone claiming to be Marisabel, Chávez's wife, denying her husband had resigned.

Had the Carmona clique worked to gain a broader base of support, had it not alienated so many potential allies so quickly, it might well have weathered this "bump in the road." But by the time Carmona realized he had to give way, it was already too late.

April 13th: The incredible shrinking coup

I woke up on the morning of April 13th to a puzzling anomaly. My clock radio woke me up to a nice spot about the history of the *arepa*. Since I was looking for news, I fiddled with the dial a bit – This Week in Baseball, dubbed, was on one station, a Catholic Mass on another, and so on.

I turned on the TV and found I had a choice between cartoons, a Major League Baseball game on channel 10, or canned day-old news on Globovisión.

Hmmm. "That's it then," I thought, "just 48 hours old and the coup's already stopped making headlines..." Politics, I mused, would be commendably boring under Carmona. At last...

But then the phone rang. It was my colleague Juana.

"*Chamo*, I don't like the way this is going down. The witch-hunt is still going on and suddenly there is no news ... who knows what's happening behind the scenes?! No *chamo*, I don't like it at all..."

Juana's call was my first intimation that the coup was in trouble. I started flipping through the radio dial more aggressively, and found absolutely no news on any station.

"What the hell?" I thought.

I had no way to know then that the infamous April 13th news blackout was on.

Late on the 12th, insiders could tell what the rest of the country could not: Carmona's de facto regime was in trouble. Word that Chávez had not, in fact, signed a resignation letter was spreading fast. Meanwhile, Carmona's pissing off of the Labor unions and much of the Army hierarchy was making it increasingly difficult for him to control the situation. Only the media, it seemed, remained solidly in the Carmonista camp.

It appears that on the afternoon of the 12th, Carmona had gathered together the nation's media owners and asked them, somewhat obliquely, to help ensure his government's stability. The owners understood the coded message clearly enough. Soon, all reporting of the collapsing coup was banned from the private media. During one of the most historically important dates in Venezuela's contemporary history, the TV channels and radio stations simply ignored the story – with the single, heroic exception of Radio Fe y Alegria, the Jesuit station, and the only station in Caracas to have broken the cartel that day.

The media owners were willing to do whatever it took to keep Chávez out of power – and believed, no doubt rightly, that their traditional influence over governance would be restored in a

Carmona regime. In this aspect, if in few others, "The Revolution Will Not Be Televised" actually gets the story right. The media elite owned the coup – and they showed themselves willing to abdicate their duty to inform in order to help sustain it.

Media owners would later claim that conditions were simply not safe enough to send their reporters out that day. As an excuse, it's not a very good one. Reporters are, by nature, aggressively curious people. Many were dying for permission to go out and report on the events of the day. Their bosses told them in no uncertain terms they could not. Some went out anyway, even going as far as to sneak into Miraflores Palace to cover Chávez's return against their editors' objections. In some cases, those editors refused to run the stories that resulted.[51]

Surely, the streets were dangerous that day, but it was hardly Beirut. There was rioting and looting in much of the city, especially in the far west, Petare and Chapellin. There were reports of Metropolitan Police excesses in trying to quell these disturbances, and I've heard stories of up to 50 looters shot dead, though it's impossible to be sure because – repeat after me - no serious investigation has ever been held.

The absence of news about the latest crises gave the situation a strange, other-worldly feel. To see your city burn is one thing. To see it burn and to see the media refuse to talk about it is quite another. The rumor mill went into unprecedented overdrive.

I was lucky that day. Since I was working as a freelancer, there was no boss around to stop me from going out and reporting, so I did. I'd heard rumors that Chavistas were congregating outside Fuerte Tiuna to demand the president's return. At about 11:30 am, Megan and I headed out with a video camera to see if we could talk to them. We somehow managed to find a taxi driver crazy enough to take us there, and we headed out.

---

[51] One intrepid reporter finding himself censored from reporting was Andres Izarra. Izarra's outrage became so famous he went on to become one of the Chief Propagandists of the Chávez government. He later served as Chávez spokesperson and, sometimes, Minister.

First we drove through downtown. The city was mostly deserted: very few cars, almost no pedestrians, and little groups of 5-15 chavistas on most corners holding pro-Chávez signs. Our cab driver radioed her colleagues to find out the situation in Catia, and quickly refused to take us there. "Too much shooting," she said. She agreed, however, to take us to Fuerte Tiuna.

As we crossed the tunnels on the way to the Fort, we got an up-close look at some of the west-side shantytowns. We saw the same thing we'd seen downtown. Small groups of people, in clumps of 5 or 10 or 15 at most, had come together on some corners to wave Venezuelan flags and hand-made signs demanding Chávez's return to power. Some cars honked at them in support.

Arriving at Fuerte Tiuna's main entrance was a bizarre experience. A set of three armored personnel carriers blocked the entrance, and a line of military police was deployed just in front of them. Behind the soldiers, there was a small but exceedingly emotional pro-Chávez crowd covering the highway overpass into Fuerte Tiuna. The crowd did not quite fill the overpass – to my untrained eye it looked to be about 1000 people or so.

They were, however, about as angry as I've ever seen anyone be angry. They were enraged at the blackout, and grateful for the chance to explain what was happening to a camera.

"We've been coming since yesterday. Yesterday the Metropolitan Police came in to disperse us … shooting. They left a whole bunch of people dead. But we're back now because Chávez is our president and we know he's being held hostage and we demand him back!" said one woman, tears rolling down her face.

We spent about an hour on that overpass, getting footage and talking to people. The atmosphere was tense and emotional – the soldiers really looked like they had no clue what they were doing there – but everyone was really nice to us. At about 1:30 we took a taxi back home. On the way, I scanned the radio for news again. Nothing.

Meltdown

By this time, the coup was crumbling fast. Most relevantly, General Vásquez Velasco had decided to strike back against the Carmona faction. In mid-afternoon he went on the air to read a communiqué. I think it's worth quoting it at length, because it really is quite an extraordinary document:

On April 11th, the Army issued an institutional statement with regards to the casualties generated that day, due to the unwillingness to open dialogue on the part of the President of the Republic and his government. Civil society, rich and poor together, marched peacefully and were repressed by the forces of order and attacked by sharpshooters around Miraflores Palace.

"The army was ordered to place tanks on the streets, without the consent of the Commander of the Army (i.e. Vásquez Velasco himself, speaking in the third person). This could not be tolerated, because it would have caused thousands of deaths. Our statement on April 11th was institutional and geared against the actions of the government. It was loyal to constitutional norms and consistent with democratic institution. It was not a military coup perpetrated by the army.

As Commander of the Army, together with the high command and many other officers, we send a message of calm to the people of Venezuela and we inform them that the army is working hard to correct errors and omissions made in this transition. We therefore make the following demands:

1. Establish a transition based on the 1999 constitution, the applicable laws, and respect for human rights.

2. Eliminate the Transitional Government decree of April 12th, 2002.

3. Reconvene the National Assembly.

4. Seek consensus with all the social forces in the nation to constitute a transition government that is representative and marked by pluralism.

We issue a call to peace and calm, and for every government action to be carried out with maximum respect for human rights...

We demand the construction of a society without exclusion, where any protest or disquiet can be manifested peacefully, without weapons, and with the full exercise of liberty within the rule of law...

We guarantee the security and the respectful treatment of Lieutenant Colonel Hugo Chávez and his family. We urge the authorities to comply with Lieutenant Colonel Chávez request to leave the country immediately and we demand live TV images of Lieutenant Colonel Chávez be broadcast immediately.

We the members of the Armed Forces guarantee the security of all the people of Venezuela.

Mayor General Efrain Vásquez Velasco

Commander of the Venezuelan Army

Some fascist he is, huh?

There are several things to note about the statement. First of all, it makes a mockery of those who would equate April 11th, 2002 with Chile's September 11th, 1973. One struggles to picture General Pinochet signing a declaration like this one. More clearly than any other document from that weekend, the statement makes it clear that, whatever April 11th-14th was, it was not a traditional Latin American *coup d'etat.*

The other thing to note was that, in some ways, the statement is the public start of the counter-coup. In many ways, General Vásquez Velasco made both the key decision in toppling Chávez and the key decision in reinstating him.

Hearing the statement, Carmona finally realized his rule was untenable. He went on TV late in the afternoon to pledge to reverse course and, in particular, convene the National Assembly – which had become the key litmus test of respect for the constitution.

By that point, it was way too late. The plan to bring Chávez back was already well underway.

The Return

Sensing that the coup was faltering, two key pro-Chávez army officers stepped forward, General Jorge Garcia Carneiro and General Raul Baduel.[52] Together, they put together an "Operation Restore Dignity" – to return Chávez to Miraflores. No one dared to fight them on this.

Garcia Carneiro was, at the time, head of the army division based in Fuerte Tiuna. He never acquiesced to the coup, though some claim he chickened out badly at one point. Story has it that on the 13th, Garcia Carneiro managed to get out of Fuerte Tiuna in a light tank which he drove through the west-side slums, urging people to rise up and restore Chávez. Garcia Carneiro has since been given his "third sun" and, despite a mediocre military record, he's now Defense Minister.

The second, more influential player was Baduel, the head of the Paratroop Brigade based in Maracay, about 150 kilometers west of Caracas. Baduel is an old friend of Chávez. In April 2002, he commanded the brigade Chávez once belonged to. Journalists who have made it into his office are always amazed by the smell of incense and the eastern religious paraphernalia he keeps around. Baduel makes no attempt to hide it: he's a proud, practicing Daoist.

Baduel had been close to Chávez for many years. He participated in the infamous 1982 *Saman de Güere* conspiratorial oath, pledging to work together for a revolution. The general soon made it clear he would not cooperate with Carmona's *de facto* regime. This is significant because the 43rd Paratrooper Brigade is by far the best equipped and best trained fighting force in the Venezuelan army, by most accounts the *only* well-equipped and properly-trained fighting force in the army. Baduel set about coordinating the operation to first locate Chávez and then bring him back to Miraflores.

---

[52] Both officers were rewarded later in the Chávez government with high-ranking government positions. However, after a few years, Baduel fell out with the government and is currently in jail, with some regarding him as a political prisoner. García Carneiro remains a loyal chavista, and is currently the governor of Vargas.

Baduel's move changed the military equation decisively. The rest of the army quickly understood that, to make the coup stand, they would have to shoot it out with the Paratrooper Brigade, something nobody wanted to do. Since Carmona had already alienated most of his natural base of support by then, the rest of the army was loathe to fight and die for him. Baduel's decision to back Chávez essentially closed the deal without firing a single shot.

Carmona never had a chance to react. By the time he realized that the Presidential Honor Guard, the Caracas Army Division and the Paratroopers were all working to bring back Chávez, his support was too narrow to stage any kind of fight back. In the afternoon, a pro-Chávez crowd began to assemble outside Miraflores. Soon enough, Carmona caught on that the Honor Guard would not act to disperse them. In a frightful hurry, he and his people abandoned Miraflores, leaving behind stacks of agendas and documents that the chavistas deeply enjoyed reading over the following weeks. Lists of potential Carmonista ministers left behind in the rush have been used again and again by the government to tar those listed in them.

As the coup collapsed, more and more chavistas felt emboldened to come out onto the streets. By 10:00 p.m. a decent crowd had gathered in front of Miraflores Palace – about four blocks' worth of Avenida Urdaneta, according to eye-witnesses. Certainly, it's quite impressive to turn out 30,000 people with no official organization and in dangerous circumstances. The hardest of Caracas' hardcore chavistas sure did turn out: they were not about to miss the momentous occasion of Chávez's phoenix-like return to power.

But even when the chavistas get it right, they have to go and ruin it with crazy exaggerations. Instead of embracing the 40,000 outside Miraflores that night, Chávez went on to claim that as many as 8 million people had come out on the streets that day. In official chavista lore, it was this massive people-power outburst of solidarity that brought Chávez back to power. Alarmingly, I've seen more than one foreign correspondent buy this line, which is demonstrably wrong.

The 8 million figure is not even believable as a send-up. Not only is the estimate at least two orders of magnitude too large, but it gets the causality backwards: Chávez did not return because the crowds came out, the crowds came out because they realized Chávez was about to return. The key decisions – both to remove Chávez and to reinstate them – were taken behind closed doors by high-ranking military men.

At about 8:00 pm, the situation turned nastier. Incensed at the absence of news coverage that day, pro-Chávez civilian groups – the famous *Círculos Bolivarianos* – activated a plan to stick it to the private channels. Riding around in swarms of motorcycles, they started touring the studios of the main TV channels, throwing stones through the windows and shooting into the buildings sporadically. The media switched, within minutes, from showing schlocky American made-for-TV movies to covering what was happening directly outside their doors. For over two hours, they cowered in terror, using the airwaves to ask for someone, anyone to come and protect them. But with Carmona having already lost control of the situation, the military chain of command had collapsed all over again. There seemed to be no one around with the authority or the desire to order the National Guard to step in and stop the violence.

By 10:00 pm or so, word got around that although the Venezuelan channels had no real news, Colombia's Radio Caracol and CNN en Español had coverage of the crisis. Since Caracol comes through the satellite-dish system in Caracas, once again the city was split between the dish-owners, who had access to information, and everyone else.

By 11:00, Radio Caracol had made it clear that the coup had comprehensibly unraveled and that Chávez was on his way back to Miraflores. The Venezuelan stations only announced as much after midnight. In an interview I'll never forget, a terrified Pedro Penzini Fleury interviewed hardcore pro-Chávez National Assemblymember Cilia Flores on UnionRadio, and I swear at one point he half-apologized to her for having overthrown her government. It was surreal.

By 3:00 a.m. the following morning, the chavistas had retaken Miraflores and symbolically swore-in Chávez's vice-president, Diosdado Cabello, as head of state. A few hours later, Chávez returned to Miraflores to an ecstatic reception from his followers. Even the most recalcitrant anti-chavista journalists I know who were at Miraflores for the event own up that it was a moving, exciting experience. "That day," one of them told me, "it doesn't matter how escuálido you thought you were. When you saw the faces on the people outside Miraflores as Chávez got out of that helicopter, you could not help but be a chavista."

A chastised Chávez gave an early morning speech, thanking his supporters and pledging to change, to *really* change after this experience. He promised to govern inclusively, and to bring critics on board.

The good intentions did not last long, but the promises fanned speculation that certain conditions had been imposed on Chávez before he had returned to office, including chiefly a change in tone. Consonant with the conditioned-return theory is the fact that the president has never again been seen illegally wearing his military uniform – a key source of friction within the army.[53]

Taking stock

This is what I know about what happened that weekend. Clearly, many questions remain unanswered, mostly because – have I mentioned this yet? – no proper investigation has ever been held.

It's worth dwelling on this a bit longer because, more than anything that happened on April 11th-14th, it's the government's subsequent unwillingness to investigate the events that seems most damning to me. Certainly, they were urged to investigate credibly from, quite literally, the very first day after Chávez's return.

On April 15th, Teodoro Petkoff wrote this in his Simon Boccanegra column:

---

[53] This is no longer true. Chávez uses military regalia regularly.

"The killings on April 11th around Miraflores Palace must not remain a mystery. Those responsible must be taken before the courts. But to find them, an investigation has to be headed by a sort of 'truth commission,' an absolutely impartial body trusted by all. In this war of accusations and counter-accusations, it's the government that stands to gain the most from a Truth Commission because suspicion today falls most strongly on some of its backers. The Prosecutors' Office must, of course, carry out its duties, but just like in some Central American countries and Argentina and Chile, the official institutions should act in parallel with a Truth Commission in order to clear up any doubt about what happened. No investigation carried out only by official institution, regardless of the evidence they put forward, will be credible. National reconciliation can only be achieved through justice, not revenge. The basis for justice is truth."

Two days later, he added:

"Everyone understands that only an impartial investigation will be credible to everyone. Turning this page, not allowing this despicable episode to turn into a tumor that attacks the entire future political life of this deeply divided country, will only be possible by establishing the truth and prosecuting those responsible for what happened."

And on April 18th, he wrote:

"What we had feared has started to happen. The sad events of April 11th have already been turned into projectiles tossed back and forth between the various political parties, who accuse each other of responsibility for the deaths. Instead of waiting for the result of an investigation from a Truth Commission, in Parliament each side went straight for "its" videos and "its" photos to sustain "its" truth. This road is totally barren and, from the start, demonstrates an unwillingness to get to the truth. Each side seems to want to keep the affair in a cloud of uncertainty, seeking to keep the events confusing enough to use as a political argument in future debates. This would be a calamity for the country."

It was only one week after this piece that prosecutors finally moved in to "secure" the crime scene. By then, most of the evidence was gone, obviously.

Writing just a week after the massacre, Teodoro showed why he is the only political analyst in Venezuela today whose judgment one can trust unreservedly. Today, almost two years later, the country has seen neither a Truth Commission nor an impartial investigation. Just as Teodoro predicted, the deaths have turned into an inscrutable mystery, poisoning an already tense political atmosphere. Physical evidence of the crimes on Avenida Baralt was allowed to decay for two weeks before *Fiscalía* experts showed up to secure it. By then, much of the evidence – bullet cases, broken windows, etc. – had been cleared away.

Meanwhile, the Puente Llaguno gunmen have been repeatedly feted by the president as "heroes of the revolution." The only people being actively investigated for murder for the events of April 11th are the Metropolitan Policemen who tried to keep the sides apart on Avenida Baralt.[54]

Just as Teodoro predicted a week after the events, the deaths from April 11th have become a political Molotov cocktail, a weapon used by each side to blame the other. In the hands of openly chavista prosecutors like Danilo Anderson, the investigation into the affair is a mockery, a slap in the face for those who were killed and wounded that day.[55]

Barely bothering to hide his partiality, Anderson first motioned to move the Llaguno Gunmen trial to Aragua State – a hotbed of judicial chavismo – and, not surprisingly, did not manage to convict any of them of anything. While Richard Peñalver walks the streets as a revolutionary hero and vows to continue to defend the revolution "with my hands, or whatever I may have in my hands", Henrique Capriles dodges an arrest warrant for trying to stop a riot outside the Cuban embassy the following day.

By now, it's doubtful whether the crimes of April 2002 can ever be solved. Barring a spectacular revelation by an insider, it's hard to

---

[54] The policemen and the commanders in charge of the force have since been convicted to thirty years in prison for their alleged crimes.

[55] Anderson himself was killed by a car bomb on 18 November 2004, a few months after this post went up. His murder was never fully solved.

imagine how even the best investigator could get to the bottom of this. It's what the government wanted.

As new cases of political violence are registered in Caracas, the government remains committed to its April Crisis game-plan when facing opposition accusations of violence: first, appoint a politically motivated prosecutor (preferably Anderson); second, wait, third, carry out a flawed investigation; fourth, convict no one. The result has been systematic impunity for anyone who acts in the name of the revolution.

The other purpose of this essay was to clear up what we know about the role of the US in this mess. I believe that US influence was decidedly marginal. The political forces tearing Venezuela's society apart were strong enough to account for what took place. The assertions of US involvement in the coup that I've seen are mostly matters of speculation or dogma, and they never seem to be based on a specific hypothesis about what the US did, when, and how.

Proving that, several months before, some US-funded organizations had given money to some of the people who were eventually involved in the coup is simply not good enough. And Chavista allegations that US Navy ships operated inside Venezuelan territorial waters hardly clear matters up: if it's so, what was their role? What were they doing? What, specifically, did the CIA do to aid the coupsters? (or the coupsters-within-a-coup?) What are the mechanics of US involvement?

I've never read a plausible answer to those questions. This is not to say the US was not involved, merely that I've never seen a good reason to think the gringos *were* involved. As a rule, those who allege US involvement seem far more interested in bashing American foreign policy than in understanding the complex events of that weekend. Plan Ávila, for instance, is never mentioned, and the cadena-during-a-massacre is always glossed over. In fact, only evidence that tends to suggest US involvement is trotted out, everything else is suppressed. This kind of selective forgetting is, to my mind, a distinguishing feature of political propaganda.

To my mind, the bulk of the evidence suggests that the decision to remove Chávez was made by the Venezuelan Army under quite unprecedented circumstances, and the decision to bring Chávez back was also made by the Venezuelan Army under quite unprecedented circumstances. Others are entitled to interpret events differently, but they must do so on the basis of evidence rather than ideological assertion.

Six years on: Usón's April 11th
Posted on April 11, 2008 by Quico

On my trip to Caracas, I picked up a copy of "Opinion Prisoner: General Usón Speaks." It's a book of interviews with Chávez's former Finance Minister and jailbird Francisco Usón, by Agustín Blanco Muñoz. What follows is drawn from Usón's recollections of the evening of April 11th, 2002.

There was a gun on Chávez's office table. A pack of cigarettes and a lighter, an ashtray with some stubs in it, an empty cup of coffee, and a gun. That's the detail that sticks out in General Francisco Usón's memories of going to Miraflores to resign his post as Finance Minister. It was about 8:30 p.m. on April 11th, 2002.

It's not the only detail, of course. He remembers people crying in the halls of Miraflores, army officers running from one place to the other like chickens with their heads cut off. He remembers Jose Vicente Rangel hanging about the scene like a sleepwalker, muttering to himself again and again that Chávez must not resign, that handing over power was unthinkable, that it had to be avoided at all cost, in a kind of loop, like a drunk you meet on an El Silencio sidewalk late at night. And he remembers Chávez's vacant, disoriented expression, how nervous he seemed, how it was impossible to tell if he was actually listening to you as you talked, the way his own speech bordered on the incoherent. The Chávez Usón saw that evening was despondent, defeated.

Mostly, though, he remembers that gun.

It couldn't have been for self-defense. When you keep a gun for protection you keep it in a holster, on your body. Usón, like Chávez, is an army man; it's not the kind of detail either of them would miss. A gun sitting on top of a table like that ... it was only ever going to be used for one thing.

The thought alarmed Usón. He was seriously worried that if something happened to Chávez that night, the country would careen toward civil war. He was concerned enough to consign his own handgun to one of the President's bodyguards before going in to see him. He even raised the importance of keeping Chávez safe as he resigned and, on his way out, went as far as to have a quiet word with one of Chávez's bodyguards, to plead with him to hide that gun when he got a chance because "nothing must happen to Chávez."

That glimpse of a suicidal Chávez is not one Usón would forget. At 8:30 p.m. on April 11th, 2002, Hugo Chávez genuinely thought his gig was up.

From Miraflores, Usón headed straight to the fifth floor of the Army General Command Center in Fuerte Tiuna, where he ran into the chaotic conspiratorial *verbena* so many others have also described.[56] The collapse of the chain of command was obvious to him right away. In the middle of the biggest military crisis Venezuela had seen in half a century, some of the assembled generals were drinking whisky.

General Efraín Vásquez Velasco, whom everyone looked to for leadership, was way out of his depth. He was the army's highest ranking officer, and the hierarchy-minded military men around him were naturally waiting for his orders. But Vásquez Velasco hadn't thought things through. He hadn't planned ahead, hadn't *conspired*. Needless to say, planning is critical to the success of a coup, and the guy everyone was looking to for leadership just hadn't done any.

Worse yet, the guys who *had* planned were pushing a disastrous scheme to impose Pedro Carmona as President. In fact, Carmona's

---

[56] A verbena is a Venezuelan version of a street fair.

presence at army headquarters that night was one of the first anomalies Usón noticed. The officers backing him – led by General Medina Gómez and Vice-Admiral Ramírez Pérez – commanded no troops. *"No mandaban ni en su casa,"* is how Usón puts it. And they weren't senior enough in the military hierarchy to tell Generals Vásquez Velasco and Alfonzo Martínez what to do.

The real "power vacuum" that night wasn't in Miraflores, it was in Fuerte Tiuna. The army leadership was making it up as they went along, trying to run a coup "by consensus." In those circumstances, it wasn't hard for the real plotters to outmaneuver the hapless top brass.

Well before midnight, General Rosendo (who'd just resigned as Head of the Armed Forces Unified Command) and General Hurtado Sucre (the Infrastructure Minister) go to Miraflores to negotiate with Chávez a handover of power. Very quickly, Chávez agrees to resign, but only if he is guaranteed safe passage to Cuba for himself and his family. It is his only condition. Rosendo and Hurtado make the deal.

But the situation is fluid back in Fuerte Tiuna. Alliances shift by the minute, and Vásquez Velasco fails to stamp his authority and impose a single course of action. So, as they try to work out the details, Rosendo and Hurtado find themselves negotiating under a constantly changing mandate. They keep having to call Fuerte Tiuna to get ever-changing instructions.

This gives Chávez the first hint that he may not be as screwed as he'd figured. He asks to speak with Vásquez Velasco directly. They speak on the phone several times throughout the night. When Vásquez Velasco speaks to the President, he goes into a small office by himself, so nobody can overhear what he's saying. The conversations continue through the night.

Little by little, Chávez starts to put 2 and 2 together. At 12:30, he calls Usón directly on his mobile and asks what's taking so long, why he isn't on a plane to Cuba yet. It's the first of six conversations between the two that night. Gradually, Chávez comes to understand it's all a bit of a bluff. Years later, in his prison cell, General Usón will have plenty of time to wonder whether he inadvertently tipped off Chávez. Maybe it was those phone calls that made Chávez realize that nobody was in overall command in Fuerte Tiuna.

Back at army headquarters, one faction has gotten into its head that sending Chávez to Cuba would be a disaster. From there, the guy would destabilize any new government, and besides, the blood that flowed down Baralt Avenue that afternoon was on his hands, and he should be held accountable. Another faction argues that it's lunacy to think you can jail a guy passionately supported by 40 to 50% of the population. Characteristically, Vásquez Velasco fails to step in and resolve the dispute.

As the early morning wears on, General Rommel Fuenmayor calls Chávez and threatens to order tanks and Air Force planes to bomb Miraflores if he doesn't leave power within ten minutes. But Fuenmayor is an army officer – and one without troops under his command at the time.[57] Fuenmayor had no authority over the Air Force or over any tanks. In the end, his threat only underscores the extent to which the military chain of command has gone to hell.

By the early morning hours of April 12th, the dazed, suicidal Chávez of the previous evening is just a memory. Sensing the weakness in the generals' position, he's well and truly snapped out of it and gone on Full Survival Mode. After all, if there's one subject he genuinely is a bit of an expert on, it's military conspiracies ... and how to survive them when they go wrong.

Just before 4:00 a.m., Chávez decides to go to Fuerte Tiuna to negotiate directly with the army brass. This is a detail that's been lost to history: Chávez doesn't *submit* to an army order to go to Fuerte Tiuna, he *decides* to go there. He needs to be there to confirm his suspicions about the coupsters' disorganization. He goes flanked by his head of security and the head of the Casa

---

[57] At the time, Fuenmayor was in charge of CAVIM, the state-owned army munitions manufacturer.

Militar.[58]Both are armed and still loyal to him. Amid the confusion, nobody finds anything strange about that.

Once he gets there, Chávez quickly confirms what he'd suspected. Rather than being met by a single officer with a single negotiating position, Chávez faces a petit comité of *militares alzados*.

They demand that he sign a resignation letter. He asks about safe passage to Cuba. They start backsliding. Suddenly, they won't guarantee that he can get out of the country right away. Chávez notes that this is not the deal he'd agreed to. He realizes his choice now is between being a head of state who's illegally detained, and being a former head of state who's legally detained. So he refuses, point blank, to sign the letter.

And the generals don't have the first fucking clue what to do next.

For General Usón, what follows is a turning point in the crisis. Faced with Chávez's refusal, the assembled generals make a decision that lays bare all their weaknesses: they excuse themselves and go off to the next room to argue about what to do next. Any pretense of being an organized force executing a carefully considered plan collapses right then and there, right in front of Chávez's eyes.

That is the instant when Chávez's fight back begins in earnest. Chávez senses that if they don't obtain a signed resignation letter, they cannot count on the support of the Maracay garrison or the junior officers nationwide, the ones in direct contact with the troops. A bit of bravado at a key moment completely throws the generals off their game and exposes how ramshackle their entire operation is. With his own eyes, he realizes the have no plan B.

Within minutes, the generals are back merely reiterating their demand that he sign, trying to intimidate him into complying.

---

[58] The Casa Militar is the presidential protection garrison. It is headquartered in Palacio Blanco, across the street from Miraflores Palace.

Even Usón, who spent years in jail due to a presidential whim and hates Chávez's guts, is forced to recognize his courage and cunning at that critical moment.

Over the following 24 hours, plenty of other mistakes would greatly aid his fight back – the Carmonada obviously being the biggest one. But it was the realization that he could send all their plans into a tailspin just by refusing to play along which made his fight back viable.

The real irony, considering the turn official rhetoric would take in the months and years to follow, is that only because April 11th *wasn't* the product of a well-planned, carefully orchestrated conspiracy – that's the main reason Chávez beat the coup.

Seeing April 11th with fresh eyes
Posted on April 11, 2010 by Quico

On the eighth anniversary of the April 11th, 2002 coup, Brian Nelson – author of the most carefully researched history of the April Crisis in print today - contributes this reflection on what happened that day:[59]

Some days you just can't think about what's happening in Venezuela. It's too depressing. But if you are reading this, then today is not one of those days for you. And that's something. Because today is the anniversary of the coup that briefly ousted Hugo Chávez in 2002. It's a time to reflect, to remember, re-see the coup, especially if you were in Venezuela at the time. I know it isn't easy, but it's important. It's important to make yourself look.

I've heard it said that everyone was a chavista once. Well, April 11th is the reason I switched from being a Chávez supporter to a critic.

I could tell (very early on, in fact) by the way that the government reacted to the coup — the way it suspended the truth

---

[59] Nelson's book, "The Silence and the Scorpion," constitutes the most detailed look at the April 11th events.

commission, fired detectives and prosecutors, by its political spin—
that it had something to hide. I wanted to find out what. Then, in
the process of talking to eyewitnesses and the families of victims,
something happened. It became very personal.

I don't mean that in a Dirty Harry way; it's not about payback. I
mean it in the way that sets a headline ("19 dead, 150 wounded")
apart from something that touches you, deeply, to the point that you
cannot look away or forget.

That's what happens when you meet five, ten, fifteen people
who have been shot. When you meet the parents of teenagers who
were killed...parents who have no legal recourse, no way to find
justice. It changes you. Especially when you go back and interview
each of them four and five times and you find all your skepticism
and detachment melting away. If you decide to let it in, then it will
change you, too. (Not letting it in is safer, and maybe even smarter.)

If you've read my book, then you know I think it is important to
understand events from all possible perspectives and that I, of
course, empathize with the victims on both sides. I even understand
why the government did what it did to stop the march. Yet a line
must still be drawn. To empathize is not to condone actions that are
clearly wrong.

So what is the Chávez government hiding? Why, eight years
later, have we had no truth commission, no independent
investigation, and why does the government refuse to admit any
delegation from the Inter-American Commission of Human Rights?
[60]

It took a very long time to figure it out—to sort through the
piles of seemingly random video clips, photographs, and
newspaper articles—to make any sense out of it. Honestly, if you'd
told me how long it was going to take when I started, I would have
given up.

---

[60] The Venezuelan government has since withdrawn from the Interamerican
Commission on Human Rights, as well as the Interamerican Court for Human
Rights.

But little by little, April 11th sucked me in; and little by little I put the pieces together. Three years into my researching and writing I would still occasionally hit a critical turning point—an "ah-ha" moment—when three, four, or five different pieces all suddenly fit together.

One of those moments was figuring out who had been killed first and where they had been shot from—critical pieces for interpreting all that would follow.

Many of the first eyewitnesses that I interviewed thought that the photographer Jorge Tortoza (who was at the head of the opposition march) was the first fatality. It was hard to know because often within seconds of being shot, many victims were picked up by friends and bystanders and carried away.

Two important sources convinced me that another opposition marcher, Jesús Arellano, had been killed first, just a few minutes before Jorge Tortoza. One source was a Chávez supporter, Douglas Romero, who accidentally wound up in the anti-Chávez crowd and witnessed the killing of Jesús Arellano first, then Tortoza. The other piece of evidence was Tortoza's camera—his last shots were of the dying Arellano. Discovering that Arellano was the first fatality was enormously important because his death was captured on film and he was clearly shot from the pro-Chávez crowd.

Pro-Chávez militants killed the first victim. The video evidence is clear. The first casualties were shot neither from the top of Puente Llaguno nor by snipers on rooftops, as conventional wisdom would come to believe, but rather from street level, from Avenida Baralt itself, just before 2:30 p.m. – when the two groups were much closer to each other than they would be for the rest of the day.

Of course, the fact that the first fatalities were caused by the pro-Chávez gunmen has tremendous implications for the ensuing coup. It completely undermines the government's narrative about a premeditated plan on the part of the opposition to cause violence as a pretext for a military intervention.

Another "ah-ha" moment was the realization that the National Guard must have been ordered not to interfere with the Bolivarian Circles as they repelled the march on Baralt Avenue.

The Venezuelan government and its apologists have tried very hard to cover this up, depicting the violence as something beyond anyone's control. For example, Greg Wilpert of Venezuelanalysis, wrote, "Chávez could rely on only a small handful of National Guard troops, who stopped the opposition's advance on two of the three streets leading to Miraflores." Baralt Avenue, where the majority of the deaths occurred, was the third street that Wilpert refers to, suggesting that if there had only been more National Guard troops, then things would not have turned so ugly.

But Wilpert is misinformed. Not only were there plenty of National Guard troops around Miraflores that day, but they were actually deployed, en masse, on Baralt Avenue. They sat there all afternoon, watching a four-hour gun battle and doing nothing to stop it. This brings new credence to reports that Chávez and his cabinet had discussed deploying the Bolivarian Circles in conjunction with the National Guard four days before the march.

It was an anti-Chávez marcher, Andrés Trujillo, who first told me that he had seen National Guard troops standing on the side streets of Baralt Avenue, and that those troops prevented people from getting out of the crossfire. I had been skeptical at first, but then a pro-Chávez eyewitness, Carolina Campos, told me the same thing.

Searching through the thousands of photographs I had stored up, I eventually found pictures of these troops. There they were, right on Baralt Avenue, sometimes only feet from the pro-Chávez gunmen, and they did nothing to stop the violence. They didn't help the police and they didn't hinder the pro-Chávez gunmen.

These are two just two important pieces of the April 11 puzzle. Obviously there are many more, and many involve criminal activity from the opposition, too. But it is clear that it is the Chávez government who has the most to hide and the most to lose from an independent investigation.

In many ways, the government's reaction to the violence is much more telling than the violence itself. The government had a choice: it could have jailed the gunmen and National Guard troops who were caught on film and in photographs shooting at the marchers. This would have provided some reconciliation for the victims and proven that the government applies the law equally to all citizens.

It did not choose that route. Instead, it began building up lies on top of lies to protect itself.

I suspect that the government feels that it has to lie, simply because the stakes are so high. After all, former Venezuelan president Carlos Andrés Pérez was impeached simply for sending campaign funds to a candidate in Nicaragua. How would Chávez look if a proper investigation were held into the violence on April 11th? This is another reason why keeping control of the National Assembly is so important. Rest assured that Chávez has thought of this. I'm sure he's also thought of former Peruvian President Alberto Fujimori, who is in jail for complicity in the killing of his opponents in Peru.

Obviously, many things are driving Hugo Chávez — his ardent belief in socialism, his distrust of the United States and the West, and his desire to become a legendary figure who can unite Latin America at least as well as his political muse, Simón Bolívar. But as someone who has studied Chávez's record on human rights, I believe his fear of incarceration is also a factor. His repeated (and finally successful) attempts to change the constitution to allow for his indefinite re-election may be viewed through this lens. Yes, Hugo Chávez wanted to end term limits so that his revolution could continue, but I believe he also wanted to end term limits to protect himself from prosecution should he lose power.

It's a crazy thing, April 11th. Eight years later it's still with us in the headlines. It's the reason Zuloaga was arrested and the excuse that Chávez will likely give when Globovisión is finally shut down.[61] Yet it is an event that most people still know very little about. I mean, what really happened down there, around Miraflores? We are still trying to put the pieces together a little bit at a time.

This strike doesn't have a chance
Posted on November 25, 2002 by Quico

The big news these days is that, last week, the *Coordinadora Democrática* (the big umbrella group that speaks for maybe 95% of the opposition) called a General Strike for next Monday, December 2nd. It's all anyone talks about around here, especially since they didn't specify how long the strike will go on for – and they've let it be known it could drag on indefinitely. I think up until now the *Coordinadora* has done a pretty good job of representing the opposition responsibly and within the spirit of democracy. But this time, I think they've gone off the deep end.

Why? Well, first and foremost because the strike will fail.

It's totally nuts to call an indefinite strike in the middle of the holiday shopping season: too many retailers and industrialists rely on December sales to balance their books for the year – especially after a disaster of a year like 2002 has been. Asking them to give up a week's worth of holiday sales seems totally crazy to me. They won't go along, couldn't go along, will go bankrupt if they go along…it's asking them to jump into some sort of sacrificial pyre for the sake for very uncertain results.

The strike's only hope for success is if the opposition can shut down the oil industry. And while many executives and managers at PDVSA seem ripe for protest, it's very doubtful whether the blue-collar workforce, fresh from signing a very lucrative collective bargaining agreement, will go along. Can you run a giant oil company for a week without any managers? I don't know the

---

[61] Guillermo Zuloaga is the partial owner of Globovisión. He was arrested in 2010, and promptly fled the country.

answer to that question, but I bet it's something along the lines of "not very well, but kind of."

The *Coordinadora* leaders claim they're just following their followers: to hear them tell it, the grass-roots pressure for some kind of radical move against Chávez is just too strong to ignore.

I hear that and I just have to shake my head: I have no doubt that among a very small, highly radicalized, militantly anti-chavista slice of the business class, there are probably some very loud voices calling for a strike. And credible polls do show that most people support a strike in the abstract. But from that to saying that there's a deafening national roar for a strike there's a big gap, and I suspect what's really going on here is that most *Coordinadora* members only talk to other *Coordinadora* members, setting up a little resonance chamber where radical anti-chavismo is taken as the only sane way of thinking. Locked up inside this circle, the *Coordinadora's* leadership has managed to convince itself that its views are a reflection of a huge popular groundswell. I don't buy it.

Of course many, *many* Venezuelans are very, *very* angry at Chávez. But 9 out of 10 Venezuelan households live on less than the $750/month it takes to purchase the Basic Consumption Basket – the government's estimates of the basic goods and services you need for an adequate middle-class life. With that many people struggling to make ends meet, and with so many who just don't earn enough to even feed themselves and their families properly, an open-ended general strike seems like lunacy.

For the upper class and upper-middle class people who lead the *Coordinadora,* calling a strike will not mean going hungry, but for millions of the people they claim to lead it does. And it's precisely that tone-deafness towards the needs and conditions of the poor that made the poor angry enough at them to elect Chávez in the first place. I dunno, I just think that by calling a strike the *Coordinadora* shows just how out of touch it is with the material conditions that most Venezuelans live under, and does nothing at all to reassure the poor that a *Coordinadora*-led government would be even a little bit concerned about their needs.

Still, the strike need not happen. The *Coordinadora* has made it quite clear that if the Elections Authorities call a national referendum on Chávez's rule before Monday, they'll call off the strike. I'm praying CNE plays along, thus saving the *Coordinadora* from itself. At that point, the strike can be kept in reserve, as a threat against the government should it even think to do anything to block a vote.

If the government did block a vote, a strike – while still far more socially painful than the *Coordinadora* leaders seem to realize – would at least be somewhat more defensible. And while it's easy to sympathize with the seething anger people feel when they see Chávez openly mock the two-million+ signatures gathered to back up the request for a consultative referendum, I don't see how the way to confront that is applying a tactic that condemns millions of people to real hardship.

Instead, it seems like a sure-fire strategy for alienating the people we should be trying to win over.

12:45 am: The Carter shuffle swings into action
Posted on August 16, 2004 by Quico

Past midnight, and the mood in the opposition is exultant.[62] The real question now is how the government will deal with the staggering defeat they're being dealt. Will they grin and bear it, or are there more tricks to come?

Union Radio reports that President Carter has just left Opposition headquarters at the Tamanaco Hotel and is headed towards the National Electoral Council. This is crunch time, *la hora de la chucurrucuticas*. The next few hours are critical.

---

[62] This post was written late in the night following the unsuccessful Recall Referendum against Hugo Chávez. Contrary to what many of us expected, we lost the Referendum by 20 points. The loss marked the end of two years of intense struggles between two factions, each struggling for political supremacy over the other.

I've said it before and I'll say it again, when all is said and done, we'll have to choose a major Caracas street to rename Avenida Presidente Carter...

Worst case scenario
Posted on August 16, 2004 by Quico

It's the worst thing that could've happened. CNE head Francisco Carrasquero, by himself, announces a set of partial results that give the government a huge advantage. The opposition CNE members immediately say the announcement was made without following proper procedures. The opposition cries foul, and announces mirror-image results. The Carter Center/OAS mission is missing in action, at least at first.

This is a national disaster. The referendum was meant to bring closure to the governance crisis in Venezuela. With results that fly in the face of exit-poll results announced on the basis of a fishy procedure, the referendum takes Venezuela further away from closure, not closer.

These are dangerous days for Venezuela, dangerous hours. The potential for violence is high. The opposition cannot, will not accept these results. And chavismo, surely enough, will not accept their reversal.

In other words, God only knows how the referendum will go down in history, but it will not go down as the peaceful, constitutional, electoral and democratic solution to the crisis that was the one chance the country had of avoiding both dictatorship and civil war.

There could, I suppose, still be a 13th hour surprise. But Jimmy Carter and Cesar Gaviria are diplomats, not miracle workers.

Pray for Venezuela, folks...it's going to get ugly.

None of it makes any sense...
Posted on August 16, 2004 by Quico

It looks very much to me like the government won fair and square. If it didn't, it'll come out in the paper-trail audit, which CNE's Jorge Rodriguez has already agreed to.

If the government did win fair and square, the *Coordinadora Democrática* has a LOT of explaining to do. In fact, if the government did win fair and square, the *Coordinadora Democrática* leadership has a lot of resigning to do.

Realities
Posted on August 19, 2004 by Quico

It would take a miracle of public relations management for the opposition to win the international public opinion battle around the referendum. As far as 99% of foreigners are concerned, what Carter says, goes. The opposition has never demonstrated any particular gift for public relations abroad – quite the opposite – so one thing is clear: five years of efforts by the opposition to explain to the world just how brutally nasty, deceitful and dangerous Hugo Chavez is were comprehensively undone on Monday. This is a battle we will not win.

Working on the assumption that there was a Si-cap fraud (i.e. the machines were programmed to cap the number of Si votes they would register) – the fraud will only be understandable by people with a solid background in university-level statistics. Chávez is a genius at this sort of thing – most of the outrages he commits are so complicated, they're impossible to explain succinctly and clearly. Just as there's no 30-second sound-byte explanation possible for the Montesinos Affair, the looting of FIEM, the April 11th massacre, the purge of PDVSA, the burning of the Fuerte Mara soldiers, or any of 5 dozen other outrages, there'll never be an understandable 30-second retelling of the Si-cap fraud. However, statistically speaking, it may well be possible to demonstrate a fraud even without looking at a single ballot paper. A statistician can easily work out the probability that the statistical "fluke" that's turning up in the data is merely a coincidence. If, as seems likely, that probability is vanishingly small, I'll have to think there was fraud, whatever the audits say.

The CNE claimed that the reason for refusing an *Auditoría en Caliente* is that it would have taken too long – the automated tallying system would have had to be stopped while paper ballots were counted, generating mistrust and confusion. If the purpose of refusing the *Auditoria en Caliente* was to bolster the credibility of the eventual results, the least one can say is that it was not a very effective strategy. Throughout, CNE acted as though holding an *Auditoría en Caliente* would be a punishingly slow task, or one of herculean complexity. This is not so, as the good burghers of Valle de la Pascua demonstrate. According to this International Herald Tribune piece, "In the town of Valle de la Pascua, where papers were counted at the initiative of those manning the voting center, the Yes vote had been cut by more than 75 percent, and the entire voting material was seized by the National Guard shortly after the difference was established."

Holding an *Auditoría en Frio* on a sample of Voting Centers selected unilaterally by CNE 12 hours earlier is about as useful as an ashtray on a motorcycle. It stands to reason that if 40% (or is it 60%?) of the country is convinced you're crooked enough to cheat them out of their votes, they're not going to trust you to choose the sample and procedures meant to demonstrate that you didn't.

As Daniel explains in his blog, a random selection of voting tables may not be a particularly sensible response to the specific fraud allegations being made. The *Coordinadora Democrática* is alleging quite specific irregularities in a specified set of voting centers. CNE – which was so adamant in checking every single signature *con lupa* – refuses to open up the ballot boxes in the specific places where the CD alleges fraud. Why? *El que no la debe no la teme*. Once again, CNE acts in a way that is at least consistent with a cover-up – and certain to be interpreted as such by doubters.

If Chávez won cleanly, CNE's refusal to conduct a hot-audit has robbed him of the possibility of convincing the entire country that he won cleanly. The country is back to square one in terms of collective schizophrenia. 60% of us live one reality, 40% live another reality. Perversely, each side is convinced that it is the 60% and the other side is the 40%. Each side is convinced the other is engaged in a mind-blowingly complex, dark, evil conspiracy to usurp power. The governability crisis continues. The epistemic gulf drags on. The only thing that's changed is that Chavez will now enjoy much greater international credibility. *Fronteras adentro*, nothing has changed.

"When you have eliminated the impossible..."
Posted on August 21, 2004 by Quico

...whatever remains, however improbable, must be the truth."

-Sherlock Holmes

Impossible: The Carter Center and the OAS conspiring with CNE and the Chavez government to willfully disregard fraud.

Impossible: The Carter Center and the OAS are so clueless they are willing to participate in a cold-audit carried out on a biased sample of ballot boxes, or on ballot boxes that have been tampered with.

Impossible: A cold-audit of 150 voting boxes, picked at random and checked in front of CC/OAS, fails to turn up evidence of the theft of millions of votes.

Improbable: Willfully or not, Sumate and Penn Schoen & Berland screwed up their exit polls.

Improbable: CNE refused the hot-audit because they actually believed that holding up a results announcement for an additional 5 or 6 hours risked destabilizing the country.

Believe me, folks, it brings me no joy to post this…

Turning Japanese
Posted on August 26, 2004 by Quico

"When you have eliminated the impossible, whatever remains, however improbable, must be the truth."

I show this sentence to Kanako, my Japanese friend.[63] She looks at it for a second, thinks about it, and in her broken Italian says, "No, it's not right."

"Hmm?"

"Maybe it's right in Europe, but somebody Japanese would never believe it. It's a very European idea."

"How do you mean?"

"I think because Europeans are monotheist, you know, there is only one God, and therefore there is only one truth. But in Japan, we don't think this way. We have so many Gods, so many spirits. And a spirit is a source of truth. So for us, it is normal to think that there are many truths, and that one spirit doesn't get to impose its truth on another. So yes, Sherlock Holmes is right…in Europe. We, we would never accept it."

"But you see, Kanako, that won't do, because either most Venezuelans voted yes or most Venezuelans voted no. It can't be both."

"Of course," she says, "but you don't understand. Yes, there is one truth on that level. But it doesn't matter. Because the truth is something we make, collectively, by believing in it. Today, maybe so many people in Venezuela believe that Yes won, and for them, that is the truth. Others believe that No won, and for them, that is the truth. They make it the truth by believing in it."

---

[63] Kanako later became Quico's wife, and the mother of his child.

"But a country can't work this way, with half the country sure the other country is wrong."

She smiles and shrugs, "maybe a Christian country can't work that way. I don't know what to say. It's a very western idea. For me, having a lot of different truths, well, it's normal, it's the most normal thing there is."

I try to make sense of Kanako's words, and I struggle. But I see that, in some sense, she's just right. There was fraud. And there was no fraud. And half the country will never believe that there was no fraud. And half the country will never believe there was fraud.

We're not Japanese. We can't think of that as normal. But maybe, who knows, maybe the Japanese are right. Maybe it is normal. Maybe it's the most normal thing in the world.

Something very strange happened in Venezuela
Posted on August 29, 2004 by Quico

Readers of this blog know I've had a very hard time trying to piece together what happened during and after the August 15th referendum. Like everyone in the opposition, I've gone through a lot of confusing, contradictory information on whether or not claims of fraud make any sense.

It's a disorienting exercise. Both sides have seemingly incontrovertible arguments, and each has to resort to fantastic allegations to refute the other. CNE has the backing of international observers not only for its official results, but also for a very-tricky to get-around consequent audit. CANTV has ratified that its machine operators and data transmission system worked as advertised. No concrete evidence of fraud has been brought forward. The opposition can only disown the results by explaining away this evidence on the basis of a massive, perfect conspiracy, a conspiracy with no visible leaks.

But the opposition also has evidence in hand that cannot be contradicted without supposing a set of equal but opposite conspiracies. Everyone knows there's no way that a professionally-run exit poll using established methodology and repeated by several different organizations comes out with a result 40 points off from the official result.

This happened in Venezuela systematically. There are state level pollsters in Venezuela that have been carrying out exit polls using the same methodology in election after election and never gotten an exit poll result more than 1% off from the announced result. This time, using the same methodology and polling intensively – as always – in poor areas, they come up with results miles away from those announced.

No "nice" hypothesis can explain the gap: it's not a matter of bias in the areas polled, because exit poll results from given voting centers vary widely from the results reported from that center. Nor can the gap be assigned to the choice of political activists as polling staff: polls run by Súmate volunteers came up with similar results as polls carried out by firms that hire college students as interviewers.

The only possible explanation for the disparity is that there's a wide-ranging conspiracy, a kind of fraud-crying cartel of any number of different organizations to diffuse false exit poll results. This sort of story is easy for chavistas to believe, after hearing years of oversimplifications and lies about the opposition. But if it is a conspiracy, it's a perfect conspiracy – one where no one leaks, no one squeals, no one made a single mistake.

Whether or not you believe there was fraud, you're required to believe a series of wildly improbable evils against your political opponents for the events of the last two weeks to make sense. Rather than providing a solution to deepening polarization, the dispute over the referendum became yet another phase in this process of increasing polarization of the country into competing camps that believe the very worst about one another.

Because, in the end, Venezuelans will believe the conspiracy theory that favors their side of the political divide and that's the end of it. And this is what's so worrying about this odd-ball situation the country's living. Each half of the country is forced to believe a conspiracy theory that paints the other half in the worst possible light. Each takes refuge in its own truth, and building an understanding, let alone trust, across the divide becomes impossible.

This is too bad, because Venezuela was badly in need of a peaceful, democratic, electoral and constitutional solution to the governability crisis, and it didn't get it.

Things that make you go hmm...
Posted on September 14, 2004 by Quico

From today's Por Mi Madre, the daily political gossip page in TalCual,

Final poll

"The final tracking poll for Consultores 21, carried out on August 13th in the nine largest cities in the country [but which could not be published due to CNE restrictions on late poll announcements -ft], showed the NO side leading the SI by 52.9% to 47.1% – a lead of 5.8 points. Official CNE returns for those same nine cities show NO leading by 53.1% vs. 46.9% for the SI. The official NO lead of 6.2% is very close to the Consultores 21 measure, and corroborates how closely matched the sides are in urban centers."

Unified field theory of non-fraud, or who exactly is Jorge Rodríguez?
Posted on September 22, 2004 by Quico

I. Suspending Disbelief

I want to address, first, my many readers who are sure there was fraud in the recall referendum last month. And I want to ask you to do something hard: I want you to consider, just for a moment, the possibility that there was no fraud.

How could that be? What story can we tell ourselves, what narrative do we need to weave, to make sense of the no-fraud hypothesis?

I think it's possible to construct such a story, and even to find some strong evidence to back it, but only if we first unlearn much of what we thought we knew about the National Electoral Council – CNE – and especially, about its key member: Jorge Rodríguez.[64]

II. Rethinking the CNE board appointments

First, we need to go back to September 2003 and the appointment of the current CNE board members. As Venezuelans will remember, the current members were named under a constitutionally exceptional situation. In normal circumstances, the National Assembly is supposed to select the five members of the board via a two-thirds vote. But since the Assembly is split 85-80, neither side could muster the 110 votes needed. Not surprisingly, compromise proved impossible and the selection process deadlocked.

The impasse was cleared by the Constitutional Chamber Supreme Tribunal – TSJ – on the basis of Article 336, paragraph 7 of the 1999 constitution, which empowers the Constitutional Chamber to declare unconstitutional an omission on the part of the National Assembly, and to "determine the guidelines for its correction." In this case, the Constitutional Chamber of the TSJ ruled that by omitting the decision on a new CNE board the Assembly had violated a constitutional mandate.

Instead of determining the guidelines to correct this omission, however, the Constitutional Chamber just went ahead and

---

[64] After leaving the CNE, Rodríguez went on to serve in most high-ranking positions inside the Chávez government: Vice-President, Campaign Chief for Hugo Chávez, and Mayor of Libertador District in Caracas.

appointed a new CNE board unilaterally. And here is where the problems started.

The call at the time, both from the opposition and the dictates of common sense, had been to try to appoint a balanced CNE – in practice, one with two pro-government members, two pro-opposition members and a neutral or apolitical chairman. If the National Assembly had deadlocked it was precisely because the government insisted on retaining a 3-2 majority.

In the event, throwing the matter to the TSJ's Constitutional Chamber did not seem like much of an advance to the opposition. The five-member Constitutional Chamber itself has a built-in 3-2 chavista majority, and a long and sorry history of highly questionable or "legally creative" rulings in favor of the government. Chief Magistrate Iván Rincón together with Magistrates Jesús Eduardo Cabrera and José Delgado Ocando have always been reliable chavistas – and for me, the biggest problem with believing the Unified Field Theory of Non-Fraud is that it requires you to believe that these people selected a CNE board that would not cheat.

Why is this so hard to swallow?

III. A short digression

Sectarianism has long been a distinguishing characteristic of the chavista experiment. Some weeks ago, TalCual ran a chilling piece on the purge of Venezuela's foremost (in fact, only) expert on the preservation of rare historic books. He was fired from his long-held job as head of the National Library's rare books division for, surprise surprise, signing in favor of the presidential recall referendum. A similar fate befell the Biblioteca Nacional's longtime head of historic cartography. Both were replaced by reliable chavistas with no specialist training for the highly specialized jobs they were asked to perform.

Now, that's only one story out of a very long list to show that Chavistas systematically demand diehard loyalty from every one of their appointees, even when quite minor positions are at stake. But if they will not trust a non-loyalist to even look after the nation's collection of historic books, or maps, what sense could it possibly make that they would appoint a genuine non-loyalist to a post as sensitive as the key position within the one agency that could eject Chavez from power? Personally, I cannot make sense of that – and it remains the single biggest obstacle to my belief in the theory I'm about to put forward.

IV. Not as advertised

The CNE board appointed by Rincon, Cabrera and Delgado Ocando was a peculiar one. The way it was presented to the public was straightforward: the government would get two members (Jorge Rodríguez and Oscar Battaglini) the opposition would get two members (Ezequiel Zamora and Solbella Mejias), while the head of the council, Francisco Carrasquero, would remain neutral.

Very quickly, though, it became apparent that Carrasquero was in no sense neutral – his statements and votes systematically sided with the government. The natural reaction in the opposition was to assume we'd been screwed, and had ended up with a 3-2 pro-Chavez council. Certainly, most key votes were decided along those lines, with Carrasquero, Rodríguez and Battaglini voting as a block, and always in favor of the government.

However, CNE watchers also started to notice another reality – while Carrasquero was the nominal head of the council, it was clear that day-to-day decision-making was not in his hands. Instead, it was Jorge Rodríguez who was calling the shots from his perch as head of the Junta National Electoral – the National Electoral Board – which could be described as the executive arm in charge of the day-to-day management of CNE.

The question of Jorge Rodríguez's integrity soon became the burning issue in opposition circles, though it was not much disputed, to be sure. Almost everyone in the opposition just assumed he was a doctrinaire chavista paying lip-service to his independent status just to cover appearances. However, well-placed sources close to the CNE (who would assassinate me if I named them) never bought this. Instead, they put forward an alternative interpretation of the CNE appointments that radically recast what the TSJ's Constitutional Chamber had been up to.

V. The Padgett hypothesis

The most complete retelling of this view in print came in a Time Magazine article by Tim Padgett. Tim is a tough reporter, skeptical and careful, and with enough distance from the Venezuelan situation to look at it with more objectivity than most of us can muster. His views, and those of the unnamed diplomats he cites, are so far removed to opposition Conventional Wisdom that our immediate impulse is to assume he just doesn't know what he's talking about. I want to encourage my anti-chavista readers, though, to make the effort to suspend their disbelief – at least provisionally – to understand the implications of this interpretation. After all, we don't own the truth – no one does.

According to the Padgett Hypothesis, CNE really was a 2-1-2 council. The reason most of us failed to see this is that the independent in the middle was not Carrasquero, as advertised, but instead Rodríguez. In this interpretation, Rodríguez was perhaps closer to the old IVth Republic model of an "independiente pro" – that is, someone with broad ideological sympathy for one side, but not actively controlled by it. Moreover, given that day-to-day managerial control of CNE was in the hands of the JNE, it made far more sense to have the one independent member as head of JNE rather than as chairman of CNE.

This, again, puts a different spin on the preponderance of 3-2 decisions in the council. From this new point of view, Rodríguez had enough ascendancy over Battaglini and Carrasquero to bring them on board on most decisions. But if Battaglini and Carrasquero were merely going along with decisions cooked up by a non-chavista JNE, then one starts to understand why the characterization of CNE as a fully-owned subsidiary of Miraflores might not hold water.

VI. Rethinking the reparos

I'm sure my anti-chavista readers are banging their heads against their desks at this point, but there's at least some evidence to lead us to believe that this interpretation could be the right one. Consider the decision to send about 1 million signatures to "reparos" all the way back in February.[65]

At the time, the opposition saw this as a clear case of a pro-Chavez CNE conniving to stop the referendum. However, Padgett's piece makes it clear that the "reparos" were not the chavistas' preferred alternative. Instead, Battaglini and Carrasquero wanted to invalidate outright the 1,000,000 signatures they'd pegged as "planas" – which would have stopped the referendum process cold.

The reparos, which caused such unmitigated outrage in the opposition, seem to have been a compromise, hatched by Jorge Rodríguez, to keep the referendum process moving forward but with added checks. This is Padgett's view, and sources inside CNE back it.

If the idea of Rincon/Cabrera/Delgado Ocando picking a true independent is the non-fraud theory's single weakest point, then this is its strongest point: if, as claimed, CNE was merely an appendage of Miraflores, the referendum process would not have gotten past February – it simply would have died as the planas were declared invalid.

The fact that CNE not only moved forward at that point but eventually agreed to a viable reparos process shows quite convincingly that Rodríguez was not simply devoted to derailing the referendum, as the opposition claimed. Instead, in a strange and roundabout way, CNE seemed to be doing what the opposition had always hoped it would – balancing the demands of both sides thanks to the leadership of someone that was controlled by neither.

---

[65] After collecting millions of signatures to recall Chávez, the CNE asked roughly a million voters – a subset of the signatures - to come back and ratify those were indeed their signatures.

In fact, it seems the closer people got to Rodríguez, the harder it was for them to dismiss him as a chavista stooge. While diplomats like Cesar Gaviria criticized the pattern of 3-2 decisions at CNE, after a year of close and difficult interactions with him they do not subscribe to a vision of Jorge Rodríguez as a cheat – as evidenced by their unambiguous acceptance of CNE's results. Even Alberto Quirós Corradi, one of the CD's two negotiators with CNE, accepted that Rodríguez had created conditions for tough but respectful negotiations, conditions he hints would not have been possible without him.

VII. Closer to Teo than to Marta

Quirós Corradi still sees Rodríguez as biased towards the government, but in a different way than Carrasquero and Battaglini. In this view, Jorge Rodríguez occupied a moderate position in the pro-government camp roughly analogous to Teodoro Petkoff's in the opposition, while Battaglini and Carrasquero were closer to Marta Colomina's extreme and uncompromising stance.

This is important because the decision on voting systems for the referendum was made more or less unilaterally by Jorge Rodríguez. As is well known, there was no public bidding process, and the SBC consortium was put together by JNE on its own. In the opposition's standard frame of mind, where Rodríguez was just as much of a chavista extremist as Carrasquero and Battaglini, his decision on the voting system looks rotten indeed. But if Tim Padgett's narrative is mostly right, Rodríguez's choice of voting software can be seen in a quite different light: as a play to adopt a technology that makes fraud essentially impossible, in an environment where attempts to commit fraud seemed likely and claims of fraud would be almost inevitable from the losing side.

The debate over Jorge Rodríguez's probity is important because if there was fraud, there can be little doubt that it had to have been orchestrated by Jorge Rodríguez himself. Similarly, if there was no fraud, it had to have been prevented by him. What you think about fraud will be determined largely by how you judge him.

If you think Rodríguez was just an undercover diehard chavista who committed a massive electronic fraud, you need to explain why it was that Rodríguez didn't just stop the recall process back in February, when he clearly had the chance to and, moreover, was under pressure from the government to do so. Conversely, if you think there was no fraud, then you have to explain how it is that the TSJ Constitutional Chamber's diehard chavista majority suddenly, on this most sensitive of decisions, took a break from its systematic partisanship and appointed a real independent to be the de facto head of CNE.

There's much that's left out of this brief sketch. But it seems to me this kind of re-thinking of what happened over the last year will be necessary to make sense of the recall saga.

The theory would have to be extended to cover the last-minute shifts in the electoral registry and the voting center staffing (who knows? perhaps there's a perfectly innocent explanation for all that) as well as quite a number of other such puzzling episodes, from the failure of the hot audit to the refusal to open up contested ballot boxes. But experience has taught me that decisions that seem incomprehensible from one point of view can turn out to have quite straightforward explanations when looked at from another – so it's very hard to be sure.

III. Final possibility

There is one final possibility, which I think is worth considering seriously: Jorge Rodríguez could be a psychopath, specifically a compensated psychopath. Perhaps the man is, like many with a psychopathic personality structure, just particularly shrewd, extraordinarily adept at lying, shorn of a normal sense of morality or a conscience, and possessed of a kind of special charisma that elicits uncommon loyalty. Compensated psychopaths can take almost anyone in – and those closest to them more than any others. At times, watching his press conferences, I had the distinct sense that I was listening to a psychopath. Unfortunately, I'm not a psychiatrist (he is!) so I'm in no position to judge this.

Yet, even as I write that, it's hard for me to quite believe it. To this litany of extraordinary character traits, we'd have to add one more: Rodríguez would have to be superhumanly competent. One month out, and after every statistician in the country has poured over the data, the opposition has still been unable to prove fraud decisively. If there was fraud, it was as close to a Perfect Fraud as one could imagine. And pulling off a Perfect Fraud, well … it's not impossible, but close.

Me? I can't really believe that you can steal an election in a way that's impossible to demonstrate – so I have to swallow hard and accept, try to accept, that the Constitutional Chamber appointed a JNE head they could not control, and that the opposition has been wrong about him since the word go. It's not a story that makes much sense to me, but for a long time attempts to come to an understanding of what happened on August 15th have come down to a judgment between the unlikely and the unlikelier. A perfect fraud seems like the least likely possibility out there. Sadly, a perfect fraud is what the opposition alleges.

The paper trail as entelechy
Posted on September 29, 2004 by Quico

Last night, I listened to the BBC World Service's report on Jimmy Carter's concerns on voting in Florida. Lyse Doucet, the legendary BBC journo, laid into the Florida official she was interviewing like only she can,

"It seems quite remarkable, then, that Florida's elections are set to go forward using electronic voting without a verifiable paper trail…after all, in the recent referendum in Venezuela the Carter Center made it quite clear that a paper trail was the one safeguard that positively had to be in place to go forward…"

Sigh.

The Venezuelan referendum has become a byword for "well-run election" in the international media. It's dispiriting, both because it's clear that Ms. Doucet doesn't really understand what happened in Venezuela and because it underlines, yet again, how effective CNE was in selling its version of events.

The paper trail has acquired a strange status in Venezuela. On the one hand, it's presented as the key safeguard vouching for the correctness of the election. On the other hand, we're not allowed to look at it. Well, not at 99% of it anyway. Apparently, we're supposed to be reassured by its existence rather than by its content. When we ask to look through it more thoroughly, CNE honcho Jorge Rodriguez accuses us of blackmail!

Paper ballots (papeletas) from 1% of the voting centers were audited on the August 18th cold audit – a cold audit that, as readers will know, has been questioned as un-random. CNE steadfastly refused to open any boxes beyond that 1% – both before and after the initial cold audit.

As mathematicians and physicists studying the referendum results zero in on a subset of tables that appear to show anomalous results, CNE affirms once more that CNE and CNE alone gets to decide which parts of the paper trail get looked at, and repeats that no further boxes will be opened. If we complain and say that that isn't a very transparent way to run an election, the answer writes itself: "Whaddayamean it wasn't transparent!? There was even a printed paper trail, that's how transparent it was!"

Follow me so far?

The paper trail has become a perfect entelechy, a kind of metaphysical imponderable. If a tree falls in the woods but no one is around, does it make a sound? If a voting safeguard is instituted, but no one is allowed to see it, does it actually safeguard anything?

Amidst all the strange comings and goings, the amazing transmogriphying REP, the illegal shifts in people's assigned voting centers, the last minute voting center personnel transfers, the bidirectional communications of the voting machines, the aborted hot-audits, the anomalous exit poll results, the dodgy "randomness" of the cold-audit, the non-binomial distribution of the vote in some states, the Benford Law anomalies, etc. CNE has a soothing retort to any question we could throw at it: "trust us, the vote had to be fair. After all, there was a paper trail...everybody knows that's the most important safeguard, even Lyse Doucet knows that..."

Mark & Doug's excellent Venezuelan adventure
Posted on April 9, 2008 by Juan Cristobal

"Exit poll results show major defeat for Chávez"

Caracas Chronicles headline, August 17th, 2004, citing a press release from Penn, Schoen & Berland.

The long anticipated departure of pollster, best-selling author and political guru Mark Penn from Sen. Hillary Clinton's campaign brought back some unkind memories. While the gringo press obsesses about the myriad ways Penn screwed up Hillary's presidential run, we Venezuelans let our minds wander back to his tour of our country between 2004 and 2006, when Penn's firm played a critical role in launching the opposition into three years of self-destruction by our misguided abstention strategy.

Mark Penn is a larger-than-life figure. Having worked - sometimes successfully, other times not so much - with the Clintons, Al Gore and Tony Blair, he is admired and despised in roughly equal measures in First-World political circles. A formidable intellect with an even more formidable ego, he's apparently the kind of person who never doubts himself.

In a keen new piece, New Republic writer Michelle Cottle describes him as:

"rough, arrogant, antisocial, controlling, manipulative, brutally ambitious, and occasionally downright abusive--a hurler of cell phones, pagers, and Chinese food."

I know that what follows will probably get me an eggroll, hurled straight at my noggin', but here goes anyway. The story goes like this.

Mr. Penn, along with his partner Doug Schoen, worked with Venezuelan opposition NGO Súmate during the Chávez Recall Referendum of 2004. Their firm advised the opposition in the run-up to the referendum and was supposedly in charge of organizing the all-important exit poll on the day of the vote. The evening of the Referendum, PSB announced that Chávez had been handily defeated, and the rest is history.

That poll was the original bit of evidence that convinced everyone that something was dodgy about the referendum. How could it be dismissed out of hand? It was Bill Clinton's pollster! To a remarkable extent, the strategy of the opposition in the coming months and years was shaped by what happened that night.

So, what was the real story behind the exit poll?

We'll probably never know, but I can tell you my version of the story, which is shared by Quico and Lucía and has been corroborated by two independent sources close to important opposition players. It goes something like this.

In the months leading up to the Recall Referendum, the polls began to change dramatically. The government had played the clock brilliantly, all the while launching the popular *misiones* social programs. Opposition elites - with few exceptions - were very slow and/or unwilling to believe Chávez's rise in the polls. They failed to understand the power of the misiones and Chávez's message and put their decline in the polls down to a mythical "fear factor" not supported by the evidence.

The opposition's umbrella group, the *Coordinadora Democrática*, failed to offer a compelling, competing message. An amalgamation of disparate political groups and NGOs, the Coordinadora failed to act effectively and its leadership was notoriously slow, disorganized and ineffective. All this is common knowledge, right?

Enter Penn, Schoen & Berland. After taking Súmate's hard-earned money, PSB told them that they simply did not have the time to design the exit poll themselves. Instead, they said Súmate should do it and kindly offered to let Súmate put the PSB stamp of approval on the results.

Súmate, an electoral NGO with no experience in polling, probably did their diligent, engineer-like best. It was probably not enough.

Exit polls are tricky to design and run under the best of circumstances. This was a well-intentioned amateur effort, from start to finish.

In the aftermath, Súmate had a lot of accomplices. There should have been tough questions asked about the reach and scope of the exit poll results. Very rural areas and unsafe urban areas, both Chávez strongholds, appeared curiously under-represented. Amid all the anger over the CNE's screwed up "hot audit", it's remarkable that nobody stopped to audit Sumate's PSB endorsed exit poll at all.

Nobody that night asked those questions with anything resembling academic rigor. The wider opposition community, including some very smart people, kept their skepticism to themselves and failed to ask the obvious questions about the exit poll. Instead, academic papers were produced at heart-stopping rates using the exit poll as the major data source, treating it like something it was not: a random sample representative of the population at large.

Opposition leaders had been treated to weeks of bad poll numbers preceding the referendum. Some of them were simply unwilling to believe the bad news. Some of them honestly believed, and still do, that the exit poll is accurate. It is not.

This period marked the beginning of the great "fear factor" myth, through which it wasn't that voters liked the new misiones, it was that they were afraid of pollsters! Most of the opposition leadership, including *Coordinadora* leader Enrique Mendoza, didn't buy this. They did understand that Chávez's numbers were rising steadily in the weeks before the vote. One has to wonder what would have happened if our leadership had adopted a more skeptical approach that night.

The belief that the exit poll had been correct was shared by the international media. Chavista media outlets were incensed that their man's victory was not being universally recognized. PSB put their reputation on the line with their exit poll, and a lot of people believed it.

The belief that they had uncovered massive fraud thanks to their polls, along with historical ties to major AD figures, paved the way for Doug Schoen to be hired by the Manuel Rosales campaign in 2006. Rosales ran an energetic campaign to unseat Hugo Chávez, yet it failed to show in the vote tallies. Rosales's defeat was somewhat of a foregone conclusion, given how a majority of the opinion polls released prior to the election predicted it.

Again, there were a couple of outliers. Only one high-profile DC poollster showed the race getting tighter, though. Who ran it? If you guessed PSB, you guessed right.

After going against the tide and predicting a few weeks before the poll that the race was tightening, Schoen was mysteriously replaced by Penn the weekend before the election.

You know what happened next: we got trounced, and Rosales accepted defeat gallantly. But if you went by what Penn and Schoen had predicted, you would believe we were robbed all over again.

For the past few months, Quico, Lucía and I have been talking to some of the people involved, and after confirming the story with different sources, this is what we believed happened: a hack-job of an exit-poll conducted by the opposition itself and rubber-stamped by a prestigious polling firm resulted in a collective belief that differed from reality and led to disastrous political decisions for the opposition in the following years.

You may choose to believe something else, but we call it like we see it. I believe there was some vote tampering the night of the Recall Referendum, but it did not make a difference overall. I also believe the exit poll was garbage.

The impact of releasing an exit poll like that at a time like that cannot be underestimated. Has this been tagged as a Súmate exit poll - which is what it was - rather than a PSB exit poll, we probably wouldn't be having this conversation. The fact that it came out at a moment of maximum tension, where it was the only piece of information available, only helped build up the myth.

Social phenomena are sometimes marked by instances where the momentum for change and for the establishment of an idea is unstoppable, a "tipping point" if you will. This concept has been been recently popularized by writer Malcolm Gladwell.

Penn, Schoen and Berland's faulty exit poll may have been our tipping point - the moment when we decided that we were the majority and that anyone who said differently was lying. We've been paying the price ever since.

VII

Our disheveled public sphere

One of the causes closest to our hearts is the rehabilitation of Venezuela's public sphere. Our public sphere has become an unfortunate casualty of the extreme polarization in our body politic. Whether by choice or as a consequence of chavista policies, we strongly feel there are things traditional media outlets simply don't say, and we hope the blog helps change that.

These posts deal with our public sphere. Many in Venezuela don't really understand the other side because there is simply no space – real, nor metaphorical - in which both sides can converge and coexist. But the public sphere did not simply die of natural causes. It was killed by all of us, mostly by chavismo.

This became evident when Hugo Chávez faced his first serious electoral defeat in 2007. Instead of accepting his defeat with honor, he trashed the winners without ever digesting what his defeat meant. This inability to see the other side's point of view was merely indicative of a major flaw in what-remains-of our democracy, and we addressed it on numerous occasions.

In this chapter, we talk about how the lack of a public sphere will likely shape future generations. We also talk about the need to understand swing voters, the fabled, quasi-mythical "ni-nis." In order to draw a contrast, I discuss the differences between democracy as exercised in Chile and in Venezuela in a couple of posts. Finally, we end this chapter with a short rant by Quico on the usefulness of a blog when "everybody already knows everything." In his post, he fails to see that some people are just tuning in, so repeating yourself may be worth it. As long as certain ideas have not penetrated, there is still reason enough to divulge them.

Still, the idea of the blog is to put contrasting theories out there, to make arguments and start conversations in a way that is deeply personal but also substantive. That is also the point of having a public sphere, a place where contrasting theories and visions can be presented and debated, all for the common good.

That is why these posts are here. In a way, that is why we wrote this book.

The public sphere is like a garden
Posted on November 16, 2007 by Quico

German philosopher Jürgen Habermas understands the "public sphere" as that realm of social life where private individuals come together to discuss public matters collectively. It is made real every single day on the pages of newspapers, at university cafeterias, around kitchen tables, in union halls and political party meetings as well as on blogs - whenever and wherever private individuals come together to talk about public affairs. At its best, deliberation in the public sphere is reasoned, focused on arguments rather than personalities, open to all, and geared towards building common understanding.

The health of the public sphere is vital to the viability of democracy. The opinion of the majority is democratically legitimate only to the degree that discussion in the public sphere operates as it's supposed to. Only then does "public opinion" embody a process of collective deliberation that honors our nature as thinking beings. *That*, deep down, is the whole point of democracy.

But there's no *a priori* reason to believe the Public Sphere will work properly all or even most of the time. Quite the opposite - the habits of mind necessary to sustain critical debate in a democratic public sphere are always fragile, ever precarious, permanently in need of attention. They can't be mandated, legislated, or imposed. They need to be fostered and protected.

I've been trying to think of an image, a metaphor to capture what's happened to our public sphere over the last few years. The other day I tried Alzheimer's. But maybe this one works better ...

A democratic public sphere is like a garden. It needs tending. It needs attention, care, fussing over. It needs somebody to protect it from all kinds of threats: insects, fungi, storms, frosts, rabbits, and weeds. Left to its own devices, it will be slowly overrun. It can't be taken for granted.

Venezuela's public sphere was never particularly tidy. Since 1958, it was always a bit ramshackle, overgrown here and there, encroached on by the surrounding wild tropical vegetation, and besieged by all kinds of plagues - petrostate clientelism, the *mantuano* discourse, general ignorance, pervasive disdain.

Nobody took the job of tending it very seriously. We treated it more like a *Conuco*, really. In spite of ourselves, it never did quite turn back into jungle.[66]

Eight years ago, Hugo Chávez sized up our public sphere and took a flamethrower to it. It's a heap of smoldering debris by now, just totally wrecked. Worse yet, many in the opposition figured that the way to fight back was to get flamethrowers of their own. They ended up scorching the parts of the garden that had somehow survived the initial onslaught.

A small minority realized all along the need to try to save what little they could of the garden, to protect it, to shield it from the devastation all around. But it's a losing battle.

Gardening takes time, effort, and perseverance. Flame throwing doesn't. What takes the gardener a year to grow takes the flamethrower a minute to burn down. Does it really make sense to try to garden while we're surrounded by people determined to burn down whatever we manage to grow?

One thing is clear to me - if we're going to build a democratic public sphere, winning in December isn't enough. Even getting Chávez out of Miraflores isn't enough, because he can keep wrecking any attempt to build a democratic public sphere just as easily from the opposition as he can from the government. We need to wrestle the flamethrower away from him...as well as from the hotheads on "our" side. And then we need to start gardening.

We need to reinvent the way we talk about ourselves ... to ourselves. We need to craft a new consensus about what is and isn't acceptable in public deliberation.

---

[66] A "conuco" is a small farm, generally owned and/or operated by a single person or a family. The technology used is bare-bones, and it is generally not productive. Much of the Venezuelan countryside is characterized by the presence of these small farms.

We need to enshrine the kind of standards Zapatero was trying (in vain) to explain to Chávez when the King lost his cool.

"Se puede estar en las antípodas de una posición ideológica - no seré yo el que esté cerca de las ideas de Aznar - pero el ex presidente Aznar fue elegido por los españoles y exijo ese respeto. Se puede discrepar radicalmente sin irrespetar."[67]

In Venezuela, getting everyone to accept those norms would require a whole new conception of what it means to "do politics." It'll be the work of a generation, or more.

One glimmer of hope: when farmers are looking to clear a field for cultivation, probably the oldest technique to prepare it is to slash-and-burn. It's just imaginable that if one day, somehow, we manage to get the flamethrowers out of our public sphere, we'll find the ground is readier for cultivation than now seems quite imaginable.

On political common sense
Posted on February 10, 2007 by Quico

Political common sense is a bit like atmospheric pressure - omnipresent, terrifically important, but normally imperceptible to us.

Political common sense is an implicit set of beliefs that sets the boundaries between views we need to defend and those so obvious they "go without saying." It structures the limits of what's politically conceivable to us, and it defines what seems obviously right and obviously wrong. Its power is all the greater because it

---

[67] In the Iberoamerican Summit of 2007, held in Santiago, Chile, Hugo Chávez insulted former Spanish President José María Aznar, calling him a "fascist." This prompted the unprecedented response from King of Spain, who fought back by asking Chávez to "shut up." The video of the confrontation quickly went viral. Spanish President Rodríguez Zapatero elegantly lectured Chávez by telling him that one can disagree with someone politically, but one needs to respect a man who was elected by Spaniards to be their leader.

feels so natural, so self-evident to us that when we use it, we don't realize that we're using it.

After arguing in circles for eight years, I think it's pretty clear that what we have in Venezuela these days are two fundamentally opposed sets of political common senses; what critical theorists would call parallel discourses.

For almost a decade, the two have been battling to establish themselves as the political common sense in Venezuela. "A symbolic struggle to re-signify democracy," was the way pollster Oscar Schemel put it.

The funny thing about this struggle is that it's taken place in a theoretical vacuum. We don't often wonder about underpinnings of our own common sense, to say nothing of our opponents'. The outcome is a lot of confusion, and a fundamental misapprehension about what is at stake.

Constitutional Liberalism

The standard rap against chavismo is pretty straight-forward: chavismo is undemocratic. It's a charge we've repeated again and again in every forum available to us. It encapsulates what we find unacceptable about his way of government.

It's also, on its face, absurd. After all, Chávez has won election after election. According to a bare-bones, etymological understanding of democracy, it's just an oxymoron to call an elected leader undemocratic.

"Not so fast," we usually respond, "he might be a 'democrat' in some ridiculously reductionist sense of the word, but he doesn't respect the separation of powers, doesn't tolerate dissent, doesn't grasp that the republic's money is not his money, can't grasp that 'state' 'government' and 'Chávez' are not synonyms, violates the constitution every other day, etc."

Turns out that what we mean when we charge chavismo of being undemocratic is a bit more complex than we realize. None of the objections we commonly level at chavismo points to a lack of democracy, understood as the legitimacy you get from winning an election. What we're really saying is that Chávez doesn't respect the arrangements we associate democracy.

When we say Chávez is undemocratic, what we really mean is that he doesn't practice Constitutional Liberalism, a specific institutional system that developed in a specific point in time in one part of the world. In our common-sense usage, we see that system as synonymous with democracy. Our political discourse sees the two as self-evidently inseparable.

Now, the charge that Chávez doesn't practice constitutional liberalism shouldn't even be controversial. After all, Chávez has explicitly distanced himself from constitutional liberalism ("representative democracy" as it's called in official phraseology) pretty much from day one. He threw a monumental hissy-fit at the Quebec City Summit of the Americas in 2001 when the rest of the hemisphere's leaders proposed to include a commitment to "representative democracy" in their declaration of principles. Rejections don't get much more explicit than that.

But what is constitutional liberalism? And why does Chávez's rejection of it rankle us so much?

On one level, it's a system of institutions, a way of organizing the state and its relationship with society. On another level, it's the system of values necessary to make those institutions meaningful.

But deep down, it's a view of humanity - or rather, human-ness. It is a political philosophy based on a given understanding of where human dignity resides.

The most basic institution of constitutional liberalism is the Constitution itself, a set of rules that constitute and delimit the state, defining what it is and what it is not, what it can do and what it can't do.

The most basic value of constitutional liberalism is the commitment to the rule of law as such, the basic belief that, as

Santos Luzardo puts it, "la ley obliga de por sí - "the law is binding in and of itself."[68]

It's clear that without a commitment to the principle of the rule of law, it doesn't do much good to have a liberal constitution. Surely, Venezuela's 1999 constitution is basically a liberal document, but chavismo's cavalier attitude towards the rule of law - its practice of behaving as though the constitution and the laws were compendia of helpful tips to be followed or ignored according to convenience - negates the values that make liberal institutions meaningful.

It's clear to us, and it's been repeated *ad nauseam*, that without a commitment to the rule of law, a formal constitution becomes "dead letter" - that evocative phrase, conjuring the helplessness of the written word in the face of the contempt of the powerful.

Beyond constitutional liberalism

So far, so banal: anti-chavista common sense distilled. The relevant question is why does Chávez's contempt for the rule of law rankle so much?

The answer might seem obvious, but asking why things that seem obvious to us seem so is what this is about. Digging a bit deeper, what is it about chavista attitudes that so offends our political common sense, our notions of dignity and freedom and human-ness?

To answer this question, I think, you need to appreciate that constitutional liberalism is a political philosophy built on a particular moral philosophy, a specific understanding of human dignity.

Rooted in eighteenth-century thinking, constitutional liberalism is the political expression of enlightenment rationalism. It's an attempt to give institutional form to an understanding of people as

---

[68] Santos Luzardo, one of the main characters in the sweeping Venezuelan novel Doña Bárbara, represents law and order in its struggle with chaos and the rule of the mighty.

rational agents, beings who are free in the sense that we can apply reason to the problems of society.

It's not only that people can think; it's that we can also talk. Because we have the capacity to communicate as well as the capacity to reason, constitutional liberalism sees human beings as able to deliberate, to reason collectively, on the basis of arguments, as a means of reaching agreements on how to further our collective interest.

What happens when we deliberate? What happens when we argue about political matters? Ideally, it goes something like this: one side puts forward a claim about the world, a view about how it works and how we can make it better. If the other side is not persuaded, he can challenge it logically, by noting contradictions between the claim and reality, for instance, or by exposing logical flaws in it. The other side takes these objections and, once again, subjects them to critical scrutiny. Both sides continue in this way, advancing towards a common understanding.

With each iteration, this process allows the sides to come to new understandings of what is true, of what is in their interests both individually and collectively, and of how best to further those interests. Ideally, deliberation leads to agreement. When it doesn't, the two sides can settle the matter by recourse to a previously agreed decision-making procedure - majority voting, for instance.

The key is that, by deliberating, participants aggregate their capacity to reason through communication.

Now, for an argument to count as a real deliberation and not just a shouting match, some conditions are necessary. We have to agree to see debate as a confrontation of ideas, not of personalities. We have to be equal, in the sense that anyone must be able to put forward a claim, or to rebut one, and that both proposals and rebuttals must be judged on their own merits, not on the merits of the person putting them forward. We have to seek to persuade the other side, but we must also be persuadable if we find, after critical scrutiny, that the other side has the better argument. We have to treat public engagement over political matters as a co-operative exercise where our common goal is to reach reasoned agreement on our response to our collective problems.

Of course, we all know that this is a highly idealized representation of what goes on in the real world. (In fact Jürgen Habermas, the German philosopher whose argument I'm following here, called it an "ideal speech situation.") We all know that parliamentarians, judges and voters have particular interests; we know people are often corruptible, pig-headed or just plain stupid. Still, when we argue, we implicitly act *as if* we believe these conditions hold. Arguing would be a meaningless pantomime if it didn't envisage, on some level, the possibility of an ideal speech situation, where claims are put forward and rebutted as if the only thing that matters is who has the better, clearer, and more persuasive argument.

The political institutions of liberal constitutionalism make sense only in this context. Having a parliament only makes sense so long as we see its members as thinking agents, able to engage in reasoned deliberations as a means of arriving at reasoned outcomes. Elections make sense only insofar as voters are seen as thinking agents, able to engage in reasoned deliberation on their way to reasoned voting decisions. The decisions of juries are legitimate precisely because they are the outcome of reasoned deliberation based on evidence; the decisions of judges are legitimate because they are the outcome of explicitly reasoned engagement with precedent and the law. It's people's capacity to reason collectively in this way that gives legitimacy to the outcomes of the institutional structures of liberal constitutionalism.

Here, I think, we start to get closer to the underlying reasons chavismo provokes such virulent rejection from its critics. On its own, chavismo's rejection of a liberal institutional order would not provoke the intense reactions it does. It's chavismo's rejection of liberal institutional values, together with its rejection of the understanding of human-ness that they are built on, that so deeply offends us.

This is most visible, I think, in chavismo's principled rejection of deliberation as a method for reaching political decisions. As we have seen with the enabling law, Fonden's unwillingness to share its accounts with the Central Bank, or any of the dozens of little outrages detailed on this blog over the years, the problem is not merely that Chávez rejects deliberation with his opponents, it's that he will not even deliberate about the nation's future with his supporters.

Chávez refuses to even couch the decisions he makes unilaterally within the frame of reasoned argumentation, opting for emotive speech again and again. Since 1998, chavistas have systematically responded to criticisms by disqualifying those who make them (viudas del puntofijismo! oligarchs! escuálidos! Gringo imperialists!) rather than by reasoned engagement with the critical ideas. In fact, the refusal to engage with criticism on its merits is one of the discursive hallmarks of chavismo, a kind of ideological badge of honor government supporters use to bolster their revolutionary credentials.

Chávez plainly does not see deliberation as a reliable basis for political decision-making. This is yet another assertion that, when you think about it, shouldn't be controversial at all.

Our political common sense can scarcely imagine a more ominous situation. From our point of view, deliberation and argument are the collective forms our individual capacity to reason takes, and our individual capacity to reason is the basis of our human dignity, the decisive dividing line between human beings and animals.

Because more than this argument or that argument, it's the *practice* of arguing itself that chavismo rejects. By systematically refusing to talk to us by reference to an ideal speech situation, by consistently attacking the messenger rather than refuting the message, chavismo strips us of what enlightenment rationalism takes as the basis of our humanity and our dignity.

This, I think, is the underlying reason for the sense of urgency many of us feel when speaking out against the government. Our passions would not be so roused if Chávez's was merely a bad government, or a corrupt government, or an incompetent government.

What riles is that Chávez treats us like animals.

On political common sense, Part 2: Their side
Posted on February 23, 2007 by Quico

I want to address the other side's common sense, its deeper roots, and the reasons it contrasts so strongly with our own.

By "revolution," Chávez seems to mean an attempt to establish his political common sense as the only valid basis for political discourse in Venezuela. The old political common sense, rooted in enlightenment thinking and committed to constitutional liberalism, has been under constant attack for eight years now. As a replacement, chavistas offer a radical alternative that discards liberal rationalism's entire conception of human dignity, upending its values and recasting reasoned debate as a mechanism of domination.

The distinguishing characteristics of chavista common sense are its radical rejection of deliberation as a way of arriving at political decisions, and its refusal to engage critically with those who dissent. We will not find an intellectual defense of this stance in the chavista movement itself, since any such defense would amount to engagement with the criticisms leveled, and the principled refusal to engage in that kind of back-and-forth is what chavista anti-rationalism is all about.

Is that all there is to say about it, then?

Not at all. A coherent, powerful defense of chavista anti-rationalism is possible, even if chavistas themselves will not put it forward. To grasp it, I think you need a bit of a detour through the work of French sociologist Pierre Bourdieu.

Bourdieu made a career out of examining the difference in tastes between rich people and poor people in France, whether in art, literature, music, food, film, or hobbies, and building a radical sociological theory on his observations. He noted the way richer people systematically preferred more "difficult" forms of art (think

Bracque, James Joyce, Bach, caviar, Lars von Trier, or bridge), while poorer people preferred "easier" forms (think dogs playing poker, Dan Brown, Top 40, McDonald's, and Hollywood). He noted the way we tend to associate aesthetic refinement with difficulty, whereas we find "easy" art crass and distasteful, and he asked himself why.

Bourdieu didn't think this was just about conspicuous consumption. Surely, refined tastes are more expensive than crass ones, so having those signals your privileged economic position, but he thought there was much more to it than that.

He noted that the things we consider refined are nearly always much more abstract, while popular tastes tend to the concrete. An abstract painting, a passage from Ulysses, a Bach fugue, an artsy Danish film - these are items that set out, self-consciously, to appeal to our minds, not to our senses.

Elite tastes revel in their own difficulty. For Bourdieu, the pleasure of consuming refined cultural items is to be found primarily in the act of deciphering them - of demonstrating that you have the intellectual and cultural capacity to understand them. Their sociological role is to distinguish you from those who don't have that capacity, the unwashed masses who are content with appeals to the senses, to raw emotion unmediated by reason.

In the Enlightenment tradition it is precisely the capacity to reason, to embrace abstraction, to think in universal categories, and to transcend our immediate sensory experience, which forms the basis of human dignity. But, lo and behold, in liberal societies, it's mostly rich people who consume, who value and share the aesthetic experiences associated with that capacity to reason.

And here, all the old Enlightenment dichotomies come back into play. Liberal rationalism is built on a series of contrast - abstract vs. concrete, conceptual vs. sensory, rational vs. emotional, hard vs. easy, spiritual vs. animal - and locates human dignity in the supposedly universal capacity to move toward the former and away from the latter. For liberal rationalism we can all become more spiritual and less animal, we can all rise through the ranks if we fulfill that potential. This, in the end, is what makes us human.

What Bourdieu stresses is that, as an empirical matter, we don't all have the same ability to decipher refined cultural goods. Some of us do, some of us don't, and which of us do and which of us don't is not a matter of chance. Those of us who are rich generally do, and those of us who are poor generally don't. In liberal societies, then, human dignity is not nearly as democratically distributed as liberal ideology likes to imagine.

What Bourdieu is getting at is that the sense of refinement, of distinction, of what is crass and what is sophisticated, helps configure a system of domination, or a mechanism the rich can use to leverage their capacity to reason abstractly not for some exalted end, but merely to assert, protect and maintain their position of dominance in society.

Now, for a far-left French intellectual, Bourdieu makes some pretty un-PC noises. He doesn't follow these arguments, as you might expect, with an impassioned rebuttal, an explanation about how the dominated poor are just as capable of abstraction as anyone else.

Just the opposite, he argues that the system of domination itself deprives poor people of the ability to reason abstractly. Poor people's experience is dominated by the need to come up with practical solutions to the problems of survival - getting enough for food, shelter and clothes are exhausting tasks that you don't achieve through abstraction. Economic precariousness and the need to scrabble together a living in a hostile environment lock the poor into a mindset where "practical reasoning" is essential and "abstract reasoning" nearly impossible.

This, he argues, is the way domination reproduces itself from one generation to the next. Liberal societies imprison one class of people inexorably in an animalistic existence, all the while insisting that abstract reasoning is the common patrimony of humanity - and, thereby, implicitly scorning those who cannot or will not attain it.

For Bourdieu, liberal constitutionalism's promise of a public sphere where the only thing that matters is the strength of your arguments is inherently part of the system of domination. The poor, pressed by the need to make a living, don't have the luxury of developing the social and intellectual skills needed to participate in political deliberation. The formal equality so carefully enshrined in liberal constitutions is meaningless when faced with these social realities.

In fact, Bourdieu goes even farther and argues that the poor, as a class, are incapable of forming truly independent political opinions. They cannot have a political position because the system of domination bars them from the cultural capacities it takes to formulate one.

Deliberation - that most sacred practice in the liberal constitutionalist imagination - presupposes the capacities that domination denies to the poor. So the stress constitutional liberals place on the practice of deliberation is just one move in a broader strategy by the dominant class to permanently establish its dominance. The poor, for Bourdieu, are unable to speak for themselves. Somebody, therefore, must speak for them.

Chávez es el pueblo. Or, more precisely, el pueblo es Chávez.

As far as I'm aware, Bourdieu - who passed away in 2002 - never wrote specifically about Chávez. But I do think his views preconfigure precisely what Chávez has tried to do.

Like Bourdieu, Chávez sees deliberation as a thinly disguised cover for the exercise of class domination. In a very Bourdieu-ian way, he sees the poor as having no independent political existence apart from the one they derived from being led by him. Like Bourdieu, he sees liberation largely as a matter of reversing the structure of symbolic hierarchies in society - of valuing that which has been devalued, and devaluing that which has been valued.

Seen from this perspective, chavismo's refusal to engage critically with the arguments of dissenters makes perfect sense. That refusal is, in a sense, the central node of the revolution.

To deliberate is unacceptable because it would mean treating arguments as though they are disembodied, disconnected from the people making them, valid in their own terms only and therefore open to refutation in terms of their internal merit only. Chavismo implicitly accepts a kind of Bourdieu-ian analysis where arguments never stand on their own, and are always valid (or invalid) only by reference to the people making them.

It's in this context that we should understand chavismo's dogged determination not to engage critically with dissenting arguments. Ad hominem attacks on those who criticize the government are not, as we so often suppose, simply a matter of chavismo's intellectual poverty. They are also the expression of a certain view of society and political power where the messenger - and his socio-political position - is always more important than the message. That, I think, is chavista political common sense condensed.

Much of what is otherwise opaque about chavismo becomes clear once you appreciate this dynamic. Specialist discourses of every kind must be rejected out of hand if the revolution is to take itself seriously. Any line of reasoning based on a specialized understanding of a subject comes to be seen, ipso facto, as an attempt to reassert the old regime's system of domination.

For chavismo, privilege always comes cloaked in a Power Point presentation.

The radicalism, the rigid dogmatism with which the government has stuck to this position, has been startling to say the least. Dismissing all deliberation and all specialist discourse as a way of managing society, chavismo is left to rely on the will of the leader alone. Under normal circumstances, such insistence would've brought massive economic chaos long ago. But the last few years have not been normal. The oil boom has provided the government with more than enough money to cover up the consequences of the myriad contradictions such a stance has produced. Surfing a massive wave of oil profits, the government has not yet had to confront the more unseemly consequences of its dogged anti-rationalism. For now, all we can do is wonder how long its luck will last.

The shit hits the F.A.N.
Posted on December 5, 2007 by Quico

It's now an established talking point in the government's response to Sunday's referendum defeat: by "graciously" accepting he'd lost, Chávez put to rest the opposition's false claim that he's some kind of crazy dictator.[69] Like the democrat that he is, he "accepted the will of the people" and moved on...

Or did he?

This afternoon, Chávez turned up unannounced at the Military High Command's press conference ... and totally freaked out. Less than 72 hours after his "graceful" election night concession speech, the all-too-predictable Narcissistic Rage response began.

He called the opposition's referendum win "a triumph made of shit," using the word "*mierda*" four times in two sentences on national TV. You know things have come to a head when Reuters has to put the journalistic equivalent of a parental advisory at the start of its write up.

And I know everybody says Chávez doesn't drink but ... looking at the video, one has to wonder.

Ahhhh...profound reflection, thine homes are many.

Before this point, he'd hinted that the No side hadn't *really* won the referendum, but said he'd been graceful enough not to demand the complete tally count that might have nudged his side to victory. He skewered the journalist Hernán Lugo Galicia, who reported he

---

[69] This post came on the heels of the first outright electoral defeat chavismo suffered. In December of 2007, Chávez narrowly lost a Referendum on a proposal to change numerous articles of the Constitution. He accepted defeat in a most ungracious manner. The defeat marked a turning point for the opposition.

had "been pressured" by the Defense Minister to accept defeat, calling his reporting (wait for it …) shit.

And then, the cherry on top: he vowed to come right back and propose pretty much the same constitutional reform to the voters all over again.

Even more than the expletives, that last part is the real insult to the Venezuelan people. The electorally suicidal decision to put the same, loser reform in front of the voters again speaks volumes about how shallow Chávez's commitment to democracy really is. "Accepting the results" doesn't mean simply accepting the brute numerical fact that the other side has more votes than your side. It means accepting the political consequences that follow from the result.

On Sunday, the will of what Chávez used to call the Sovereign People was clear: keep your reforms out of our Constitution. In any event, the Constitution's article 345 explictly bars him from from putting the same proposal for constitutional reform to the people for a second time in the same term of office. A politician with a sounder grasp of reality might take the message, but the layers of abject sycophancy now insulating the president from the world around him have grown so thick, he's no longer able to make even minimally sensible decisions.

Chávez is treating his referendum defeat the way I might treat failing a driver's license test: it's embarrassing, sure, but no biggie. I just try again a few months later. Even if I failed the first test "fair and square", there's no question of giving up. After all, I need a driver's license.

The only difference is that, as far as Chávez can see, he wasn't the one who failed the exams, it was the voters who goofed. His message to them? "Wrong answer! Go back and vote better next time!"

That's not respecting the will of the people. That's is a deep, dark contempt for the will of the people.

Seriously, the guy is loony tunes...

"Revolution" as conceptual bulldozer
Posted on November 4, 2006 by Quico

"If anyone forgets we're in the middle of a Revolution, we're going to beat it into them: this company stands with Chávez."

-Rafael Ramírez, PDVSA chairman and Minister of Energy and Mines

More and more, Rafael Ramírez's recent speech to PDVSA management has made me think about the way chavismo uses the word "revolution" to flatten the distinctions between state, government, homeland, *pueblo* and leader - conceptual distinctions vital to a free society.

"Public employees are at the service of the State and not of any partiality," the Constitution tells us. But a Revolution cannot think of itself as a "partiality" - it must think of itself as the quasi-mystical political incarnation of the people, its essence and its interests. The Revolution is the state.

It makes no sense, within a revolutionary mind frame, to posit a distinction between Chávez's interests and the interests of the people, the homeland or the state. They are all one and the same.

This explains why chavistas, when they read Article 145, don't see what you or I see. They read the same words we read, but what they understand is different: "public employees are at the service of the Revolution and not of any partiality."

In a Revolution, state = government = homeland = people = leader. If you accept that, it follows that dissenting from the leader is tantamount to treason against the state. Once you've conflated these ideas into a single, undifferentiated soup, you pull out all the conceptual stops that restrain a government from tyranny. In this way, the word "Revolution" has become a trump-card, a conceptual bulldozer plowing over all spaces for legitimate dissent.

Ramírez is explicit about this: "we were put here by the Revolution, we were put here by the *pueblo*, we were put here by President Chávez." You can't pick and choose between them, because they're basically the same thing - a kind of revolutionary Holy Trinity. There's no room in this vision for NiNis, for "light" supporters. To be "a little bit revolutionary" is to be a little bit of a traitor. It just won't do.

According to this thinking, anything short of total, unthinking support for the Revolution makes you an enemy of the people. Your conscience doesn't belong to you, it belongs to us ... well, to him. And if you hold back, even a little, if you don't quite surrender your will in its entirety, you become suspect, an enemy to be liquidated.

It's a road that leads to tyranny, and nowhere else.

How do NiNis make a living?
Posted on October 22, 2005 by Quico

Businesses know that it pays to know your market. Rule one of marketing is "know your customers." How old are they? How much money do they make? What's their gender? Where do they live? How educated are they? How do they make a living? How does your product relate to their needs, wants, and fantasies?

You need clear answers to these questions before you can put together a sensible marketing strategy.

What I've been trying to say in the last few posts is that the traditional opposition's failure has been a failure of political marketing: they didn't know their customer!

Watching a lot of opposition leaders speak, they don't seem to have any clear idea of who they were talking to, or should be talking to. They failed to think through carefully the demographic groups they needed to win over and to craft their message accordingly. Not surprisingly, they made all sorts of rookie mistakes. They put out messages that alienated people they needed to attract, that ignored the concerns of those they wanted to represent, that contradicted those they needed to cozy up to, etc. etc. etc.

One reason to think Venezuela de Primera could do better is that they're led by a businessman, and one from a business – mobile telephony – where marketing is everything. Fortunately, Venezuela de Primera has learned some key lessons from the traditional opposition's political marketing failures. And make no mistake: it will take real marketing savvy to put together a message that can attract an electoral majority in the wake of the traditional opposition's implosion.

There's one key bit of political marketing data I don't have, though, and really wonder about. We know that roughly half of Venezuela's workers are in the formal economy and half in the informal sector. But how do political attitudes vary between those two groups? What percentage of chavistas have formal work? More importantly, what proportion of NiNis work informally? How do NiNis make a living?

My guess – and this is only a guess – is that NiNis are less likely to have formal work than either chavistas or antichavistas. If my hunch is right, then marketing to the political center means marketing to the needs of the informal worker. If so, it shouldn't be hard to put together a political message that is specifically geared at the very serious problems of informal workers as such.

Because, when you think about it, informal sector workers have all kinds of problems the government has done very little to address over the last seven years. With no prestaciones, no pensions funding, no sick leave, no vacation leave, no collective bargaining, no health insurance, no help for pre-school education and no workplace health and safety protections, their position is incredibly precarious. The government has done nothing for them on these fronts – largely because it's failed to stimulate formal sector work – and the opposition almost never talks about these themes. The specific needs of informal workers are ripe for the picking, politically speaking.

What's more, as I wrote at mind-numbing length in this essay, some very interesting recent research suggests that putting informal sector workers at the center of a developing country government's concerns could serve as a catalyst for development. So, by making a pitch specifically at the informal sector, you could also be laying down the foundations for success once you get into office.

Hmmmmmmm…

A postcard from the end of the world
Posted on January 16, 2005 by Juan Cristobal

It's 11:30 in Chile, and I'm watching TV.

Pundits and politicians are hard at work breaking down the triumph of Michelle Bachelet in today's Presidential elections. Instead of wondering why results are still missing in spite of very expensive electoral machinery, Chileans had official results with 99% of the votes counted by 9 pm local time. Instead of claims of fraud, they are breaking down the vote by gender line -in Chile, men and women vote separately, so it's possible to break down voting patterns- and by counties. All the information is already on the government's website. All this thanks to a transparent system based on a piece of paper, a pencil, a glass urn and an impeccable voter registry – a system that, in spite of being handled by the Interior Ministry, is impartial and trustworthy.

Is it healthy envy to ask myself why? Why can Chile have a working electoral system that everyone trusts, while Venezuela's citizens have en masse been forced to abandon the vote as an alternative? How can two countries with similar cultural circumstances have such different systems, with such vastly different outcomes? Only Jorge Rodríguez and his conscience can answer this.

In the meantime, I am amazed to see the international chavista brigade celebrate Bachelet's triumph as another swing to the left in the continent. Ms. Flanker, in the comments forum, has gone as far as saying that, since Bachelet's platform was based on modifying the private pension system, this is enough to place her bust on the lefty mantelpiece. These arguments show a deep, unabashed ignorance of what Chile has become and the type of policies that have driven its success.

Chile is the only Latin American country firmly on the way to development. It is developing thanks to many of the neoliberal policies that lefties decry. This is a country where a socialist President has inaugurated thousands of kilometers of ultra-modern highways built and managed by private companies in record time. Here, foreign businessmen come and build private parks that effectively cut the country in half (Google Douglas Tomkins for more details) and the discussion centers on whether or not the country has the right to build a road through his land. Chileans have access to modern health-care and pensions thanks to the participation of private industry. The system is not without flaws, but it is miles away from Venezuela's make-shift, state-run system.

The country's main industry, copper, is wide open to local and foreign private investment. Tuition in public universities runs in the thousands of dollars per year, but this socialist government (and the coming one) have understood that effective subsidies are those that target the person in need, not those that provide free-for-alls that allow people who don't need them to benefit. This has helped put Chilean universities at the vanguard in the sub-continent.

This is a socialist government that has pledged to run a fiscal surplus, and Bachelet has pledged to continue on this path and promised not to raise taxes. Chile's socialist government has partnered private industry, and has signed free-trade agreements with the US, the EU, South Korea and China. Japan and India are soon to follow.

Sure, there are problems in Chile. The pensions system is not working well, but Bachelet's reforms involve lower fees, more competition and tighter regulation. It has never crossed her mind that private industry should be shoved out of the system. Likewise, educational achievement has been lagging. But instead of blaming private education, the rich or the Catholic Church, like He-who-must-not-be-named has recently done, solutions are more innovative: vouchers, increased testing, teacher education, investment in "target" public schools. Income inequality is alarming, but she does not blame it on the rich.

So PSFs, here's some advice:[70] try and not look so ignorant. Ms. Bachelet will preside over a government more "neoliberal" than any Venezuela has ever seen. More than CAP's, more than the second half of Caldera's, more than anything that Primero Justicia is proposing. She will also preside over a more successful government than anything Venezuela has seen.

As I read Venezuelan news from afar tonight, my nostalgia mixes with rage. In spite of this, I am happy that my daughter could go vote with her Chilean parent today and learn what democracy is about.

Some day when she is older, I will tell her about how in Venezuela we had a democracy and we let it go to waste because we did not address its many flaws. I will also teach her to love Venezuela in spite of all her failures. I will teach her that the struggle for democracy is the noblest task our people face.

And I will teach her that this includes her as well.

Santiago Chronicles
Posted on December 10, 2006 by Juan Cristobal

Santiago on a Sunday is an unusually subdued place, boring even. One of my first shocks upon moving here was hopping over to the Restaurant district of El Bosque Norte on a Sunday for lunch and finding restaurants empty or, in some cases, closed. The contrast to the hustle and bustle of Las Mercedes on a Sunday was startling.

This being a long weekend, the city was even more subdued, until the news came out: former dictator Augusto Pinochet had died. I decided to step out to the places where each side was gathering, to mingle with Chileans and try to grasp what this meant for a divided country.

---

[70] PSF is a "Pendejo sin Frontera," roughly translated as "douchebag beyond borders." It refers to clueless foreigners who expect to come to Venezuela and provide anything more than a cursory explanation into the country.

In a city of six million people, the man's death left no one indifferent.

My first stop: Plaza Italia, meeting place of those celebrating the dictator's death.

The place was brimming with cops, and the mood was festive. A huge banner advertising Andrés Bello University made me feel a little less out of place, even though I was the only one there carrying an eighteen-month old toddler.

Several banners made sure I knew not everyone there felt happy about the man's death. The first read "Death defeats justice", while the second pair claimed for divine justice and lamented that "El tata", as his supporters used to call him, is now playing poker with Hitler in hell.

A woman curiously resembling Pres. Michelle Bachelet was so happy that she took her top off and started dancing in the streets in jubilation. Well, at least her bra was black.

As I immersed myself into the crowd, the signs got more rustic, and way more raw.

I was not surprised to find among the many flags being waved, my own Venezuelan tri-color, or at least what used to be my flag with the seven stars. We have definitely become part of the landscape of the Latin American left.

I had never witnessed street celebrations for a person's death. And while the mood was contagious, the common presence of Ché Guevara T-shirts and hammer-and-sickle flags made me question the commitment to human rights of many in the crowd.

I took a parting shot of the crowd, with the San Cristobal mountain's statue of the Virgin Mary in the background, as if imploring "Can't we all just get along?"

I drove a few miles to the East to the Military Hospital, where the General had died a few hours earlier. The crowd there was equally numerous and equally enthusiastic, chanting military songs mixed with anti-communist and anti-Bachelet cheers.

The women in the crowd showed a special fondness for the General, coming out in droves with military headgear and framed pictures of Pinochet accompanied by small children. It reminded me of other pictures of military strongmen appearing alongside children to soften their image.

As I drove home, I glanced at the modern office buildings in the El Golf neighborhood, with the Ritz Carlton hotel in the foreground. These gleaming monuments to Chile's dynamic economy stood in sharp contrast to the reminders of Chile's painful past that I had witnessed just a few kilometers down the road.

One city, torn apart by the actions of politicians and men in uniform. The wounds are still open in this divided country, and the passing of one man will do little to heal them.

During the course of the afternoon, my baby girl drew coos of admiration from rabid Pinochet supporters and from communist *pasionarias* alike. And even though she experienced the smell of marijuana for the first time in the anti-Pinochet rally, I'm glad I brought her along. Her bright-eyed innocence made me wish for a world without military strongmen, without divisiveness. My hope is that when she is older, both Venezuela and Chile - her native countries - will each be able to stand as a single nation.

Hugo Chávez's hidden tax hike
Posted on May 4, 2012 by Juan Cristobal Nagel

One sign of how screwed up Venezuela's public sphere has gotten is the fact that, in the last few years, corporate tax rates have just about doubled and you, who are an actual Venezuelan politics junkie, hadn't heard about it until 10 seconds ago.

In fact, the story of the way chavismo has managed to disguise a series of huge tax hikes through a variety of seemingly unrelated new laws, attracting virtually no public dissent in the process, stands as a kind of monument to our broken national debate.

First, it's good to remember that, though Venezuela is often viewed as a classic petro-state with a government lavishly funded by oil and little else, in reality 54% of Venezuela's tax income comes from the non-oil sector – mostly Income Tax and Value-Added Tax (VAT).

While Hugo Chávez has greatly increased the tax burden on oil companies, he has largely left non-oil income tax rates untouched. Instead, he's pioneered a whole new set of taxes, hidden deep inside seemingly unrelated laws, which fly almost entirely under the radar.

Take the INCES Law, intended to foster technical (and "socialist") training for the nation's workers. You wouldn't peg it for an appropriations bill, would you? Except the INCES Law includes a new 2% tax on all salaries paid - not profits, mind you, but salaries paid.

How about the new Sports Law? Sounds benign enough…but it too includes a provision for raising the tax rate by 1% in order to finance sports activities.

The new Science and Technology Law slaps a seemingly small new 0.5% tax on companies. Well, it seems small until you get to the fine print and realize that's 0.5% of gross income – not profits, but gross sales - like it's some sort of royalty on every commercial activity in the country.

Anti-drugs laws? They got taxes in there. Laws to build new housing? Yup, they snuck some new taxes in those too! The Municipal Law? 2% of gross income goes to municipalities.

So, as my beloved grandmother used to say, how much is much?

Together with some colleagues from ODH, a Caracas consulting firm, we set out to investigate how these laws changed the tax burden of firms. Because official data is impossible to obtain, we simulated the balance sheets of different sized firms, and incorporated the effect of the new legislation on their total tax bills.

The results were astonishing.

In Venezuela, corporate tax rates vary according to the size of the company. For small firms, the corporate tax rate starts at 15%, while for larger companies it is 34%. But once you add the new chavista laws, a completely different picture emerges.

Take, for example, a medium sized firm producing *alpargatas*. Suppose your firm makes 52 million BsF. in yearly sales, and the profit before taxes is something like 3.2 million BsF. Apply the 34% corporate tax rate, and the firm pays 1 million BsF. in taxes, with 2.1 million BsF. in after-tax profit.

The different laws affect our Alpargata-maker's tax liability differently. In the end, with all the new legislation, that same company ends up paying 605 thousand BsF in corporate taxes (because some of the other taxes are deductible), and a whopping 1.4 million BsF. in other taxes. The total taxes the company pays are double what they would be under the old regime – a jump from 34% to 64% of net earnings.

Including the effects of the different laws raises the tax burden – the percentage of profits that go to paying taxes – to 61.4% for small companies and almost 75% for large companies. If you simulate this for different sized companies, for different scenarios, the answer is always about the same.

So we've had a sea-change in corporate taxation, and all that with barely a ripple in public opinion, or even elite awareness! Under the guise of promoting science, fighting drug trafficking, promoting sports, or giving greater autonomy to municipalities, the chavista legislature and the President himself have instituted crippling tax hikes on an already obscenely over-regulated private sector. And let's not even mention where that money is going, 'cause we didn't even look at *that* aspect of the problem.

The fact that this is barely discussed in the Venezuelan public sphere points to just how bizarre a political phenomenon chavismo is. We obsess over gossip about the President's health, we analyze the absurd rants of corrupt wayward judges, and yet the important stuff falls right through the cracks.

While they distract us with outrageous, extraordinary events, they keep on pushing their equally outrageous agenda.

Which is, I guess, exactly how chavismo would want things.

Venezuela's thriving democracy
Posted on March 20, 2012 by Quico

First things first: I know it's a losing game trying to distinguish between "democracy" and "constitutional government." I'm well aware that that's too clever by half, that it's the kind of nuance that regular newspaper readers just won't get. I get it that headlines like the one above this post are almost made to be quoted out of context and will come back to bite me in the ass.

And yes, I also grasp that, in contemporary usage, "democracy" stands in for a whole bunch of practices that go well beyond electoral competition. That when people call a country a "democracy" they imply that it respects minority rights, and honors due process of law and the separation of powers: things that, strictly speaking, have everything to do with the rule of law and very little to do with "democracy" in a strict sense.

I know all that.

And yet…

The more I think about it, the more I think you have to lean on the distinction, because nothing about Venezuelan politics makes any sense these days until you grasp both aspects of what our country has become: an Unconstitutional Democracy.

Take the second term first. Competition for electoral support has come to color just about everything political that happens in the country. You see democratic dynamics playing out day in and day out, in the thousand little ways that both chavismo and the opposition curry favor with voters, from the populist-goodie giveaways (not just by the national government), to the billboards trumpeting the name of every Podunk politician who ever filled in a pothole anywhere in the country, to the relentless endless propaganda...everywhere really. This is just not the way actors behave in a political system where what normal people think doesn't matter.

In that sense, democracy is thriving in Venezuela. Politicians on both sides face major incentives to fight hard for regular people's support, and the dynamics that that incentive structure generates permeate the whole public sphere.

Competition for voters' favor is now one of the basic, defining characteristics of Venezuela's political system, much more than it was, really, in the pre-1999 era, when basic standards of co-existence lowered the stakes for AD and Copei in their struggle for votes. After all, in 1983, Rafael Caldera didn't fear that Copei would be eradicated as an independent force forever if Jaime Lusinchi won the election. He didn't have to – and that basic assurance of cozy *bipartidismo* lowered the frantic, desperate tone that electoral competition has acquired since.

Of course, the fundamental unfairness of the conditions under which Venezuelans compete for votes is the other basic, defining characteristic of Venezuela's system. And this you also see all around you: in the collapse of the conceptual distinctions between state, government and party, in the openly incestuous relationship between State TV, the *Fiscalía*, and Miraflores; in the government's increasing unwillingness to even pay lip-service to principles of equal justice under the law. Even the pretense of fair play has been left for dead in Venezuela these days.

It takes an obdurate determination to refuse to see what's right under your nose to miss quite how screwed up the system is.

The paradox is that unlike in other illiberal democracies, where the collapse of constitutional governance usually leads to the withering away of competitive dynamics (the prime example here is Russia), in Venezuela what we've seen is a deepening of democratic dynamics hand-in-hand with the total collapse of constitutional governance.

These strands aren't supposed to go together...but, in our country, they do.

It's these contradictions that make the Venezuelan case so fascinating to watch at this point. Venezuela's outlaw state is, today, more dependent on what its people think of it than at any time in the past. As the conditions of electoral competition grow more unfair, the competition intensifies rather than slackening. These are not normal-country dynamics – and really, I don't think I know of any close parallel to this kind of system either in our history or elsewhere around the globe.

It's really weird what's happening in our country. Riveting, really.

The naïve economics of speculation-led inflation
Posted on April 2, 2012 by Quico

I have a morbid fascination with "speculation" as an explanation for inflation. It's one of those shibboleths that get thrown around the Venezuelan public sphere all the time, and it usually goes unchallenged. People sort of nod knowingly, as though the whole trope wasn't – how to put it politely? – totally insane and moronic.

Sometimes – usually in the middle of an insomnia attack – I'll sit there trying to puzzle through the implicit economics at work here. There is some sort of widely shared but never clearly stated understanding of what-causes-what in economic life that accounts for the baffling fact that people who blame inflation on "speculators" aren't immediately laughed out of the room, out of their careers, and out of any possibility of holding a role in public life.

My best guess starts with a fallacy of aggregation: "speculation" sort of makes sense, intuitively, when you invoke it as the reason why one good might get unduly expensive in one shop, right? The damn *portu* down the street can mark up a good or two outrageously at his *abasto* in a speculative bid to see if some shoppers still bite.[71] And if that's good enough to explain any one price rise, why wouldn't it be a good enough explanation for every price rise?

Even to pose the problems in those terms is to think at a higher level of abstraction than the followers of the speculation school of inflation seem capable of, but let's just follow the logic down that rabbit-hole for a second here – which, conveniently, is about how long it takes for the whole flimsy edifice to come crashing down.

For speculation to account for inflation, it's not one or two *portus* who have to be speculatively trying to see if they can make some extra cash – it's every *portu*, marking up the price not just on one product, but on goods in general.

Now, there are only two ways prices can stay above their equilibrium level for any length of time. The first involves monopoly, where sellers face no competition and so can pretty much name their price.

As a general description of the Venezuelan economy, that one really makes no sense. Even now, after 13 years of trying to stamp out competition, there are thousands and thousands of sellers of most mass consumption products.

And so we're left with the alternative explanation: a massive, sprawling *portu* conspiracy, a sort of generalized cartel of all those thousands of sellers plotting secretly to raise their prices above the equilibrium price, in tandem, forever.

The key thing to understand is that a conspiracy such as this would also need to be perfect. Any single defector could bring the whole thing down in a moment. If it's possible to sell a given good at a profit for BsF.10, but all shopkeepers conspire to hike the price up to BsF.11, any single shopkeeper willing to buck the conspiracy could make off with basically the entire market, making huge windfall profits in the process.

---

[71] Many Portuguese immigrants came to Venezuela after World War II and set up small mom-and-pop grocery stores and bakeries, or abastos. Some, such as Central Madeirense, went on to become some of the largest supermarket chains in the country.

The conspiracy would be inherently unstable.

Set aside from the moment that, in this hypothetical *portu* conspiracy world, you would have excess supply of goods piling up on store shelves finding no willing buyers (rather than the shortages we actually live with) and ask yourself this: what would a real capitalist speculator, motivated by profit and profit alone, do in a world where he could sell profitably for less than BsF.11, but all his competitors are selling for BsF.11? What speculative price point might he speculatively try for, just to see how it goes?

The answer is more than obvious: BsF.10.99! When he does that, he breaks the cartel, capturing huge rents to himself, all through a speculative bid to test the prevailing price.

Of course, *los portus* tambien juegan. Eventually, one of his competitors, seeing the bottom falling off of his sales, is going to try to go one better, pricing at BsF.10.98, only to for his competitors in turn to take up the baton and drop the price to BsF.10.97...and so on and so forth until the prevailing price in the market comes all the way down to BsF.10 ... all through the speculative behavior of heartless, capitalist shopkeepers!

For reasons clear to exactly no one, though, the possibility of this form of "speculation" simply never enters the Venezuelan public sphere. The notion appears to be too sophisticated for us, even though the whole thing was first worked out by a 19th-Century Frenchman named Josephy Louis François Bertrand. In *chavenomics*, speculation only ever puts upward pressure on prices, never downward pressure.

"Speculators", in the chavista formulation, are a very queer breed of "capitalist" indeed: one gripped by an obsessive, single-minded mania to raise prices at all places and all times, regardless of what the competition is doing. In other words, a speculator in the chavista mold is somebody willing to lose money to indulge his price-raising obsession, or at any rate someone unwilling to cut prices even when doing so would make him more money.

Another way to see this is that the naïve economics of speculation interprets every market as monopolistic and every capitalist as enjoying monopoly rents…just because. The assertion doesn't stem from any kind of examination of what actually goes on in markets, but from a kind of definitional conviction that capitalism is monopoly.

The irony, of course, is that chavismo has managed to brand all capitalist as "price gougers" even though one of capitalism's chief attractions is actually just the opposite. Well-functioning competitive markets make price gouging unprofitable. In any event, the proper response to speculation is certainly not more controls, but more competition!

There's an element of setting-up-a-shooting-gallery-at-a-barreled-fish-market to this post, I realize, but I've just never really been able to get my mind around what exactly chavistas – and Venezuelans in general – have in mind when they blame inflation on speculators. It's a view so primitive, so childish, so trivial to debunk, that you really have to pinch yourself to believe you still have to argue against it.

And then, as I'm sitting there tossing and turning at four in the morning, that lurking question just won't go away. Is it really imaginable that the people who run our economy, people like Finance Minister Jorge Giordani and BCV chief Nelson Merentes, don't understand the first-semester economics outlined in this post? Or is it that they do understand it, but have chosen to pretend not to in a bid to further their careers?

I honestly don't know which it is…and I honestly don't know which I'd find scarier.

Rediscovering the whys and wherefores of democratic institutions
Posted on June 1, 2010 by Quico

Teodoro Petkoff has an enlightening piece on the conflict in Polar, where workers are coming to the defense of their company. Reading it, it occurs to me that maybe, just maybe, Venezuela needed *chavismo*.

We needed it so workers could rediscover, from lived experience, why they need independent labor unions.

So students could learn, first hand, why the right to organize is important, not in the abstract, but to their daily lives.

So politicians could feel, in their bones, why freedom of speech is sacred, why justice is a lie if judges are not autonomous, why politicizing the elections' body is unacceptable.

Just as it took Pinochet and Videla to convince Southern Cone leftists that "human rights" weren't just some reactionary slogan, that they had a stake in principles that could at times seem like purely airy abstractions, the traumatic experience of the Chávez era is serving to drill into young Venezuelans why the abstractions of democratic theory are vital for their everyday lives.

The kids whose political consciousness is being formed today – the generation that's going to fight out the presidential election of 2040 and beyond – are going to carry the lessons they're learning now throughout their lifetimes.

They will know that a government which takes away workers' rights to organize and defend their interests is a clear and present danger to the rudiments of political freedom for everyone. And they will know that deeply, intimately, in the flesh. They will know it in the way a child who's been burned knows to not put her finger on a hot stove again.

Forty years of corruption in the labor movement under the *Puntofijo* system had blunted these understandings. It was, in 1998, easy enough to dismiss the labor movement as nothing more than a cesspool of petty corruption and patronage.

That's not a mistake our leaders in 2040 are going to make.

Everybody already knows everything
Posted on March 27, 2010 by Quico

[Note: If you came looking for fresh insights or proper analysis, you might as well move along. This one's just one long rant.]

"Three new political persecutions in one week, with more certainly on the way. The regime is working to routinize repression, to establish it as just part of the normal 'way things are' that those who criticize it publicly can expect to go to jail."

What can you say about a statement like that? It's grave, certainly. It's deadly serious stuff. It's also evident – determined to impose itself on our collective consciousness with all the subtlety of a sledgehammer. It's something like the opposite of insightful. It takes no special insight to grasp it. The governing elite has decided the time for subtle messages is over.

Any questions?

I don't know how to shake this sense of the sheer useless repetitiveness of continuing to write about it, the raining-on-wet-pavement sense that the cards are now fully on the table, that power now acts at its most basic, at its most naked in Venezuela, and that the evidence all around makes further comment just plain depressing.

I keep remembering the meta-narrative in Nanni Moretti's *Il Caimano*, which is less a film about Berlusconi than it is a film about making a film about Berlusconi while being fully aware of the sheer, soul-crushing pointlessness of making a film about Berlusconi. At one point, one of the characters, played by Moretti himself, explains why the project is so ridiculous:

"A film about Berlusconi? Oh no! Everybody already knows everything about Berlusconi. Those who wanted to know, know...and as for those who'd rather not understand...well, come on! What else do you want to tell people about?...everything's out in the open."

This, *mutatis mutandi*, is pretty much where we are now in Venezuela.

The challenge, I suppose, is to keep the sense of outrage going, to fight the routine so that each new injustice burns as bright as the ones before. Some people are better at this than others. I only envy them. Personally, I struggle with the sense of despair, with the sense that all this bullshit is making the blog too predictable and boring. Or, what's worse, solemn.

That last bit, in particular, gnaws at me.

My ambition all along has been to craft a blog that's serious, but not solemn. I wanted an antidote to the dreary, plodding, narcosis-inducing drone that takes up so much of the official Venezuelan public sphere. I always thought Caracas Chronicles makes an implicit promise to its readers: come here and, day after day, we're going to keep it fresh.

Sassy.

Fun.

We're going to point your attention to stuff you need to know about Venezuela without preaching or getting all solemn and boring and sanctimonious. Hopefully, we're going to make you laugh along the way.

Could the sheer dictatorial excesses on the ground be forcing us to renege on that promise? At what point does sprinkling a blog with sarcasm become just plain obscene?

It may just be that the time horizons of the Internet world are too compressed for the task we face. That blogs, written daily, or Tweets, written in just a few seconds, create an illusion of immediacy that blinds us to the Long Game. That postmodern dictatorship can't be demolished, but can be slowly worn away at, corroded little by little by the sheer bloody-minded determination to keep on keeping on. That every tiny act of defiance is useful – if on a microscopic scale – and that the only way the regime wins is by psyching us out – by feeding the despair that leads to the inaction that is its only hope.

It could well be like that.

Still, it's a fight you have to fight every day.

Earth edition

www.earthedition.org

CPSIA information can be obtained at www.ICGtesting.com
Printed in the USA
BVOW082343090513

320353BV00003B/36/P